PRAISE FOR THE COMPLETE GUIDE TO ACT

"An excellent introduction to ACT—easy to read and easy to implement. Packed full of powerful tools, techniques, and strategies to foster profound and meaningful changes in your clients, this step-by-step guide is an invaluable resource for any type of health practitioner. Highly recommended!"

—**Dr. Russ Harris,** author of *ACT Made Simple* and *The Happiness Trap*

"Writing an easy-to-digest introduction to ACT that holds strong to the rigorous scientific work that supports the model is something many have tried but few have pulled off. Dr. Borushok does it here in this primer that belongs on any ACT clinician's shelf."

—**Jacob Martinez, MA, LPC,** theactmatrix.com

"*The Complete Guide to ACT* offers a fresh, inspiring, and creative perspective that is sure to enliven the clinical hour for both therapist and client. Whether you are new to the model or a seasoned clinician looking for some new inspiration, this book needs to be in your hands. Jessica Borushok has gifted us with an innovative metaphor, the playbook, that is guaranteed to bring the processes to life, either as written or customized and adapted to suit your needs. There is a depth to Jessica's clinical examples and guidance that reassures us that we are learning from someone who is immersed in the work."

—**Dr. Sheri Turrell, PhD,** clinical psychologist and psychoanalyst, coauthor of *ACT for Adolescents* and *The ACT Relationship Skills Workbook for Teens*, and creator of the Choose Your Life online self-help course for teens

"*The Complete Guide to ACT* is an impressively well-crafted, hands-on guide that seamlessly bridges ACT theory and practice. This book doesn't just teach ACT—it trains you in it. With engaging exercises, clear explanations, and practical tools, Dr. Borushok makes psychological flexibility more than a concept—it becomes an accessible skill clinicians can integrate into their work immediately. Whether you're new to ACT or a seasoned practitioner, this book will sharpen your skills and deepen your impact. A must-read for any clinician committed to meaningful, effective therapy."

—**Daniel J. Moran, PhD, BCBA-D,** ACBS-recognized ACT trainer and author of *Finding Your Why and Finding Your Way*

"Dr. Borushok has achieved something remarkable here—a book that doesn't just teach you about ACT but trains you in it. *The Complete Guide to ACT* is clear, concise, and a joy to read. Dr. Borushok creates engaging opportunities to practice new skills by deftly weaving together real therapeutic conversations with thoughtful exercises. If you are new to ACT and want to develop your skills, this is the book you've been looking for."

—**Jennifer Kemp, MPsych,** clinical psychologist, author of *The ACT Workbook for Perfectionism,* and coauthor of *The Neurodivergence Skills Workbook for Autism and ADHD*

"*The Complete Guide to Acceptance and Commitment Therapy* lives up to its name—an insightful, comprehensive resource. Jessica Borushok masterfully presents both the original ACT model and its extensions in a clear, engaging, and highly accessible manner. What sets this book apart is its interactive approach, allowing therapists to not only grasp the concepts but also to immerse themselves fully in the experience of ACT. This guide fosters a deep, functional, and flexible understanding of ACT therapy, making it a valuable resource for any practitioner. I wholeheartedly recommend this book!"

—**Jennifer L. Patterson, PsyD,** author of *The ACT Workbook for Behavioral Addictions*

"ACT is a cutting-edge, well-researched therapeutic approach for making life more fulfilling, yet it is often challenging to implement because it goes beyond just using words and thinking. In *The Complete Guide to Acceptance and Commitment Therapy,* Dr. Jessica Borushok does much more than list ACT techniques—she provides a clear understanding of how the principles work. The concepts are brought to life through engaging case example dialogues, practice exercises, and concise chapter summaries. The sometimes-technical jargon of ACT is presented in a natural way that makes it easily digestible for therapists and clients alike. Whether you are new to ACT or a long-time practitioner, you will find much to value in this book!"

—**Richard Sears, PsyD,** author of *ACT with Anxiety* and *The ACT Flip Chart*

THE COMPLETE GUIDE TO ACCEPTANCE & COMMITMENT THERAPY

An Interactive Skills Manual for Clinicians to Learn and Practice ACT

Jessica Borushok, PhD

THE COMPLETE GUIDE TO ACCEPTANCE AND COMMITMENT THERAPY
Copyright © 2025 by Jessica Borushok

Published by
PESI Publishing, Inc.
3839 White Ave
Eau Claire, WI 54703

Cover by Amy Rubenzer
Interior by Emily Dyer
Editing by Marisa Solis

ISBN 9781683737070 (print)
ISBN 9781683737087 (epub)
ISBN 9781683737094 (ePDF)

All rights reserved.
Printed in the United States of America.

To Bill. Thank you for introducing me to ACT.
You have changed the trajectory of my life
in a thousand tiny ways.

TABLE OF CONTENTS

Introduction ix

PART I • UNDERSTANDING ACT

Chapter 1. The World Through the Lens of ACT 3

Chapter 2. The Psychological Flexibility Agenda 21

Chapter 3. Core Processes in ACT 35

PART II • GETTING STARTED WITH YOUR CLIENT

Chapter 4. The Role of Diagnosis in ACT 63

Chapter 5. Intake Assessment 71

Chapter 6. Treatment Planning and Relationship Building 81

PART III • FILLING YOUR ACT TOOLBOX

Chapter 7. Psychological Flexibility Tools 97

Chapter 8. The Playbook: A Functional Analysis Tool 111

Chapter 9. Language and Metaphors 125

Chapter 10. Embodied Experiential Work 145

PART IV • CREATING AN ACT FRAMEWORK

Chapter 11. Incorporating Other Skills Into ACT 169

Chapter 12. Furthering Your Practice 179

References 183

Acknowledgments 187

About the Author 189

INTRODUCTION

Why ACT?

As a therapist, you may struggle with the thought that you can't save your clients from the pain of living. As I write this, there are dozens of client examples running through my head: the client whose partner left them; the client who witnessed something horrific; the client who didn't get the job; the client who experienced something awful; the client who wasn't chosen for the program; the client who realized their parent would never change. And if I could, I would take away all of their pain. My guess is you would too. Unfortunately, that's not how therapy—or life—works.

Pain hurts. It *makes sense* everyone wants to avoid pain. And yet, to live our life, not just survive it, involves pain. To love someone, to have dreams, to strive for anything in life makes us vulnerable to loss, failure, and heartbreak.

While we can't erase the experiences our clients have, the vital work we do is not entirely hopeless. Our work instead turns to helping them develop new ways to respond to the tough stuff that shows up in life. The end goal is not to take away a client's pain, but to help them experience the pain that is a part of living. To learn to sit with the heartbreak and sadness and anger and trauma instead of constantly fighting it until it becomes so huge that it is unescapable. Until it takes them away from the life that is happening right now. That's where *acceptance and commitment therapy* (ACT) comes in.

The unofficial motto of ACT (*act* said as one word, not the letters A-C-T) is to alleviate human suffering. Lofty, I know, but a worthwhile endeavor to strive for. ACT aims to do this through increasing *psychological flexibility*. Psychological flexibility focuses on how to be open to our full experience, even the unpleasant stuff, notice patterns that are no longer serving us, and be intentional in pivoting toward what matters to us even in the presence of pain.

People create suffering through trying to pick which life experiences can be in their world—usually the happy ones—and attempting to avoid all others. The problem is that we don't always have control over which life experiences we have. We focus so much effort on trying to change what is *out* of our control that we don't have any energy or focus left for what is *within* our control: how we show up to this moment. So in order to not experience pain, we also miss out on people and experiences that truly matter to us.

In our attempts to avoid pain, we create suffering. Think of someone with panic disorder who avoids driving for fear of having a panic attack while operating a vehicle. As a result, this person rarely gets to spend time with their friends and turns down every job opportunity that would require a commute. They *may* be reducing panic attacks by avoiding driving, but at what cost? And even if they manage to avoid panic attacks, they are constantly anxious over a future scenario where they might have a panic attack. As a result, their life is smaller, and in the end, they're still suffering—it's just become a different kind of distress.

ACT helps clients identify the *internal experiences* (thoughts, feelings, urges, memories, physical sensations, beliefs) they are trying to avoid, recognize the patterns of avoidance this creates in their life, and realize how unworkable these patterns are in the long term. Once clients notice the patterns, they can develop skills and strategies for creating a different relationship to those painful experiences. They begin to change how they respond when the pain shows up, instead choosing to take steps toward what matters to them. The cool thing is this happens even in the presence of pain.

The goal of ACT is not to reduce a specific symptom. Rather, it is to teach people through experiential work how to respond in the presence of their symptoms in a way that helps expand their life instead of narrow it. I like to think of ACT as an additive approach, not a subtractive one.

If your background training is in a more symptom-reduction agenda, it is understandable that this concept may seem vague or not workable.

ACT Research

ACT has been studied for over 30 years, and as a result, it has accumulated quite the evidence base. To date, ACT has more than 1,000 randomized control trials. While we won't be going over every study, it's useful to highlight some areas of particular strength.

The American Psychological Association (APA) considers ACT an empirically supported treatment for obsessive-compulsive disorder (Soondrum et al., 2022; OCD), chronic pain (Trindade et al., 2021; Lin et al., 2019; Veehof et al., 2011), depression (Bai et al., 2020; Jiménez, 2012), mixed anxiety disorders (Bluett et al., 2014; Twohig & Levin, 2017; Arch et al., 2012), and psychosis (Jansen et al., 2020; Tonarelli et al., 2016). In addition to this, ACT has growing evidence in a variety of domains and presenting problems, including stress, addiction, weight loss, health behavior change, and sports performance.

Studies have also explored many of the components of ACT in more depth. For example, the core processes of acceptance and cognitive defusion create session-by-session improvement and overall reductions in symptom severity, while values work leads to greater improvements in quality of life overall (Villatte et al., 2016). In comparing treatment as usual and control conditions, ACT is more effective than waitlist, control conditions, and psychoeducation programs, and as effective as cognitive behavioral therapy (CBT) for a variety of presenting problems (A-Tjak et al., 2015).

One reason ACT has such a strong evidence base across so many areas of specialization is that it is inherently a transdiagnostic model: ACT was not designed for a specific treatment, such as exposure and response prevention, first created to treat OCD, or dialectical behavior therapy, originally designed to treat borderline personality disorder. Nor is ACT a remedy to reduce certain symptoms, like, for instance, cognitive behavioral therapy. If we think of ACT as more of an approach or framework for understanding and interacting with our own mind, it can be applied to any population, presenting problem, or environment. The goal is to be fluid and adapt to what shows up in the moment. ACT clinicians work with clients to increase their awareness and expand how they can respond to pain, no matter what that pain is.

What You'll Learn

My goal in this skills manual is not to teach you ACT but to *train* you in ACT. By the end of *The Complete Guide to Acceptance and Commitment Therapy*, my hope is that you will be able to flexibly bring ACT to your work with clients. This approach differs from many ACT books out there, as they tend to be didactic in nature. They teach ACT to therapists through describing the main components and providing experiential work only through exercises that a therapist would use with a client. This leaves many seeking more hands-on experience in training or workshops in order to feel comfortable actually implementing ACT with their clients. This book bridges that gap.

Information may change our attitude toward something, but not always our behavior. It is not enough to take in information—we must interact with it. The old adage of see one, do one, teach one is a perfect lens from which to explore ACT. Throughout each chapter in this book, you will learn and see how this work applies to your clients. Then, you will practice these skills yourself. This truly is an interactive book. Feel free to write directly in these pages, or, alternatively, you can download the worksheets on the companion website* to practice over and over again. On this website, you'll find practice worksheets for both you and your clients, scripts for the various exercises, and additional information for further learning.

Throughout *The Complete Guide to Acceptance and Commitment Therapy*, there are ample exercises designed to train your framework for understanding ACT. You will have the opportunity to reflect on your own practice or approach as well as follow therapist-client scripts with sidebars that explain the skills, tools, and approaches the therapist is using. This way, you not only see what ACT can look like with a client but also understand the process behind the scenes. At various points, you'll also find strategies for overcoming common pitfalls and roadblocks in your ACT practice.

My hope is that this book will not only introduce you to ACT and its foundational principles and philosophies but also guide you in a functional approach to ACT that is context specific and flexible. With the following pages as a guide, you'll go out in the world and teach ACT to your clients, helping them develop a new framework for exploring and interacting with their experience. Your goal is to teach your clients the skills and approach to flexibly adapt to any situation they are in, so eventually they don't need you to be a filter through which they funnel their experiences. Rather, you will act as a mentor who slowly takes off the training wheels of support and gives them more control over their lives.

The chapters in this book are grouped into four parts. Part I: Understanding ACT focuses on understanding the overall approach of ACT so you can use this lens as you dive deeper into the book. These

---

* You can find the downloadable content from this book at https://www.theacttherapist.com/ACTskillsmanual.

initial chapters emphasize the basic foundational knowledge, particularly the six core processes in ACT that lead to psychological flexibility. You'll also learn how to explain ACT to clients and create buy-in for therapy. By the end of part I, you will have a strong understanding of functional contextualism and what ACT is and is not. You'll be able to introduce ACT to your clients, set up creative hopelessness, and formulate a case conceptualization based on a functional understanding of your clients' behaviors and values.

Part II: Getting Started with Your Client reviews the transdiagnostic model and more concrete skills for therapists. This includes 1) conducting intake assessments that are consistent with ACT, and 2) adapting current intake assessments so they are still compliant with your setting requirements. You will explore the role of diagnosis in ACT, exploring what your own personal stance is based on your background, setting requirements, and boundaries. You will also learn ACT's approach to relationship building and self-disclosure in therapy. Finally, you will create treatment plans for your clients based on a variety of presenting problems and explore how to make them more consistent with ACT. This will include examples and practice opportunities. Special consideration will be taken for navigating your setting requirements in an ACT-consistent way.

Part III: Filling Your ACT Toolbox explores the various frameworks and diagrams that have been developed to conceptualize and explain ACT. This includes the ACT matrix, fACT, the choice point, DNA-V, and my own adaptation of the ACT matrix, the Playbook, which is an interactive tool for exploring the six core processes and conducting a functional analysis with clients. In addition, you will learn how to create your own metaphors that connect with your clients and explore ways to bring more embodied work into ACT for those clients who struggle with the intangible and abstract nature of ACT. By the end of part III, you will have a deep understanding of the components of psychological flexibility and an idea of the tools available to you.

Finally, in Part IV: Incorporating Other Skills into ACT, we will discuss how to adapt skills from other disciplines and integrate them into an ACT framework. You will practice these skills and create your own adaptations that fit with your own settings and populations. You'll also learn how to pivot when work with a client isn't "working."

It is easy to binge this book without engaging with any of the material, coming away with a lot of new information but no additional confidence in your ability to implement ACT with your clients. My recommendation is to view this book as a four-month challenge. Take one month to work through each part at a time. Read through each chapter, pausing to ensure you understand not only the words but also how the exercises, scripts, and tools function. When you read through a script, study the sidebar explanations and talk yourself through what is happening. Relate it to the work you are doing with your clients and think about how it might work in your sessions. Take opportunities to explain a concept in your own words. Practice explaining the concepts in different ways. Use metaphors. Explaining what you are learning with loved ones, especially those not in the mental health field, can be a great way to determine whether you understand it. Because unlike clients who may nod along, your loved ones will hopefully question you if something doesn't make sense.

Once you've finished the book, take a moment to reflect on what you've learned. Consider the ways you can bring in pieces of what you've discovered into your everyday life and work with your clients. Then, challenge yourself to include a specific exercise, core process, or explanation in a session, where appropriate. Focus on what feels uncomfortable and lean into that. If you're already familiar with ACT, you may choose to read this book in one sitting, and then go back and spend extra time on areas you struggle with. The choice is yours. However you choose to use the book, my hope is that approach includes curiosity, flexibility, and compassion for yourself as you embark on learning something potentially new to you.

My Story

I've been in the "other" chair in a therapist's office multiple times throughout my life. At each of these moments, I was stuck. Figuring out how to ensure OCD didn't take over my life. Deciding whether to get back together with my terrible ex-boyfriend. (Don't worry, I didn't.) And processing some of the darkest moments of my existence. Throughout all of it has been a thread woven through the fabric of my very being. That thread kept tugging me toward my values and the life I wanted to live for myself, but I didn't quite know how to follow it. I didn't always have the term *values* to give it a name, but I knew that thread represented the core of who I was and what was important to me. Over the years, I've been able to identify each strand of the thread: authenticity, creativity, curiosity, kindness, and so on.

When I was in the midst of posttraumatic stress disorder (PTSD) and depression, I felt as if I had folded in on myself until I was just a tiny spark in the center of a dark cloud. Fearful that I would never make it out again. Yet even then, I could feel the tug. ACT gave me the framework for understanding my own experience. ACT taught me how to take the steps forward to follow that thread. And as I sit here now, living a life fully immersed in my values and surrounded by the most incredible people, I am so grateful that graduate school brought me into contact with ACT.

I hope you can feel the tug of your own thread even if you can't name all the strands yet. And that this book and ACT in general can make it a little clearer how to follow your own thread. Part of furthering our ACT practice involves exploring it for ourselves in our own lives. The best part is you don't have to do it alone.

ACT Terms at a Glance

While we will go more in depth on various terms and concepts in future chapters, for now, here's a quick reference guide you can refer to as you go through the book.*

Acceptance: The process of being open to our full experience, including those that cause us pain. A common question for clients is "Are you willing to experience X in order to move toward what matters to you?"

Cognitive fusion: The act of believing a thought to be literally true and narrowing our behavioral repertoire, meaning what we can do in the presence of that thought.

Committed actions: The process of taking steps toward our values. These can include both observable and cognitive behaviors.

Creative hopelessness: The process of realizing that our attempts to escape and avoid painful experiences do not work in the long term and end up causing more suffering. The process of creating buy-in for ACT.

Defusion: The process of noticing when our attachment to or buying into a thought as literally true limits our options for showing up to the world (narrowing our behavioral repertoire). Cognitive defusion exercises help us create space between hook and response in order to create choice around how we want to respond.

Disconnecting from present moment: Engagement with the past or imagined future. Not intentionally focusing our attention.

Experiential avoidance: Attempts to erase, control, or escape painful experiences.

Functional contextualism: What works in a given situation. The focus is on both short-term and long-term impact.

Lack of clarity or connection with values: Unclear values or not feeling engaged or connected with values.

Lack of engagement with values: Engaging in actions without thought, often for short-term relief. Default reactions to experiences instead of actions that serve values.

Present-moment awareness: The process of connecting with the here and now. The action of noticing when our mind has wandered and intentionally checking into the present both internally (thoughts, feelings, memories, physical sensations) and externally (five senses, observable world).

---

* This reference guide is also available as a printable download at https://www.theacttherapist.com/ACTskillsmanual.

Psychological flexibility: The ability to come in contact with our full experience in order to interrupt patterns that aren't helpful and engage with what matters to us in the present moment. The six core processes make up psychological flexibility: present-moment awareness, values, committed actions, self-as-context, cognitive defusion, and acceptance.

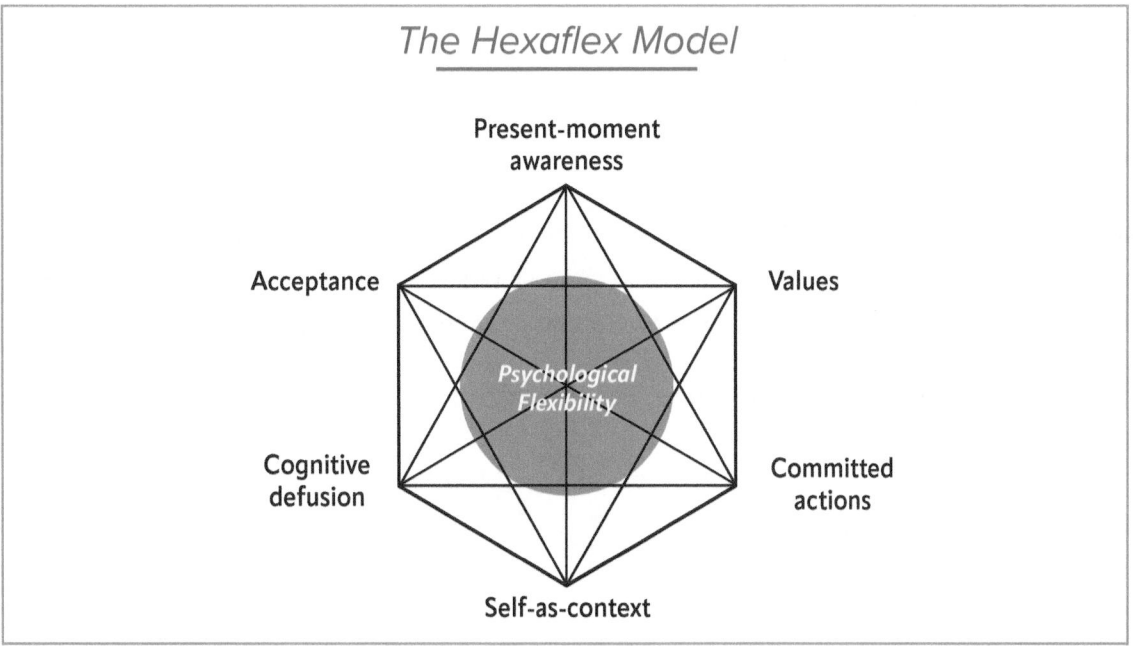

Psychological inflexibility: The inverse of psychological flexibility and the six core processes. It includes: dissociation from present moment, lack of clarity or connection with values, reactivity, self-as-content, cognitive fusion, and experiential avoidance.

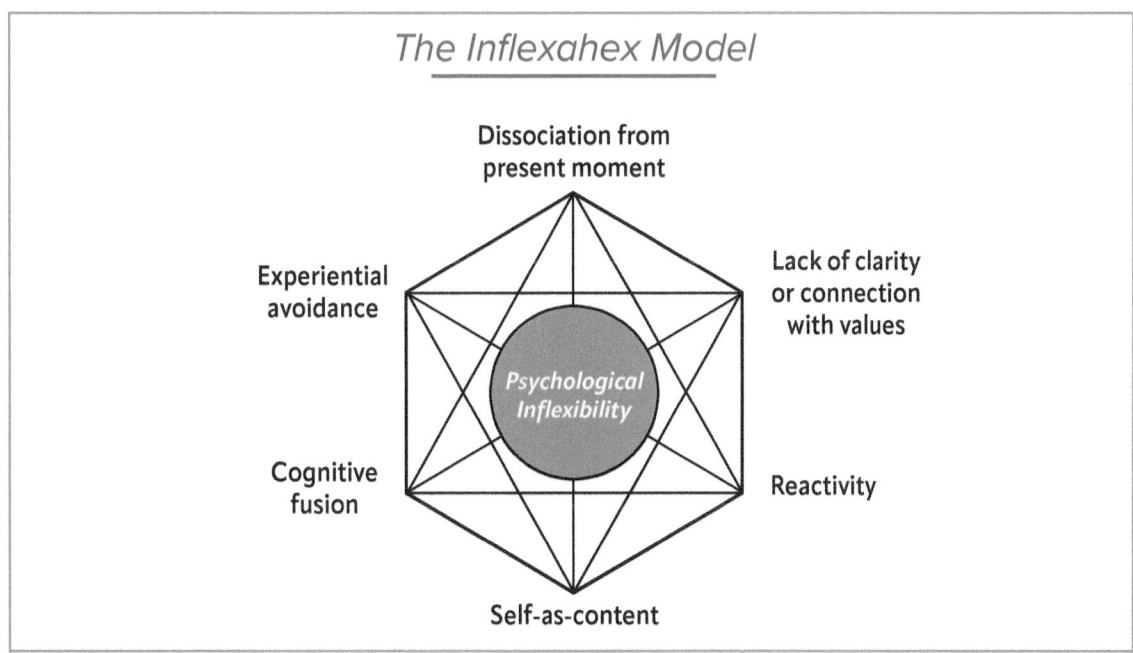

Self-as-content: This is the inverse of a core process (self-as-context). It means being rigidly adhered to roles and labels. This fusion with identity or a fixed self narrows our behavioral repertoire (the options for how we can show up to a moment) and makes our life small.

Self-as-context: One of the six core processes. It aims to increase our awareness of our own perspective and uses deictic frames to explore other perspectives across space and time. The purpose is to loosen the rigidity we have around rules, labels, and roles, and instead, practice showing up to each moment as a constant self (observer self) who is witness to what is happening internally and externally, thereby increasing our behavioral repertoire.

Starting assumptions: The starting point for beginning ACT. It involves focusing on what works in a given setting (functional contextualism), setting realistic expectations for therapy, getting informed consent, and not promising or prioritizing the reduction of symptoms but rather increasing engagement with values.

Values: The who and what that matters to us. The characteristics or qualities that we want to embody as we show up to each moment.

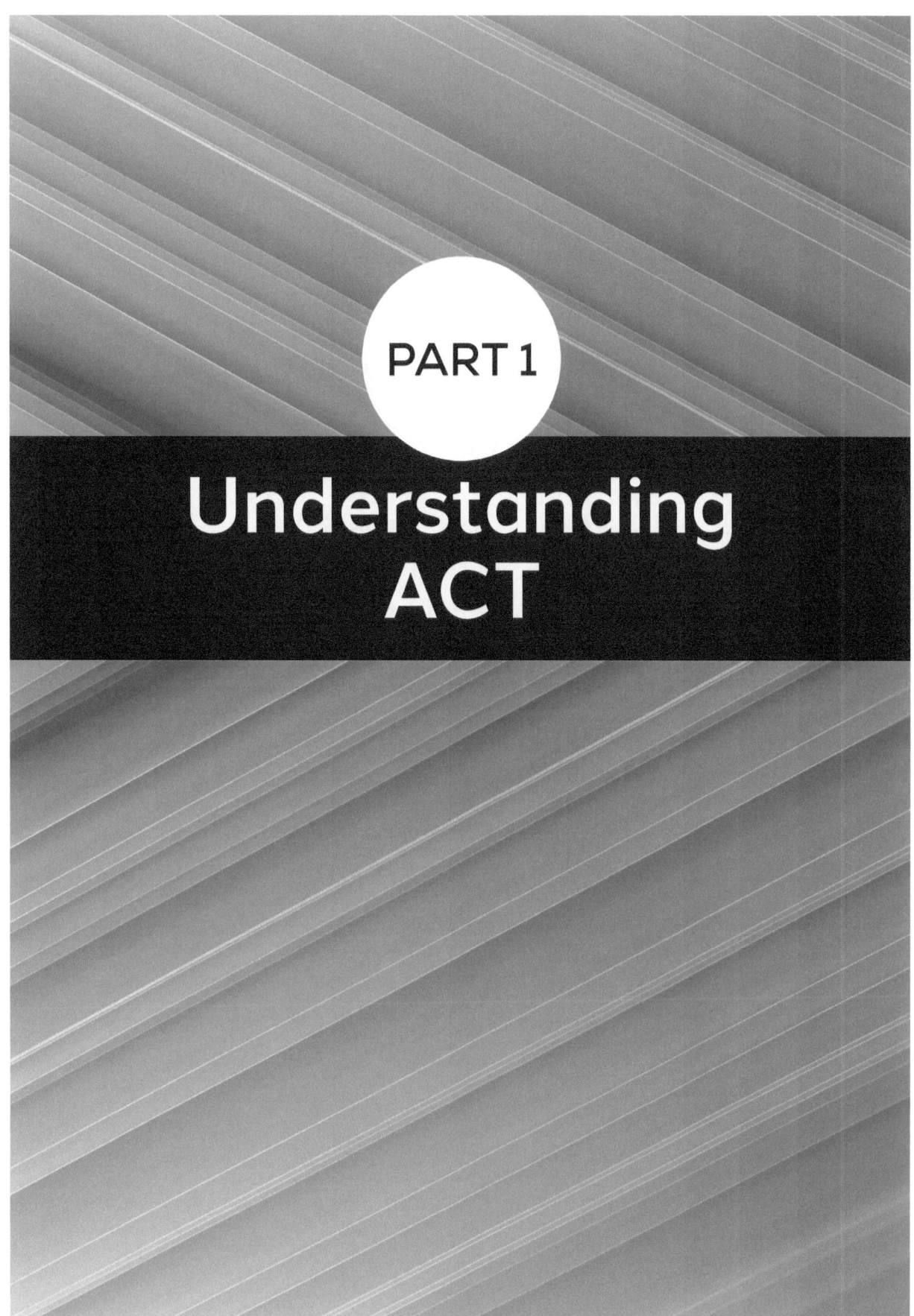

CHAPTER 1

THE WORLD THROUGH THE LENS OF ACT

Acceptance and commitment therapy (ACT) was developed by Steven Hayes and colleagues with the aim of increasing *psychological flexibility* in clients. At its core, ACT helps clients to 1) engage with their full experience in order to understand and interrupt patterns that are no longer serving them, and 2) pivot toward what matters most in the moment. ACT comprises six core processes that contribute to psychological flexibility: present-moment awareness, values, committed actions, self-as-context, cognitive defusion, and acceptance. In chapter 3, we will break down each of the processes in detail. But since ACT is grounded in *functional contextualism*, there's no better place to start our discussion of this therapy than with its philosophical foundation for understanding human behavior.

The Functional Contextual Philosophy

At heart, I am a functional contextualist. It is my belief that we cannot intentionally *do ACT* in the absence of a foundational knowledge of functional contextualism. Without it, ACT is simply a series of metaphors and exercises without context. Functional contextualism is the philosophical underpinning of ACT.

So what is it? And how does it differ from other theoretical orientations? Functional contextualism asks us to look at how something functions in a given context. Or, said another way, how something works in a given situation or environment. Because we live in a world of right or wrong, good or bad, we often struggle to pause and look at the function of a behavior. What we often find is that it's not as cut and dry as we default to.

The best way to describe functional contextualism is in contrast to CBT's approach to the mind. Many therapies today, including CBT, focus on an ontological approach. This assumes there is a "capital-T Truth," as in thoughts being labeled as good or bad or right or wrong. Many therapies operate under the assumption that the content of thoughts are the problem. Therapists then work with clients to attempt to change these thoughts to be more in line with a person's reality. The hope is that if a person's thought can be changed, their mood, and subsequently how they behave, will begin to change as well. This is where strategies such as *cognitive restructuring* come from.

A lot of great skills and tools have come from these methods, but the difficulty with a more mechanistic approach like this is that that's not how our brain works. We can't, on a whim, delete thoughts. And trust me, I've tried. You've tried. Our clients have tried. We especially cannot erase thoughts that we regularly recall over and over again.

If we take a step back and look at how we first take in information and then encode it, we can begin to see some faults in a fully symptom-reduction and thought-elimination model. The more that we recall thoughts and interact with them, the stronger that network in our brain becomes. Imagine, for example, that you have the thought *I'll never succeed at anything*. Maybe that thought shows up at random, but maybe you also recall it after every moment of failing, falling short, or struggling. Each time you interact with that thought, and each time you connect it to a pivotal moment in your personal or career development, the stronger the association you have with that (often painful) thought.

These types of thoughts—the recurring ones that are linked to a thousand difficult moments spanning decades of experiences—are nearly impossible to erase. Every time we recall information and reflect on it, the connection becomes stronger, not weaker. In comparison, we rarely remember what we had for breakfast thirteen days ago unless something truly profound happened that morning to encode the information into a strong network. Those inconsequential thoughts *do* get deleted. The problem unfolds when the thoughts and memories we don't engage with are the ones that get weeded out of our mind, while the ones we desperately want to get rid of are the ones that get stronger and stronger every time we interact with them.

In ACT, instead of replacing or changing thoughts, we work to build skills that help us *change our response* to those thoughts. Rather than attempting to delete these thoughts, we broaden our behavioral repertoire (our potential responses) in the presence of the antecedent, or trigger (an intrusive thought popping up). Essentially, we have more options of what to do after a thought or feeling shows up instead of just our default response, which generally isn't—and hasn't been—super helpful in the long term.

In cognitive restructuring in CBT, for example, we often introduce the exercise of taking one thought and replacing it with a thought more aligned with reality. From an ACT perspective, we can't replace thoughts. However, if we approach cognitive restructuring as creating a new response to that thought, we begin to look at each step as a new behavior. It's not replacing the initial thought or removing the anxiety. It's changing our response to it, which may help us take more values-aligned steps.

Perhaps the thought *I'm a terrible therapist* pops up for you. When this happens, you typically eat a whole pizza, skip a peer consultation out of embarrassment, or research alternative career options. Those choices may help you feel a little better in the short term, but in the long term, they don't erase that feeling or thought. It still shows up. You still feel insecure.

So, what if, through practice or maybe therapy, when that thought shows up, you learn to pause, create space for that thought, acknowledge that it makes sense that thought is popping up because being a good therapist really matters to you, and either resume what you were doing before or pivot toward a values-based behavior (maybe picking up this book)? Maybe in response to that thought, you tell yourself *I'm working hard to be the best therapist I can be*. When that difficult thought pops up again and again, you are each time engaging in various skills to add a new way of responding to the equation. And with practice, that new thought (*I'm working hard to be the best therapist I can be*) can build a strong connection with being a therapist so it also pops up more frequently.

Over time, these adaptive ways of responding become the default. But functionally, we are not erasing the initial thought. It'll likely even pop up from time to time. The thought is not the issue. Our response is. In ACT, we work to interact with the thought differently, which ultimately changes how the thought impacts us.

The Un-Truth of the Matter

ACT takes an *a-ontological* approach: the idea that there is no absolute "Truth." From this comes the understanding that it is not so much the content of our thoughts that are the issue, but rather the way we respond to those thoughts. Do we buy into a thought as true? As a result, do we narrow our behavioral repertoire? Or are we able to notice that it is simply a thought and choose what we want to do in the presence of that thought? This is where processes such as *acceptance* and *defusion* come in (see chapter 3). The content of the thought is less relevant from an a-ontological perspective. Instead, we look at what happens next. When an internal experience pops into a moment, what do we do?

Let's say I have the thought *I am ugly and no one will ever want to date me.* If I believe that thought to be one hundred percent the truth, it really limits my options for how I show up to the world. If ugly people can't date and I'm ugly, then I'd likely never date. It would be a futile attempt. Or I could refute that statement and look for evidence that I'm attractive. Or, if by society's standards I'm an ugly duckling, then I could look for evidence that ugly people can date and find partners. Or I could spend all of my time, money, and energy trying to be attractive. All of these are pretty miserable options. And all of these efforts, while they may feel like they are addressing the thought, keep me stuck in a cycle where my appearance is at the forefront of my mind, steering all my decisions. Moreover, even if I get married or get all the plastic surgery in the world, my mind will *still* whisper *You're ugly and no one will ever date you.* When we believe the content of the thought, we have fewer options for what's next.

Instead, in ACT, we take the stance that a thought is a thought. It doesn't have to be grounded in reality. It's not all-knowing. It's just a thought that popped into our mind. That thought may be painful, but it doesn't limit how we can show up to the world. The thought isn't the issue; it's how we respond to it that causes suffering in our life. If we're able to take a step back and notice our thought—and maybe recognize that it's showing up because there is some value tied to it that's causing us to care—then the thought simply holds less power over us, because it isn't the truth. It's just a thought.

If I am able to acknowledge that my thought is painful and then pivot toward what matters to me *even in the presence of that thought*, I have a lot more options for how I can live my life. And most importantly, I can be myself, find hobbies I enjoy, build a career and community that I love, and maybe meet someone to spend my life with. All in the presence of the thought *I'm ugly and no one will ever date me.*

But what if our thoughts are true? I get asked this all the time by clients. And sometimes the content of that thought *is* true. Maybe the client really does struggle in school compared to others. Maybe they are truly in a lot of physical pain due to a condition they cannot change. If someone's life was forever changed by a car accident resulting in a physical disability, the thought *My life will never be the same* is accurate. It is a reflection of their reality. An unchangeable, uncontrollable factor. And it sucks.

But in ACT, we are not focused on the content of the thought, but rather how it functions. This is the really cool thing about ACT. There's a reason why ACT for chronic pain has such a robust amount of research backing it. If our main objective is to change or delete the content of a thought (the actual words or meaning of the thought), we are screwed if the thought reflects reality. But by accepting the thought, particularly in these harsher circumstances, validating that those are our client's realities can be extremely liberating for them. To know that they don't have to pretend everything is fine and perfect and great. Because sometimes it isn't and it won't be. So how do we help this person?

Ending the Struggle

We help our clients by getting them to focus on how their response to painful thoughts is serving them. Is sitting around all day and thinking about the ways their life has changed or all the experiences they're going to miss out on helping the client? Probably not. It's likely making them feel extra awful. It's what we call *dirty pain*, or "suffering." This is the extra pain that gets added onto the pile from our attempts to fight, avoid, or sink into the experience. I once had a supervisor who would call this "shit on shit." Stuff stinks, and then we just keep piling it on. I imagine someone walking around a farm and stepping in a pile of horse manure, getting upset, and spending so much time ranting and raving that they aren't paying attention to the moment and stick their other shoe in it. Now they have two dirty shoes. Their attempts to not feel any pain helps no one, and it certainly doesn't clean off their other shoe.

Clean pain, on the other hand, refers to the pain that comes from living. The loss and heartbreak and low moments that everyone experiences. The cost of living.

Again, horse manure isn't the issue; it's the act of railing against it over and over again that is. Having a life-altering experience can be awful. Perseverating on how awful it is and refusing to make any changes doesn't usually help. In fact, it leaves us with very few options for moving forward.

ACT and functional contextualism encourages us to ask these questions: *Is the way we are responding to the internal content of our experience helpful? Do our actions help us live the life we want? Does it move us forward in life? Does it improve our understanding of others' perspectives? Does it help?*

Spoiler alert: Most clients come to therapy because the answer is no.

The Function of Our Behaviors

Let's look at substance use. On internship, I worked in a hospital that had a residential substance use program. It was a 28-day program and every other week, I'd come in for an hour and give a little talk. Folks in the program would often lament that this was their second or third time. They'd talk about the long-term consequences of their drinking and would often end with a statement about how nothing would ever change if it hadn't already.

Given so many consequences to their actions, why couldn't they stop? We talked about it. I would draw out a functional analysis on a whiteboard with the group. We took a step back from the narrative that alcohol was bad and instead looked at how it was serving them. The answer: It helped them escape. While alcohol consumption and the behaviors surrounding it are the main focus of alcohol use disorder, alcohol itself is a by-product. People drink for a reason. This applies whether someone drinks socially, once per year, or an entire bottle in an evening. Alcohol may have different functions for different people, but there is always a reason for drinking it.

What is often missed in conversations about alcohol use disorder is that alcohol is really good at helping people escape. It works in the short term. It helps people numb pain, both physical and emotional. It helps them fall asleep. It helps them space out. It helps them feel anything other than what they are feeling at the moment. If we view alcohol use from this perspective, then our questions begin to shift from "Why can't they get their drinking under control?" to "What are they escaping by drinking?" That's why many residential programs have chronic pain and trauma services. If we take alcohol away and don't develop new tools for navigating their other symptoms, it is much more likely that people may relapse.

Exercise: What the Function?

Let's explore function. Consider the subject of work. On the lines below, write down some of the reasons that people may work overtime. What function does working overtime serve? When answering, don't just pull for "negative" reasons; list anything that comes to mind.

_____

_____

_____

_____

There are an infinite number of responses. People might work overtime to provide for their family (financial security), to avoid going home, because they enjoy the work, in response to impostor syndrome thoughts (*I'm not as good as everyone else, so I have to work harder or else they'll realize I don't know anything*), because they're afraid of saying no or setting boundaries, or because it's a social outlet. The list goes on. Two people in identical offices doing identical work could have wildly different functions for their behaviors.

Now let's do the same, but for the idea of *exercise*. How could exercise function for someone?

_____

_____

_____

_____

People might exercise to feel strong, in response to health-related fear, to improve cardiovascular endurance following a health event, to lose weight, in response to a self-conscious thought (*No one could ever love me how I am*), due to body dysmorphia, or to run around with their grandkids.

Helping Your Client Understand Patterns of Behavior

We can't always delete or erase thoughts. We can't always change a client's circumstances, and we certainly can't change their past. However, we can help them begin to move toward what matters to them no matter what their context is, both internally and externally. The path they take may not be what they had always imagined or hoped, but there will always be a path forward toward what matters.

Humans are more responsive to short-term, immediate reinforcers. This makes it hard to create long-term change. A functional analysis of a client's behavior can help us understand what is maintaining their behavior (praise from others, avoidance of pain or discomfort, immediate good feeling). It can also be the start to a client recognizing their own patterns. Our goal in ACT is to train clients in a functional understanding of their patterns so they can identify for themselves if something isn't working or if something is working in the short term but won't take them toward their goals in the long run. Then, we work together to build concrete tools for interrupting those unhelpful patterns. We'll review tools to facilitate this process in part III.

For now, the ACT inquiry process can start with a simple question: *How is that working for you?* The following dialogue shows a therapist beginning a functional analysis with a client:

CLIENT: I'm so tired of feeling this way. My friends keep inviting me to go on trips with them, and I keep having to say no. I just want to be normal.

THERAPIST: Panic attacks can really make our life smaller. I'm so sorry it's getting in the way of connecting with your friends. I know they're important to you. [*validates how client's fear of panic attacks is narrowing her behavioral repertoire; highlights client's value of connection*]

CLIENT: They are. I also just want to be free. To go wherever I want without having to research and plan and freak out over it.

THERAPIST: That sounds like a good goal to work toward: going out to dinner or lunch with a friend without any preparation beforehand. [*identifies a committed action*]

CLIENT: I just don't see how that's going to happen.

THERAPIST: Well, let's look at what you've tried so far. [*begins functional analysis*]

CLIENT: Everything! I have tried literally everything. Meditation, exercise, positive self-talk, only driving on side roads, planning routes to different locations beforehand, bringing a friend with me.

THERAPIST: Okay, and how have those worked? [*asks about how those behaviors functioned in the past*]

CLIENT: They all sucked.

THERAPIST: All of them? None have helped even a little?

> During a functional analysis, when clients say nothing has helped, this can be helpful for capturing the idea that many of their behaviors are useful in the short term even if the effects don't last.

CLIENT: Fine, so exercise helps me feel a little better. Going with a friend I trust makes it a little easier, but now I feel like that's not working as well anymore. Meditation helps when I'm not already worked up.

THERAPIST: Awesome. So you have some tools that help a little or help for a period of time, but none of them truly stop panic attacks or make the fear of having one go away? [*highlights that the client has tools that work to increase engagement in values but they simply are not one hundred percent effective and do not permanently erase panic from her life*]

CLIENT: Exactly. They don't work.

THERAPIST: What if that's the point? It seems to me that you've been trying really hard to manage your panic attacks. You've done a ton of reading, attempted to put a lot of these skills into practice, and panic attacks are still there. And it seems like your world is getting smaller. [*validates the client's hard work; shows that if there was a magic pill, the client would have found it by now*]

CLIENT: It is.

THERAPIST: What if avoidance isn't the answer? What if you could learn to move through these intense feelings and thoughts? [*shifts focus from symptom reduction (see chapter 4) to the possibility that the client can live her life without eliminating panic*]

Creating a Functional Analysis

One of my favorite things to do with a client is to create a *functional analysis*. A functional analysis allows us to break down a complex situation into trigger and response, watching closely for patterns that emerge.

For example, for a client with PTSD, I might start with their fear of having nightmares. Our first step is to identify the situation, trigger, thought, or emotion that first sets off the cycle; this is called the *antecedent*. The following dialogue shows a therapist discovering their client's antecedent:

Therapist: How has your sleep been this past week?

Client: Honestly, pretty terrible.

Therapist: I'm sorry to hear that. What's been going on? [*keeps the question broad in order to not accidentally steer or pull for a specific response*]

Client: I'm fine all day, but then when it starts to get dark out, I notice I get nervous.

Therapist: Okay, is this nervousness more of a thought or a sensation in your body?

> If the therapist had the goal of practicing acceptance or defusion, this could be a great point to lean into experiencing the feelings, but here, the goal is to break down what exactly the client is initially experiencing to begin a functional analysis.

Client: It's kind of both. I start worrying whether I'll have a nightmare tonight and then I get all tense.

> In this case, the antecedent the therapist is focusing on is the intrusive thought: *What if I have a nightmare tonight?* Next step is exploring exactly what happens next for the client, both internally and observably.

Therapist: And what happens after that?

Client: I start panicking. I just start thinking over and over how I'm so tired of this and I just want one night of good sleep. I had a big presentation yesterday at work, and I was so scared that I would be exhausted for it. Of course I was.

Therapist: So your mind jumps immediately into what-if thinking about the future?

> The therapist translates the client's experience into a behavior; in this case, the client is engaging in a cognitive behavior, meaning it happens in their mind instead of in their environment.

Client: Oh yeah, I feel like I get so wound up and the fear gets bigger and bigger the closer it gets to bedtime.

THERAPIST: What do you do when the fear gets bigger? [*asks questions to identify what the client does in response to thoughts or feelings*]

CLIENT: I just scroll on my phone. I honestly think I spend like four hours per night on TikTok.

> Now the therapist has a clear picture of a couple of these steps. The next step is to evaluate the function of these behaviors in the short term.

THERAPIST: Does scrolling on your phone help ease some of the fear? [*checks for short-term function*]

CLIENT: While I'm doing it, yeah, but I feel like it also keeps me awake for longer.

> Some clients will say no to this question. If that is the case, it may be useful to ask what happens during and immediately after they engage with these behaviors.

All we want to do here is establish that it makes sense that the client would engage in a behavior. Sometimes clients will tell you that it isn't helping in the short term at all. In this case, they may need some help understanding why that behavior persists. Shame is a big part of avoidance. Many clients express feeling shame, embarrassment, and guilt for engaging in behaviors they know aren't helping them in the long run but they continue to engage in. Walking the client through the "why" of their behavior can help to alleviate those heavy feelings. Because even if they don't like doing something, it makes sense to want to alleviate pain, escape discomfort, or avoid rejection or disappointment. And if it makes sense to you and the client, there can be space for a little more compassion. An action might only reinforce or provide an escape for a split second, but sometimes that's all we need to reinforce this pattern—kind of like when we eat past fullness because it tastes so good and then the moment we put the fork down, we feel a little ill and maybe angry at ourselves because "I know better!"

Let's return to the dialogue: The final step in this process is to highlight how it's working in the long term:

THERAPIST: Makes sense! So scrolling on your phone helps for a bit just to get through the night, but then once you stop the feelings come right back? [*summarizes while also highlighting that this is temporary*]

CLIENT: Honestly, I'm not even sure they ever go away. My brain is constantly running in the background.

THERAPIST: How is it helping with the nightmares? Have they gotten better over time, stayed the same, or gotten worse? [*explores long-term function*]

> The therapist may already know the answer to this, but it's helpful for the client to think about it and answer themselves. This is a skill they are building.

CLIENT: Gotten worse, if that's even possible. Sometimes I just stay up all night until I'm so exhausted I pass out. But even then, I'll have nightmares and feel like crap the next day.

The therapist in this dialogue highlights the main points, but it's the client's own words they are using. The client is the one acknowledging whether something is working or not. That's important because we aren't doing a functional analysis *on* them, we are doing one *with* them. Our goal is to train them to look at their own behavior in this way and notice patterns. This process will be discussed further in chapter 7, but I want to give you a taste of it here, as it's a foundational component of ACT.

At the end of the day, if we continue to come back to what the function of a behavior is, we will always be able to regroup, create clear goals for therapy, and choose the right ACT processes and skills to build up in our clients.

Exercise: Test Your Knowledge

Below are three brief client summaries. Read each one carefully and then respond to the prompts based on what you think the function of their behavior is. Take your time. At the end of the exercise, compare your responses with the answer key.

1. Sasha has been with her boyfriend, Jack, for three years. They met shortly after Sasha's mother passed away, and Jack was really there for her when she needed someone. She has pretty limited social support outside of her boyfriend, as her father lives in another state and has thrown himself into his work following his wife's death. Sasha also doesn't have many friends, as she spends all her time with her boyfriend. Over time, Jack has been less thoughtful and supportive. In fact, he regularly criticizes Sasha, often making jokes at her expense, both in private and in front of his friends, which embarrasses her. Sasha shares that she knows she's not good at many things but tries her best to make him happy, and yet, it never seems enough. Lately, he's been yelling at her, calling her names, and throwing household items in her direction. She emphasizes in session that he has never hit her. Sasha has come to therapy to work on herself so she can be a better partner to Jack and not disappoint him so much. They live together in the home that he purchased before they met. Jack makes more money than Sasha and often brings up how she should do more around the house because he covers more of the mortgage.

    a. Why does Sasha stay with her boyfriend?

    _____
    _____
    _____
    _____

b. What is reinforcing her for staying in the short term?

_____
_____
_____
_____

c. What would be the short-term consequences if she left?

_____
_____
_____
_____

2. Blake has been struggling at his new job. He's always been someone who completes tasks at the last possible moment, but this new job is so much more intense than internships he's had in the past that he's falling behind. He has come to therapy to work on strategies for procrastination and to prevent burnout. Blake feels as if he's constantly working and yet getting nothing done. When asked what he usually does during the day, Blake shares that he feels "all over the place" and that it is "hard to work on his upcoming project." Blake notes that his job pays well but has a steep learning curve. He finds himself spending a lot of time doing busy work instead of the actual harder work he needs to get done because he's worried he'll make a mistake. He tells you that everyone around him seems so competent, and he feels as if he's "drowning." Despite receiving only positive feedback from his boss, Blake is convinced that he will be fired when they view his work on this new project.

a. What is maintaining Blake's procrastination?

_____
_____
_____
_____

b. What is the function of his behavior?

_____
_____
_____
_____

c. What would he have to experience or come in contact with in order to complete his work in a timely manner?

_____
_____
_____
_____

3. Samuel has been feeling kind of empty lately. Since the pandemic, he's been working from home. He shares that his life feels meaningless. He notes that the days seem to blend together, as he gets up, eats breakfasts, showers, completes work, watches TV or plays video games, and then goes to bed only to repeat everything the next day. Samuel tells you that he can go days without leaving his apartment. He lives at home with his two cats. All of his coworkers live in different states and are much younger than him. He feels out of touch with everyone. Every week he tells himself he will get outside and go for a walk or call one of his friends, but he never does. He shares that he's worried about bothering others, even though they reach out to him, stating, "They probably don't want to talk to me anyway. They have busy lives." Samuel has come to therapy to "figure out" his life and find his purpose.

   a. What is the function of Samuel's isolation?

   _____
   _____
   _____
   _____

   b. What is maintaining it?

   _____
   _____
   _____
   _____

Now, let's turn to long-term consequences:

What do you expect will happen to 1) Sasha, 2) Blake and 3) Samuel if nothing changes?

   1. _____
   _____
   _____

2. _____

3. _____

What might be important to each of them that they'd want to move toward?

1. _____

2. _____

3. _____

How could their life be different if they moved in this direction?

1. _____

2. _____

3. _____

Answer Key

1. **Sasha**
    a. *Why does Sasha stay with her boyfriend?*
       Jack was "really there for her" when she needed someone after her mother died.
    b. *What is reinforcing her for staying in the short term?*
       Sasha loves Jack; she fears having no support; Jack provides financial security; he hasn't hit her; she blames herself for their problems.
    c. *What would be the short-term consequences if she left?*
       Sasha is burdened financially; she has limited social support; she receives more emotional and verbal abuse from Jack; she feels sad.

2. **Blake**
    a. *What is maintaining Blake's procrastination?*
       Blake waits until the last moment to complete tasks; he knows he's always gotten work done in the past; he avoids his tasks.
    b. *What is the function of his behavior?*
       Blake's procrastination allows him to avoid the unpleasant feeling associated with doing his tasks until the very last minute.
    c. *What would he have to experience or come in contact with in order to complete his work in a timely manner?*
       Blake worries that he'll make a mistake; he fears that everyone else is better than he is; he is a hard worker. He'll have to come in contact with these fears.

3. **Samuel**
    a. *What is the function of his isolation?*
       Isolation allows Samuel to avoid coming in contact with rejection from others.
    b. *What is maintaining it?*
       Samuel believes his friends "probably" do not want to talk to him; he fears that his friends are too busy for him; he feels life is meaningless.

What do you expect will happen to 1) Sasha, 2) Blake and 3) Samuel if nothing changes?

1. Jack probably ends up physically abusing Sasha; nothing changes in their relationship; she feels even more isolated and dependent on him.
2. Blake falls further behind and fails out of his internship or doesn't get a job offer from them.
3. Samuel loses further contact with his friends as they may stop reaching out. His depression likely worsens.

What might be important to each of them that they'd want to move toward?

1. This is unclear at the moment. Currently, Sasha's focus is on what's best for Jack.
2. Blake places importance on his job—and doing well at his job.
3. Friendship and connection are important to Samuel.

How could their life be different if they moved in this direction?

1. Sasha could build a support network of friends. She could find a partner who treats her well. She could prioritize herself and find things she loves to move toward.
2. Blake could get his work done in a timely manner. It may still be difficult, but it would leave more time for learning and improving.
3. Samuel would spend time with friends, go outside, and engage with things he enjoys more. He could create more meaning in his life.

One Goal of ACT: Don't Get Hooked!

When we look at ACT through a functional contextual lens, we can begin to see clear goals for therapy emerging. (Don't worry, we'll break this all down in later chapters.) To reiterate, this begins with a functional analysis. In this process, we are helping the client learn to understand what is driving their behavior. Behaviors can be both observable and cognitive, and we explore these patterns with clients in session. They will evaluate how a behavior functions in both the short term and long term, and they'll let us know whether it's working or not. Then we send them out into their real lives to observe.

I often describe the initial thoughts, feelings, memories, and physical sensations that clients want to avoid as *hooks*. Everyone has hooks. Unfortunately, we don't get to choose the ones we get. But we can learn not to bite them. Think about a client like a fish taking bait from a hook: When clients bite down, they can become hooked (engage in avoidance behaviors) and get taken off into a direction they wouldn't have chosen for themselves. They are no longer in control of what happens next. This experience of *notice hook* then *bite hook* can feel almost instantaneous. This default reaction to feel pain and try to make it go away is so automatic that it's extremely difficult to even separate the two as different actions. That's why a functional analysis can be helpful. While clients can't control if hooks show up, they can begin to learn strategies to pivot away from biting the hook and toward their values.

My goal at the beginning isn't to modify their response in any way. It's simply to notice. I always tell my clients, "We can't change what we can't see." So, their first job is to see the patterns that aren't working. Then we take a step back and look for similarities. Usually clients will tell me that they begin to notice so many more hooks and subsequent patterns of behavior that aren't serving them. From here, we break those patterns down. We identify what trigger or hook is showing up and the client's response. This can also lead to identifying actionable treatment goals. And then we work backward. We identify the ACT core processes they need to build up to increase their ability to notice these patterns, interrupt them, and engage in more values-aligned behaviors. That is the process of ACT in a nutshell. It is a fluid, flexible approach that has a clear direction: teaching clients to be open to their full experience, even painful stuff, in order to notice what is and is not working for them, so they can choose how they engage with the world and themselves. And in ACT, we hope that choice is values-based.

My hope in teaching you the functional contextual foundation of ACT is that it serves as your anchor. When you get stuck, lost, or defeated, you have something to reorient to. It also is a great practice for understanding your own behavior in session.

Exercise: What Are My Hooks?

It is worth taking time to evaluate your own hooks. Are you uncomfortable with silence and talk to avoid it? Do you rush through explanations when clients don't seem to understand? Do you abandon an exercise when it's "not working" the way you thought it would? There can be much knowledge gained from taking a moment to explore your own patterns in session. Here are some starting points to begin exploring:

What is one *observable* behavior you know you struggle with in session? This can be talking or staying silent, avoiding certain topics, rushing through when clients are expressing big emotions, and so forth.

_____

_____

_____

What are the thoughts, feelings, memories, urges, or sensations that show up in these moments right before you engage in the behavior?

_____

_____

_____

What happens to you in the short term? For example, this might be relief or avoidance of an uncomfortable experience.

_____

_____

_____

What happens in session in the short term? Specifically, think about how this behavior impacts therapist-client interactions, your next steps in the session, and how the client behaves or responds.

_____

_____

_____

What happens to you in the long term? Do these thoughts go away? Do these feelings get bigger?
___
___
___
___

What happens to your clients in the long term? Are there certain skills they don't learn? Do they tend to leave therapy? Do they come away with a belief that is incorrect?
___
___
___
___

What happens with your practice long term? Do you avoid certain populations? Do you feel more confident working with a specialized group? Do you take more or fewer trainings?
___
___
___
___

When you think of the type of therapist you want to be, what comes to mind? If your clients were to describe you, what would you want them to say?
___
___
___
___

What would a step in that direction look like?
___
___
___
___

The first step in any change is noticing what's happening. You have to understand what's not working in order to create a plan to fix it. Your clients must also understand what's not working, and be willing to make changes to how they approach their lives. The next chapter will explore how to get buy-in from your clients. How to help them understand what isn't working. How to increase their willingness to make changes. As you go through this book, I hope you keep function and context at the forefront of your mind.

Chapter Takeaways

- Functional contextualism is how something works (functions) in a given situation (context).
- ACT focuses on changing the response to thoughts, not the thoughts themselves.
- ACT acknowledges that living comes with some pain ("clean pain"). Our focus is to reduce suffering ("dirty pain"). Suffering comes from our attempts to try to control, escape, or delete "clean pain."
- Substance use is a common tool to decrease pain. It can be effective in the short term but often causes long-term problems. Sometimes this is the only tool our clients have to feel some relief.
- Hooks are the thoughts, memories, physical sensations, and feelings we don't like. When we bite the hook, we are engaging in an avoidance behavior. These behaviors can be observable or cognitive.

CHAPTER 2

THE PSYCHOLOGICAL FLEXIBILITY AGENDA

Now that you have a solid foundation in functional contextualism, let's dive into what ACT aims to target: *psychological flexibility*. As you learned in the introduction, ACT's primary goal is to increase psychological flexibility so that clients can be open to their full experience, even those unwanted thoughts, feelings, and sensations. Psychological flexibility allows our clients to more easily pause, tune into their values, and choose actions that serve them—even in the presence of pain.

This is in contrast to a *symptom-reduction agenda*. In fact, one of the hardest shifts for practitioners beginning ACT is moving away from this perspective. In symptom-reduction therapies, everything we are taught revolves around making "bad" symptoms go away—the assumption being that the only way to reduce suffering and improve well-being is to decrease experiences that don't feel great: negative thoughts, trauma memories, panic symptoms, and so on.

This leads to another problem: Clinicians are so committed to reducing suffering that we set up expectations that inevitably fall short. Sometimes this goes unnoticed by clients because they are developing skills and tools to move forward in life and their goals change naturally. Other times, however, they feed into a cycle of self-blame and low efficacy and hopelessness. I've had a number of clients come to see me after working with a different therapist. They mention how they felt like failures when they weren't getting better. How they would lie to their therapist because they didn't want to let them down or be seen as a "bad" or "problem" client. Or they took it as a self-failing. If their therapist said this would work, or maybe the skills even helped while they were in therapy but stopped working once therapy was discontinued, they took on the blame for therapy "not working."

The profound reality is this: Many of our clients come to therapy because their attempts to escape or reduce the pain they are feeling in their life actually creates more suffering. Furthermore, eliminating pain is not what we really notice on a day-to-day basis of transformation in our clients. This is why ACT promotes an agenda of psychological flexibility.

Psychological flexibility looks like the OCD client who still has intrusive thoughts and yet talks about how they know it's OCD now and doesn't listen to what the thoughts are saying. Or the client with panic disorder who can notice the panic symptoms and instead of being afraid, acknowledges that the symptoms are uncomfortable and engages in values-based behaviors anyway. Or the burned-out client with perfectionistic tendencies who pauses when her mind says she "should" do more and is able to step back from the moment, notice where that narrative is coming from, acknowledge that she doesn't want that story to lead her life anymore, and make a different decision. This ability to be flexible in our thinking and behaviors is at the core of ACT.

Stepping back from a symptom-reduction agenda doesn't mean we tell clients to suck it up or let them know they will always feel this way. It's all about setting up expectations for outcomes as well as highlighting our focus in ACT. So how we do that? With a very useful buy-in tool called *creative hopelessness*.

What Is Creative Hopelessness?

Creative hopelessness generally refers to the process of walking clients through experiences and exploring how their attempts to erase, delete, or avoid painful thoughts, feelings, memories, and physical sensations are not effective in the long run.

It also helps them to create space for new, more workable approaches to dealing with difficult experiences—in other words, it promotes psychological flexibility. The *creative* aspect derives from fostering openness to new, potentially more effective ways of relating to difficult thoughts and feelings. The *hopelessness* part refers to letting go of the hope that controlling or eliminating unwanted internal experiences will lead to a better life.

This is a collaborative process with the client. We use their own experiences and conclusions about their success to inform our plan of action moving forward. In a nutshell, the process entails three steps:

1. The therapist helps the client examine their history of attempts to control or avoid unwanted internal experiences.
2. Together, they explore how these attempts have worked in the short term and long term.
3. The client is guided to recognize that these strategies, while well-intentioned, have often led to more suffering or limitations.

Creative hopelessness is about creating space for new, more workable approaches to life's challenges. It's a foundational process that paves the way for the core ACT processes, which will be addressed in the next chapter.

Getting Buy-In for ACT

As good as creative hopelessness sounds, it can take some convincing before starting the process. That's because, frankly, therapy is hard. While it can also be enlightening or even a place of joy at times, it is difficult at its core. Terrifying, in fact. We ask clients every day to examine their deepest fears, sit with their strongest distresses, and approach their greatest discomforts with a stranger. Experiences they are scared we may judge them for. Thoughts and feelings that cause intense anxiety or shame. Sensations that feel as if they're dying.

And yet, we need to give clients a reason to not avoid. They already know it's not working. They wouldn't be coming to you otherwise. Unless, of course, it's mandated. Our job is not to tell them we can wave a magic wand and make life better. Nor is it to promise any specific outcome. Because we can't. It is to build enough trust and insight into the journey that they are willing to try it. An experiment. If they are coming to therapy and are willing to do exposure work, process trauma, or build new behaviors through letting go of security blankets, then we are responsible for ensuring they know what to expect.

Your approach, process, and even definition of ACT should be part of informed consent.* Remember that for clients who have either been to therapy before or have been to a medical provider in the past, reducing symptoms is their assumed focus of therapy. Without true informed consent, you can find yourself struggling down the road as you attempt to correct course when clients are frustrated that their intrusive thoughts aren't gone or that you can't guarantee their panic attacks will never return. By setting up appropriate expectations early, therapy has fewer bumps.

Here are three examples of how I explain ACT directly to my clients during informed consent:

> *In therapy, I primarily use a type of therapy called acceptance and commitment therapy, or ACT. ACT helps us look at the full picture of our behaviors. It teaches us to step back and notice the patterns that are serving us and those that aren't. Together we'll work to understand the thoughts, feelings, memories, urges, and physical sensations that show up and make it hard to engage in the life you want. Then we'll develop skills to get some space from those feelings so you can live a meaningful life—whatever that means to you. In ACT, we call these values.*

> *To me, therapy is all about looking at how we interact with the world and ourselves. My role is to help you get a clear picture of how you interact with others, how you move through the world, and what's going on inside your head, heart, and body. We work to engage with the present moment, focus on what is within our control, and take steps toward our values. This may include developing skills to pause and get space from difficult experiences or processing how you think about yourself and the world and how that's impacting how you react to it. The type of therapy I primarily use is called acceptance and commitment therapy, or ACT.*

---

* For a downloadable list of what to include in your therapeutic informed consent form, visit https://www.theacttherapist.com/ACTskillsmanual.

Oftentimes people come to therapy to escape from experiences that make them feel awful. It is very human of us. The trouble is, we aren't always in control of the feelings and thoughts that show up. I like focusing on what is within our control. To go beyond simply not feeling a certain way to understanding why we're reacting the way we are and developing skills to interrupt patterns that are no longer serving us. I like focusing on what is important to you. To what you want to be moving toward. Then we will look at how these past experiences are getting in the way of that and how you can learn new ways of responding to them. This way, even if life is really hard right now, you can still take steps toward the life you want to live instead of waiting for a feeling or thought to go away. The type of therapy I use is called acceptance and commitment therapy, or ACT.

Exercise: Getting Buy-In for ACT

Take a moment to consider how you would introduce ACT to your clients and write your statement. Write as if you are speaking to a real person, not defining a technique. What kind of language do your clients resonate with? How straightforward is your style? We'll continue to come back to this throughout the book as you learn more about ACT. You may find yourself wanting to highlight different aspects as you learn.

_____
_____
_____
_____
_____
_____
_____
_____
_____
_____
_____
_____
_____
_____
_____
_____

The Mind as a Threat-Detection System

Many clients come to me asking why their minds seem to be working against them. Why are they like this? Why can't they just let it go? To me, this is a great opportunity to change the way they relate to their mind and encourage some additional buy-in with clients. After I explain what ACT is, I often talk about how our mind is a threat-detection system. I will say something like this:

> *Our mind is designed to notice and anticipate threats. Our mind is not designed to create a meaningful life. It is designed to stay alive. Let's take a moment to think of our ancestors. Their concerns were immediate and grave, such as finding clean drinking water, building shelter, deciding what was safe to eat, and escaping predators both animal and human.*
>
> *Times have changed, but the way our mind operates has not. It's always scanning for danger and never stops trying to protect us. So even if the immediate present isn't fraught with life-altering decisions, the mind wanders. It travels to the past to try to squeeze out more lessons. It travels to the future to try to prevent or prepare for possible scenarios. Sometimes this feels like an endless loop of what-if scenarios. It's exhausting. It brings pain into the present moment.*
>
> *But remember, our mind isn't broken or out to get us. It simply operates on default, but since our environment has changed so drastically, it's not always useful anymore. Imagine that you used to live somewhere that was always cold. Your default was to always put your coat on before you left the house. But now you moved to a place with four seasons: Sometimes automatically putting on your coat is helpful, but other times, it's setting you up to be way too hot.*
>
> *At the end of the day, your mind isn't bad. It's doing its job. Your job is to decide whether to listen to it or not. We do that by looking at its function.*

This is where creative hopelessness comes into the therapy. We help our clients naturally come to the conclusion that we already know: It's not that they aren't trying hard enough; they simply are not able to control the future, change the past, or live a life completely void of pain. Despite their best efforts, the endless what-if scenarios they engage in take them out of the present moment but can never guarantee the future.

Our aim with clients is to help them learn to notice when their mind is time traveling, identify whether this is useful or not, and then develop strategies for interrupting that process so they can focus on making their present moment amazing. I often use this as a way of leading into a functional analysis to take a look at some of the moments when their mind time travels. A substantive part of the ACT process entails showing our clients how to go from being reactive to being intentional when their mind detects a real or perceived threat.

Going from Reactivity to Intentionality

"You may not always be able to control what pops up in your head or your body, but you can be intentional with how you respond." This is what I say to my clients when introducing them to ACT and leading them down the creative hopelessness process for the first time. This helps greatly with buy-in. You see, many clients are used to engaging in the world reactively. How they feel on the inside dictates how they engage with the world on the outside. With ACT, we are asking our clients to identify how they want to show up to the world and then simply choose how to behave, while at the same time having uncomfortable feelings. We are asking them to engage with more intentionality.

This comes up in conversations around anger and sadness. In depression work, *behavioral activation* is a helpful tool. The phrase "follow your feet" is often touted within this work—the idea being that even in the presence of sadness or depression you are able to take small steps toward the life you want to live. In ACT, we simply take that a step further by emphasizing values-based steps. In anger management and couples work, clients may struggle to differentiate between the feeling of anger and acting from anger. We as therapists are not telling people how to feel. In fact, we literally have no control over that. What we are working toward is one tiny pause.

In ACT, our goal is to create space, *a pause*, between what shows up inside us and how we respond to it. A pause is simply a moment in the present when we can choose a response. At the beginning, it may feel impossible. It may seem out of our control. Like we discussed in chapter 1, we might feel as if we're getting hooked and have no control over what happens next. We often attempt to make the hooks—the shiny pain points connected to our values—go away. But that is not within our control. We all have hooks. To care about something inevitably invites fear of losing it, being betrayed by it, or not living up to it. And so, to live a meaningful life, it must involve pain at times. But with practice, we can learn to notice and create space for the pain without compromising our values. Over time, we can begin to identify patterns of behavior. Covering all of these points at the outset with your client is key.

At first, our clients notice what isn't working in a kind of postmortem analysis. They may not be able to catch it in the moment, but they know afterward that they bit a hook. Later, and in possibly the most frustrating phase for clients, they will notice it happening in real time. And like those slow-motion moments when words leave our mouths just as we realize we should have definitely not said that thing, so too will they notice the pattern playing out in front of them.

Eventually, through your work together, clients begin to see the hooks, notice how and why they would usually bite it, and create a pause. Then they get to choose how they want to show up next. Sometimes clients still choose to bite the hook. Yet this time, given its intentionality, it doesn't lead to as much suffering. Instead, it comes with more settling in and acceptance of the consequences of their actions. Other times, they know what they want to do but just aren't sure how to accomplish it. You will work on this with them in therapy. There will also be moments when they are able to pivot away from the hook and choose to engage in an action that is consistent with their values.

We can't choose our hooks. We can't decide when they show up or how shiny and enticing they will be. We can work to notice patterns, develop skills to create a pause, and then pivot toward our values. That is what this work is about. That is the hope we give our clients. And it is entirely in their control.

Validating the Client's Experience

Another aspect of the creative hopelessness process is to validate a client's experience. Acknowledge that it makes sense why a client feels the way they do. Many clients will talk about feeling broken or angry toward themselves for not being able to make the changes they know can make a difference in their lives. It can be a frustrating and shameful experience. Helping to acknowledge both their feelings and how normal their experience is matters. It helps to bridge the gap between not dismissing or undermining their experience while also acknowledging what needs to change. It creates hope.

Not to mention, clients often fear judgment. I've had clients shamefully admit when they haven't done their homework. Or share that they did an assignment only so they didn't have to lie to me. Many want to be seen as a "good client." They want you to like them and be proud of them—which makes sense. The patterns clients experience in their own lives are often replicated in the therapy space. Validating their experience helps with this. It allows space for a discussion about what is within their control and what isn't.

It's also a great training opportunity for understanding the function of behaviors. Just because behaviors hurt us doesn't mean they don't make sense. They do. That's why I always include clients in a functional analysis instead of simply telling them about their behavior. This way, they receive the validation of their experience from me, but they also get the experience of exploring their behavior and coming to that conclusion on their own. People tend to believe things they decide themselves rather than those they hear during lectures. Let clients use their own language to describe their experience. Follow along and ask clarifying questions as needed to explore short-term and long-term functioning. And remember that all behavior makes sense. Even if it makes us feel awful.

Short-Term Versus Long-Term Analysis

As we lead into a functional analysis, one of the important components of getting clients on board for therapy is understanding how their behavior operates in the short term versus the long term. Let's look at another therapist-client dialogue that illustrates this discussion:

THERAPIST: Let's break down what happens when you want to take lead on a project. What is the first thing you experience?

CLIENT: My mind just starts racing and telling me all the ways I'm going to mess up.

THERAPIST: Okay, so it's trying to protect you from making a mistake or embarrassing yourself. Are there any feelings or sensations that you experience with the racing thoughts, or is it mostly in your head? [*highlights the function of the behavior; helps set the stage for the idea that the mind is trying to be helpful even if it isn't; prompts the client to identify thoughts, feelings, and sensations*]

CLIENT: No, I start feeling panicky, like my heart is racing and I feel like I'm going to faint. It's awful.

THERAPIST: That sounds awful. What would I see you doing next? [*validates and then identifies the next step*]

CLIENT: Nothing. I literally just don't do anything and often go to the bathroom to calm down.

THERAPIST: Does that work? [*begins to explore function*]

CLIENT: Eventually. But I feel so exhausted afterward. Sometimes I start crying and then I have to hide that I've been crying and it's super embarrassing.

THERAPIST: Okay, and just to clarify—by "literally don't do anything," do you mean that you don't speak up or ask to take the lead?

CLIENT: Yeah. And then my coworker Matt gets it, which is so frustrating because he's terrible to work with and way too arrogant.

THERAPIST: Okay, so what I'm hearing is that when you get the opportunity to lead a team, it brings up a lot of loud thoughts that turn into uncomfortable physical sensations, and in response, you decline the opportunity. It seems like in the short term this is mostly working for you in that those thoughts and feelings go away. Does that sound right? [*summarizes through identifying each antecedent-response; highlights that this pattern works to alleviate more distress in the short term—client's default behaviors are being reinforced*]

CLIENT: I mean, I feel terrible afterward, but like exhausted and mad at myself, not panic-attack level.

THERAPIST: Okay, fair. So in the immediate short term the panic goes away, but you still feel exhausted. And then a little after that you feel mad at yourself and frustrated that Matt got the position. [*breaks down step-by-step what client is experiencing*]

CLIENT: Exactly! I hate it. Why can't I just stop?

THERAPIST: Well, it goes back to what we were talking about before. Your mind is trying to protect you from rejection and embarrassment. It's acting as though not doing a good job on a project is equivalent to being chased by a lion. So it's trying to help you. It's just really bad at it.

CLIENT: No kidding.

THERAPIST: And from what you've told me, listening to your mind and escaping the situation does help decrease that immediate panic, but even then, you feel terrible. So it's really not doing a great job overall.

CLIENT: I think my mind is broken.

THERAPIST: [*laughs in sympathy with client*] I don't think it's broken. I think it's simply really, *really* good at avoiding rejection and all the feelings that come along with it. The problem is, that doesn't really help you. It doesn't seem like avoiding these situations is really making your life better. [*validates client's experience; highlights that by listening to the threat-detection system in their mind, the client cannot move toward their values and doesn't really feel any better*]

CLIENT: No, it's for sure making it worse.

THERAPIST: And I know you've been trying so hard to manage panic and social anxiety. But the more you avoid, it doesn't seem to make it any easier. [*highlights that this strategy is not effective in the long term*]

CLIENT: It honestly just gets worse.

THERAPIST: Okay, so is it fair to say that avoiding these uncomfortable sensations and thoughts has worked a little bit in the short term, but in the long term, it's keeping you from progressing in your career in the way you'd like and isn't really making you feel good overall anyway?

CLIENT: One hundred percent.

THERAPIST: What if avoiding it isn't the answer? It's clearly not working, and I can tell you've been trying hard. What if the way you move forward toward becoming the type of professional you want to be is learning how to come in contact with that panic? Even when your mind is freaking out that it's a lion. [*introduces creative hopelessness*]

CLIENT: Can't you just make it go away?

THERAPIST: I wish. But honestly, there would just be some new worry that takes its place. Your mind is going to continue to default to trying to protect you. Removing the feeling doesn't change that.

CLIENT: I know, I just hate it.

THERAPIST: Fair, you definitely don't have to like it. But we can run it like an experiment. You know what to expect when you do what you've been doing. Let's try something different and see what happens. Are you willing to give it a shot? [*determines client's willingness*]

CLIENT: Sure.

Let's break down what happened in this exchange. The therapist identified one experience the client is struggling with and broke it down into a functional analysis. It starts with the scenario, then what internal experience showed up, and how the client reacted in the short term and long term. This helped the client realize that even if their avoidance helps reduce panic in the short term, it's getting in the way of a much more important goal in the long term: their professional development. The end result is a client more willing to learn how to navigate their panic and face potential rejection in order to take steps toward what matters to them. Sometimes I will draw this out with a client on a whiteboard. I'll go over what that looks like in chapter 8. But you can also do this simply through talking.

Notice too that the therapist didn't tell the client what they were thinking or feeling—the therapist *asked*. The client used their experience to lead the functional analysis with guidance from the therapist. Next, they looked at short-term impact, both the immediate impact and the shorter-term but not-as-instantaneous response. Finally, they explored the long-term impact, with the therapist again letting the client share their experience. The therapist highlighted that the strategy of avoidance or trying not to feel a certain way not only wasn't going away in the long term, but was also getting in the way of the client's professional goals.

And finally, the question of willingness. In this script, the therapist framed the buy-in as an experiment. This makes it feel low-stakes. It's a reminder to the client that they can always go back to the way things were if it's too much. Highlighting that it's a choice they can back out of at any time can help increase willingness because it doesn't feel like such a large leap of faith. These willingness questions are genuine. Clients don't have to believe it'll work. They just have to be *willing* to try something different for a period of time. That's all. Your job is to build up those skills, encourage your clients, and help them notice the outcomes both in the short term and long term. Willingness is an incredibly important part of ACT and will be discussed further in chapter 6.

Metaphors to Use for Creative Hopelessness

Metaphors play a crucial role in ACT, serving as a powerful tool to convey complex concepts in an accessible, memorable way. They are particularly helpful when a client tends to overthink, needs help engaging with their emotions, or struggles with understanding abstract ideas. Metaphors facilitate cognitive defusion, promote psychological flexibility, and help clients grasp the often counterintuitive approach of accepting rather than struggling against difficult thoughts and feelings—all core processes of ACT.

Later in this book, we'll go through an entire chapter on metaphors. You'll be able to use your client's experience to come up with metaphors on the fly that relate directly to their interests or background. But in the meantime, it's worth learning some metaphors that are often used for creative hopelessness. Some of the following metaphors were created by others, and others are favorites I've created or modified to use with my clients.

Squeezing a Lemon

This metaphor is a favorite of mine because it's so simple. When clients are getting stuck in a mental loop, I often use the lemon analogy to highlight the workability of their cognitive behavior:

When we get stuck in our mind analyzing, planning, reviewing, reflecting, and generally overthinking, I like to think of lemons. Specifically, juicing them. A lemon only has so much juice to squeeze. Imagine you have a lemon in your hand and you're squeezing it. After a certain point, you can keep squeezing, but no more juice will come out. At first, going over something may be useful (you get juice!) but after a while, it's no longer serving you (no more juice and a cramped hand!).

I then ask a client if they want to "put down the lemon" and focus on something else. (They aren't actually holding a lemon, but they get the gist.) Once we've discussed this, I can ask a client at any point, "Are you still squeezing the lemon?" or "Is there any more juice in that lemon?" and clients are easily able to recognize that they are engaging in a behavior that isn't serving them anymore. Then they can "put down" the metaphorical lemon and we can refocus on another task that may serve them better.

The Person in the Hole Metaphor

This is a great metaphor for exploring the futility of putting more effort into the wrong thing (Hayes et al., 1999). Clients often think the answer is "try harder." When in reality, we want our clients to recognize that what they're doing isn't helping, and they should instead pivot to an approach that will. Here's how you might introduce this metaphor:

Imagine you're walking through the forest and suddenly you fall through the leaves and into a large hole. At first, you attempt to climb or jump out, but it's too tall and the walls are too smooth. In a panic, you see a shovel leaning against the side of the hole and begin to dig. Every time your mind tells you that you're stuck or you feel afraid, you dig. You dig wider and deeper until your arms ache and sweat pours from your face. And yet, you're not any closer to getting out of the hole.

This is how avoidance works. When we feel scared, uncomfortable, or in pain, we react to escape from that pain. Just like the person in the hole digging. And yet, the avoidance only lets you escape for a moment. But shoveling helps you feel useful. It makes you think you're being productive and solving the problem. But you're still just as stuck. Plus, tired and sore. And even worse, after a while, the feelings come back. Sometimes with friends. Or sometimes even bigger than before. The answer is to pause, learn to work with the pain, and pivot toward a different solution—instead of continuing to do the same thing over and over again.

Name Your Mind

Naming your own mind is a common defusion exercise. The idea is if we give our mind a name, like Barbara, it helps to externalize the intrusive thoughts and feelings that seem to be working against us. It makes it easier for your clients to defuse from those thoughts by interacting with "Barbara." Plus, it creates a shorthand for identifying your client's defaults: "When 'Barbara' says that, what do you usually do next?" A therapist might introduce "Barbara" like this:

> *Let's try an experiment. I'd like you to give a name to the voice in your head. Whatever name comes to mind that resonates with that voice, as long as it's not the name of someone in your life. Barbara? Okay, awesome! Now I want you to think of Barbara as misguided but well-intentioned. She's trying to keep you safe and wants to be a faithful companion. Possibly has been around for years or even decades. But unfortunately, Barbara is simply not very skilled. She isn't helping you create the life you want, and she oftentimes gives you terrible advice. So when she pops up, you can say, "Barbara, thanks for trying to help, but I'm going to try something different." or "Barbara, I hear you, but I don't need help with this." Do you think you can try that this week?*

Mental Lion Versus Real Lion

At the beginning of this chapter, we talked about the mind as a threat-detection system. One of the ways I introduce this idea is through lions. The purpose of this metaphor is to highlight to clients how our mind reacts to imagined scenarios as if they are real threats, which isn't very helpful:

> *I've mentioned before that our mind is a threat-detection system, and its sole focus is on keeping us alive—which is great in some scenarios. For example, you're alive today because your ancestors were probably really great at noticing threats. If they heard rustling sounds in the grass and their mind said, "Maybe it's a lion," they took that seriously and lived to tell the tale. The problem is when we aren't confronted with dangers like real lions, our mind goes looking for the metaphorical mental ones.*
>
> *And unfortunately, metaphorical lions can be anywhere: in the past, in the future, in an alternate timeline. Sometimes it's hard for your mind to distinguish from a real lion right in front of you and a metaphorical lion in your head. So every time a what-if scenario pops up, you try to avoid or escape it. But unlike real lions, metaphorical lions follow us everywhere we go. Trying to escape them is a losing battle. Instead of constantly fighting off metaphorical lions, maybe there's a different way you can interact with your mind to spend more time in the present enjoying your life.*

Chapter Takeaways

- Our goal in ACT is to set appropriate expectations and refrain from implying that we will remove all the client's unwanted feelings or thoughts. Be sure to include an explanation of ACT as part of informed consent.

- Be sure to get buy-in for the work you are going to do. It sets a shared reality from which your client can build.

- Creative hopelessness is a process by which a client comes to the realization that they cannot permanently erase painful experiences. Instead, you create buy-in to help them set aside their symptom-reduction agenda and be willing to try something different (ACT).

- Creative hopelessness is a collaborative process between you and your client. You want them to come to the conclusion on their own through exploring their patterns of behavior and both the short-term and long-term impact.

CHAPTER 3
CORE PROCESSES IN ACT

Suffering is the reason our clients come to us for help. With ACT, we aren't promising to eliminate pain or even the thoughts that contribute to pain. Rather, we are providing clients with strategies and tools to respond to their suffering in more effective ways. In this chapter, we'll look at six of the most common problems clients present with: dissociation from present moment, lack of clarity or connection with values, reactivity, self-as-content, cognitive fusion, and experiential avoidance. These experiences represent the inverse of the six core processes of ACT that make up psychological flexibility. We represent this inverse in a diagram called the *inflexahex*. Then we'll review the six core processes—present-moment awareness, values, committed actions, self-as-context, cognitive defusion, and acceptance—that can transform their relationship to pain. We often show the six core processes in a *hexaflex* diagram. The hexaflex and inflexahex are a perfect mirror of each other, demonstrating the common ways we suffer and the processes that help us respond differently to our pain.

Psychological Inflexibility: A Great Way to Prolong Suffering

ACT sees psychological inflexibility at the root of a lot of suffering. The following image shows a quick rundown of what your clients might be struggling with. Then we'll look at the core ways ACT addresses those issues.

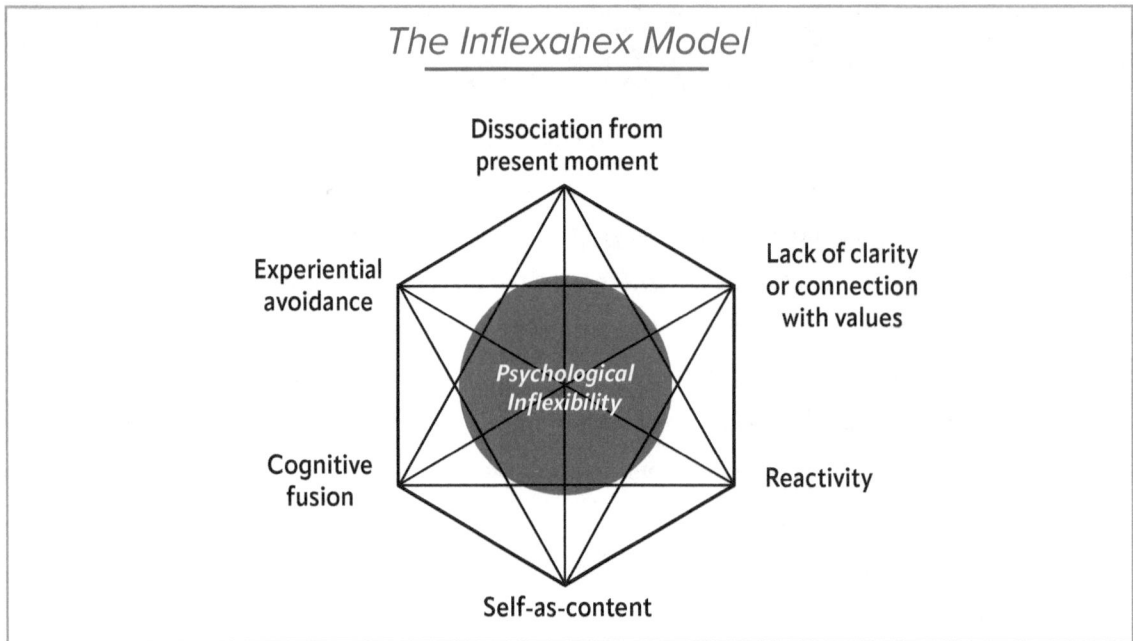

Dissociation from Present Moment

I like to think of this anti-core process as the *time traveler*. Our default in times of relative peace or neutrality is to time hop to the past or the future. Essentially, from a survival perspective, it is not useful to stay present when there is no crisis. So our mind tends to go to the past to reflect on experiences and learn from them in order not to repeat past mistakes. Conversely, it can also fast-forward to an infinite number of potential what-if scenarios in order to reduce uncertainty and prepare for anything. In either way, we tend to dissociate from the present. Our mind is here, but it is muted to our senses in some way.

Basically, our mind has a lot of readily accessible options for nope-ing out of the present. In fact, these are our defaults. They aren't bad, per se, but it can be problematic when we aren't in control of where our attention goes. Not to mention we miss cues. Time traveling makes it harder to connect with our values and enjoy our life. Because life only happens in the present.

The following are some indications that your client may struggle with dissociation from the present moment:

- Feel very disconnected from their life and the people in their life
- Tend to engage in a lot of cognitive behaviors, such as analyzing, planning, and ruminating

As an intervention, you may target the present moment awareness core process. These clients may benefit from mindfulness practices (see chapters 10 and 11), grounding exercises (see chapter 11), and defusion strategies (see chapter 9).

Lack of Clarity or Connection with Values

In ACT, we view values as the north star or compass we use to guide our behavior. There are many ways a client can struggle with their values. Clients who don't know what their values are may feel lost or stuck in their life without any clear direction. Sometimes a client may feel pressure from their family, culture, faith, or community to prioritize other qualities, characteristics, or concepts. These don't necessarily have to be in direct contrast to their true values, but they may serve as competition, taking away from the time or energy needed to move toward what matters to them. Other clients may simply feel disconnected from their values. They may have struggled to achieve certain goals that relate to their values, or they feel that where they are in their life is a place they can't possibly move from—in this instance, they may not even try to move in the direction of what matters to them.

The following are some indications that your client may struggle with a lack of clarity or connection with values:

- Have difficulty setting goals
- Set goals that lack meaning
- Are caught between what they want and what they have been told they "should" want based on their family, culture, community, faith, and the like

These clients would benefit from values clarification and self-as-context work (see later in this chapter).

Reactivity

If a client is operating on autopilot and engaging in a lot of experiential avoidance, chances are that they are not engaging in committed actions. In fact, they may be doing the direct opposite of values-based behaviors. Clients who struggle in this way may tend to respond impulsively or without thought in the moment. Their actions are guided by a desire to avoid uncomfortable feelings and seek immediate reward. A client who is reactive will engage in actions that are not helpful for creating a meaningful life, and furthermore, may lack direction or purpose. Essentially, they are focused on the short-term outcome of avoiding pain rather than the long-term outcome of engagement with their values. These clients are often aware that how they are living isn't working, but they are unsure of how to change or in what direction to move. If this is the case, working with clients to identify their values, and then working on functional analysis to identify fused content and patterns of experiential avoidance, may be a good starting point.

The following are some indications that your client may struggle with reactivity:

- Feel very stuck and frustrated that they are not making progress toward their goals
- Report a cyclical pattern of motivation and intense progress followed by difficulty to maintain changes
- Have difficulty articulating what is important to them and may seem to contradict themselves at times

These clients may benefit from functional analysis (see chapter 7), assignments geared toward noticing patterns of avoidance (see chapter 7), in-session work on values clarification, and goals that take small steps toward what is meaningful to them (see chapter 11).

Self-as-Content

Instead of viewing ourselves as continuous observers of our experiences, with *self-as-content*, we are tightly bound to the roles or labels to which we ascribe. This can limit our ability to engage in perspective taking and, therefore, empathy. It also makes it harder to understand the nuance of context. How we show up to the world changes based on the context we are in. If we hold onto our identities too tightly, we may not be as flexible.

To be clear, there is nothing wrong with associating with labels. Most people have many roles they feel connected to. Perhaps we see ourselves as parents, or siblings, or therapists. Problems arise when we hold so tightly to these labels as our whole identity that we are unable to move through the world in the absence of them. Parents often experience this when their children leave home. Many older adults experience this as they enter retirement, particularly if their occupation was a main part of their identity. When we use our role to understand how to move through the world or what rules to follow, we can struggle greatly in the absence of or change to that role.

Similarly, we face this in therapy when clients overidentify with a diagnostic label. It is not that the label is incorrect or that we want them to throw the label out, but rather, they would ideally take a step back and recognize that that role or label is only one aspect of who they are.

The following are some indications that your client may struggle with self-as-content:

- Going through a change to their main role or identity and struggling to adjust (retirement, transitioning into parenthood, have become empty nesters, laid off from their job)
- Describe having no purpose in life now or being resistant to change because they don't know who they would be or what they would do with their life if they didn't have access to this role

These clients would benefit from values clarification (see later in this chapter), perspective taking and self-as-context exercises (see later in this chapter), and defusion practices (see chapter 9).

Cognitive Fusion

Fusion is the process of combining, attaching, or otherwise melding together. In ACT, we fuse together thoughts with reality. *Cognitive fusion* is the act of becoming so enmeshed with a thought that we believe it to be literally true. It becomes our reality. Our mind might jump to more extreme versions of this, like hallucinations, delusions, or flashbacks. And yet, we become fused with thoughts all the time.

Here is an example of some common negative thoughts:

- *I'm ugly.*
- *No one could ever love me.*
- *Nothing will ever change.*
- *I'm lazy.*
- *I can't do anything right.*
- *No one cares about me.*
- *Life isn't worth living.*
- *I deserve this.*
- *This is my fault.*
- *I'm having a heart attack.*
- *Something is wrong.*
- *It's not good enough.*

While not a catch-all, I often listen for the "shoulds" in my clients' language. Many of these negative self-talk thoughts are followed by how they "should" act or what they "should" be able to do. Anytime I hear a "should" I want to pluck it from my client's mind, crumple it up like a piece of paper, and throw it in the garbage. They are useless—the "shoulds" that is, not my clients. My clients are awesome.

In response to thoughts like those in the previous list, our clients' options for what to do next are quite limited. Even more frustrating? These options are often not aligned with their values.

The following are some indications that your client may struggle with cognitive fusion:

- Have thoughts they have struggled with since childhood or adolescence
- Feel hopeless or helpless that anything will change

These clients may benefit from education on the mind as a threat-detection system (see chapter 2), defusion skills (see later in this chapter), present-moment awareness and self-as-context exercises (see later in this chapter), and self-compassion.

Experiential Avoidance

Experiential avoidance is the unwillingness to come in contact with the full experience of our thoughts, feelings, memories, and sensations. In doing so, a client will resist or avoid something painful in the present moment. They may try to distract, escape, erase, or dissociate from their experience instead of coming in contact with it. Anything can be an avoidance behavior, so your task is to determine the function of that behavior in order to discern if it is an avoidance behavior. Remember that it all comes down to the context.

When we spend all of our time engaging in experiential avoidance, not only is it not effective in the long term because we can't actually permanently erase or avoid painful experiences, but it also uses up all of our attention and energy toward that aim. We then end up not having much opportunity to engage with what else is happening in the moment or to move toward our values. Essentially, we are prioritizing the short-term reward of moving away from these painful experiences at the expense of our long-term mental health. When we engage in experiential avoidance, we are negotiating to temporarily find relief from pain in exchange for long-term suffering. This process is often very automatic. It can feel like an instantaneous default reaction.

Most clients come to therapy because even if they cannot pinpoint why what they are doing isn't working, they are aware that it's not helpful.

The following are some indications that your client may struggle with experiential avoidance:

- Engage in short-term behaviors that either distract them, attempt to change their feeling, or completely escape feeling (television, eating habits, overworking, exercise, drugs, alcohol, social isolation)
- Are aware that their behaviors aren't helpful

These clients may benefit from doing a functional analysis and tracking patterns of experiential avoidance, especially highlighting short-term versus long-term impact.

Psychological Flexibility: A Great Way to Manage Suffering

Fortunately, each of the struggles we've just covered has an ACT counterpart designed to *decrease* suffering. These are acceptance, cognitive defusion, present-moment awareness, self-as-context, values, and committed actions, which are all components of *psychological flexibility*. The following chart illustrates each of these components in relation to their counterpart, *psychological inflexibility*.

Psychological Inflexibility *Behaviors that Promote Suffering*	Psychological Flexibility *Tools that Promote Healing*
Experiential avoidance	Acceptance
Cognitive fusion	Cognitive defusion
Dissociation from present moment	Present-moment awareness
Self-as-content	Self-as-context
Lack of clarity or connection with values	Values
Reactivity	Committed actions

We can also look at the following hexaflex diagram to better conceptualize how these six core processes interact to improve psychological flexibility. The cool thing about the hexaflex is that even if a client only increases or improves skills in one core process, it impacts the whole model, thus increasing psychological flexibility. Keep this in mind as you are working with clients. There is no starting point for ACT in terms of the core processes. Your goal is to identify which core process a client could benefit from growth and work from there. We can use the hexaflex to explore treatment planning and the inverse of psychological flexibility, the inflexahex, for case conceptualization.

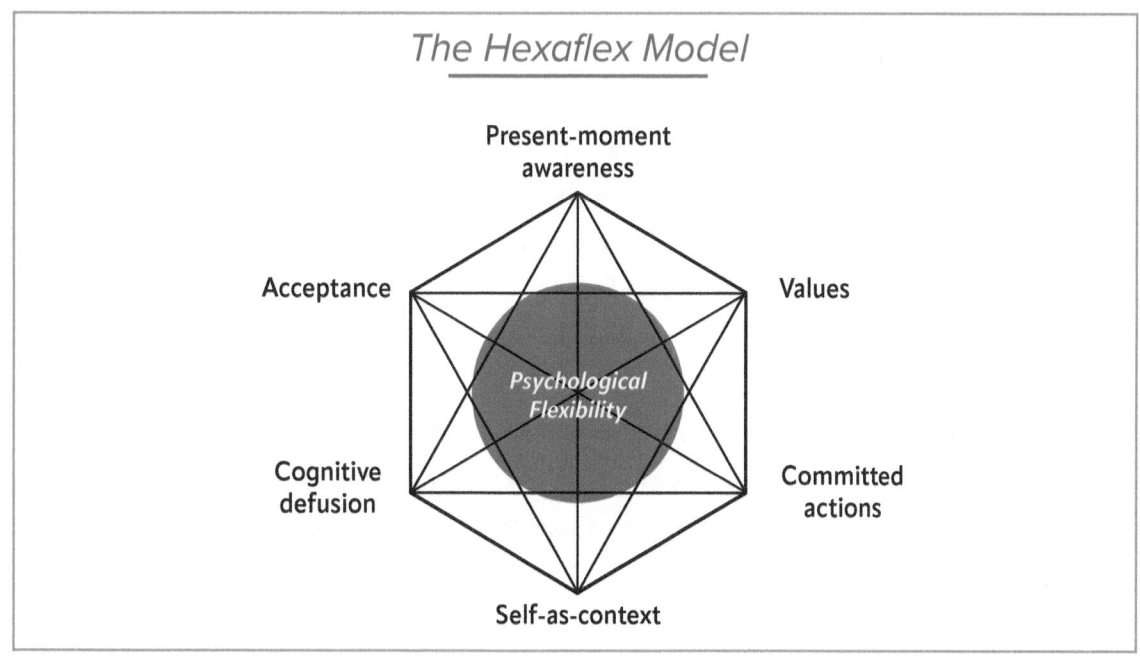

There is one thing to keep in mind as you are developing your approach and style with ACT. It is very easy to default to a set way of "doing ACT." Maybe you guide clients through a workbook or always start with values identification. Regardless of protocols and the order of operations you create, you must remain flexible. If you are approaching every client in the exact same way, you are not responding to the context. Every person is different and every struggle is unique. Take time to think through what each specific client needs in this specific moment.

One way I like to combat getting too rigid in my practice is finding new ways to introduce or describe processes or skills. There are certain terms, concepts, and exercises I tend to do with 90 percent of my clients. If I'm starting to feel stagnant, I will challenge myself to adjust how I introduce a concept to a client. This forces me to step back, think about the function of what we are doing in session, and approach our work together in the present moment. In this way, I am practicing psychological flexibility in my work.

Other ways to incorporate flexibility into your practice is challenging yourself to create metaphors specific to each client. We will cover how to do this in chapter 9. If you have the opportunity to hold varying session lengths, you can also think through what a 60-minute versus 30-minute session on the same topic would look like. However you approach it, remember to be sensitive to the context. Challenge yourself to be present to the person or persons sitting across from you in the therapy room (or screen). The more you can show up to the moment, the more opportunities to respond there are.

Now let's look at the six core processes of ACT shown on the hexaflex model.

Acceptance

I like to think of *acceptance*—a somewhat controversial word even among ACT practitioners—as an openness and willingness to come in contact with our full experience. We all have internal experiences we wish we didn't. Thoughts, feelings, memories, physical sensations, and urges can be beautiful and awe-inspiring or they might be straight-up terrifying. Usually they're somewhere in between. People come to therapy because of these painful internal experiences. They want to make the pain go away.

Yet, that's not always possible. Our attempts to try to not feel, think, or remember can lead to more suffering. We end up piling onto the misery. So in ACT, we help guide clients through allowing what they are already feeling to exist. They don't have to be happy about it. They don't have to think differently about it. They don't have to forgive, reconcile, or let go. We simply ask them to acknowledge that it's here. So then we can talk about what we're going to do now that it's here.

Acceptance or willingness can also be a yes or no question. As in, "Are you willing to come in contact with this right now in the service of your values?" No is a perfectly valid answer to this question. The work we do in therapy is hard. Clients share pains and secrets with us that they have not told anyone before. Or they are bravely telling you something after someone else has already dismissed them. Informed consent for therapy means creating space for *no*. Acknowledging that it is an insightful and intentional answer at times.

As you begin to approach acceptance with clients, it can be easy for many of your discussions to feel rhetorical—especially as you set up creative hopelessness with the intention of highlighting how the work you are doing is the obvious next step (see chapter 7). Please hold space for what you are asking of your clients. Create the kind of environment where they feel safe to say, "I don't want to go there right now." One straightforward way to do this is to add on "And no is a perfectly acceptable answer" when you ask them a question that feels rhetorical. Some of your clients may not have known that was an option.

Okay, now that those general basics are out of the way, how and where does the acceptance core process show up? Everywhere!

When we are helping our clients move toward acceptance, it is because they are typically struggling with experiential avoidance, an unwillingness to come in contact with their full experience. As a result, they resist or avoid painful thoughts, feelings, and sensations. As I mentioned previously, acceptance does not mean enjoying, liking, or even being okay with our full experience. It is simply acknowledging that it is here. This gives us the space to then decide how we want to respond to it.

When working with the process of acceptance, creative hopelessness is really important. Also important—I'd venture *necessary*—at the beginning of therapy is engaging in a functional analysis with your client to help them explore and come to the conclusion that their attempts to avoid or escape their pain may provide temporary relief but comes at a long-term cost (see chapter 7). If your client is still in a state of believing that there is a way to ensure they never experience pain, then why would they ever be interested in learning to create space for that pain and allowing it to simply exist? They wouldn't.

So how do we begin to introduce acceptance into our work with clients? The following dialogue shows a therapist discussing willingness and acceptance: (This dialogue uses the tips introduced in chapter 2 as well as the tools you will learn in part III.)

CLIENT: So what you're telling me is I just have to suck it up because these thoughts are always going to be there?

THERAPIST: No. Sucking it up sounds absolutely awful. Our goal is really just a pivot. You have tried basically everything to try to stop the intrusive thoughts and images from popping into your head. And from what you've said, the thoughts that aren't around as often anymore did not really stop because of anything you did—it's almost as if your mind just decided it was done with that thought for now, does that sound about right? [*sets up creative hopelessness; highlights efforts client has tried that have not resulted in long-term impact*]

CLIENT: Yeah, I feel like I have to hit an absolute breaking point for my mind to say, "Just kidding, I don't care about this anymore."

THERAPIST: [*laughs a little with client*] Exactly, your mind is going to do whatever it wants and change its mind on a whim—which does suck. So let's take the stance for now that we don't get to control when the intrusive thoughts show up. And it's probably fair to say they are never going to be benign things you don't care about because your intrusive thoughts are always going to be tied to things that really matter to you. [*takes an experiment approach to buy-in; "Let's take this stance for now" emphasizes the client can always go back to doing what they have been*]

CLIENT: Which is just the absolute worst.

THERAPIST: Agreed. But if that's the conclusion and you find that engaging in compulsions, avoiding certain situations, and ruminating on the thoughts doesn't make it better, then we have to come up with a new plan. Are you open to trying something different? [*asks about client's willingness; begins acceptance process*]

CLIENT: At this point, I'm willing to try anything.

THERAPIST: Right now your thoughts feel like they are consuming every waking moment you have like blinders that narrow your vision only to them. [*holds her palm up in front of her eyes to represent the thoughts and how the client is engaging with them*] And we've established that those thoughts are going to be there sometimes. So what if we practice [*lowers hands to her lap*] walking through the world with those thoughts and learning to not engage in battle with them? [*begins defusion exercise*]

CLIENT: That would be amazing, but how do I do that?

THERAPIST: [*describes exposure work, what to expect, and what the first steps would look like*] Would you be willing to give it a try?

CLIENT: Yes.

More than any other ACT process, acceptance is an answer to a question. It is answering yes over and over again, moment by moment, to the question "Are you willing to come in contact with this in the service of your values?" The second part of that question is really important. We are not asking clients to come in contact with pain for fun. We are asking them to come in contact with their full experience so they can more easily notice their patterns and what works and doesn't work for them. We are exchanging the illusion of control that comes with experiential avoidance for actual control over the response they have to pain.

The ultimate goal is to notice what they are experiencing and then respond to that with a behavior that is consistent with their values. For the client in the previous dialogue, that might mean engaging in a defusion exercise to create some space from the intrusive thoughts and images they are experiencing. It could also be choosing to continue with what they were doing instead of engaging in a compulsion. For example, that might look like pausing, acknowledging the thought *Stab yourself in the hand*, exhaling, and then continuing to chop vegetables in the presence of that thought.

Acceptance is at the cornerstone of every process. Cognitive defusion exercises help us learn how to create space for those thoughts, feelings, and sensations once we come in contact with our full experience. We need a willingness to come in contact with pain in order to engage more fully in the present moment. And as we just touched on, in order to take steps toward our values through committed actions we need to be willing to come in contact with our full experience. Not to mention that values are often the flipside of our pain, so if we can truly acknowledge and sit with our pain it may give us better insight into our values.

Cognitive Defusion

Defusion is a fun made-up word that your computer might try to autocorrect to "diffusion" with infuriating frequency. What does it mean though? If we break up the word into two parts, "de" and "fusion," we can begin to parse out what is happening. As we learned earlier, cognitive fusion is the process of buying into our thoughts as the absolute truth. With defusion, our job is to separate or create space from the stuck thought. Our goal is to *de-fuse*. When someone buys into a thought as the truth, their options for how to respond narrow. If a client buys into the thought *Life will always be like this*, they have very few options for how to respond. If "nothing will ever change," then why would they try to make changes in their life? Why would they put energy and effort into therapy or build skills or try something new? If it were the case that their mind was omniscient and that was the literal truth, then they would be right not to try. But just like we can't make certain promises to our clients, they can't predict the future.

Instead, we work toward getting some space from our stuck thoughts so we can choose how we want to respond. A functional analysis ties in nicely with defusion skills. It can help you and your client identify fused content. It also helps them to recognize automatic, default responses and explore whether they're working for them. And if you're talking about it in therapy, the response usually isn't helping your client in the long run. Defusion helps your client choose a different response than the one they typically do.

For example, if in response to the thought *I'm a burden to others*, your client tends to retreat, avoid asking for help, or pretend that they are fine, and as a result, feel lonely and disconnected, that is an unhelpful pattern. They are having the thought *I'm a burden to others*, believing that thought to be true, and then responding accordingly. But what if it's just a thought? What if it's one of thousands of random thoughts their mind throws out every day? What if it shows up because they care about their community? Or maybe they really value their independence and that's not as accessible right now? If they can defuse from that thought to create a little space, then they can walk themself through a different process: "Right now I really want to stay home so other people don't see how much I'm hurting. But every time I do that, I end up feeling even worse and more alone. Honesty and community are really important to me. So even though it feels awful, I'm going to ask for help."

Hold up, what if the thought *is* true? What if your client is conventionally unattractive or their life does suck right now? It doesn't matter. I don't mean this in a flippant "who cares" kind of way. Rather, they should take a step back and recognize that how they are responding to that thought isn't serving them. Does their life suck right now? Sure! Does ruminating on how awful their life is and how nothing ever goes their way and how this is how their life will be forever help? Does it make them more likely to make changes in their life that may change their circumstances? No.

An easier way to look at this is through the lens of a chronic or terminal illness. Imagine you are working with a client who has a terminal illness and the thought they are fused with is *I'm going to die*. That thought is true. To be fair, it's true for every living human, but it is true in a much more tangible sense to this person. And it is heartbreaking, unfair, horrible—all the things. When I hear that thought, I also hear all the other thoughts that come attached to it.

I'm going to die . . .

    . . . so what's the point?

    . . . it doesn't matter anyway.

    . . . I should just get it over with and save my family the cost.

    . . . and I don't want to. I'm not ready.

And a million more.

Yes, this client will die. And that is *horrible*. Take a moment to sit with them. Help them to practice acceptance or acknowledgment of a really sucky truth. Once you can help them create space to acknowledge reality, they can begin building from there. They can process why it's so scary. You can help them identify who they want to speak with and what they want to experience beforehand. They can begin to navigate some of the more concrete difficult questions, such as a living will, do-not-resuscitate orders, power of attorney, and those who will handle their affairs afterward. When we can hold space for the hard truths, we can begin to explore all the options we have in response. In ACT, we look toward the client's values to inform what would be meaningful for them to focus on.

Later in this chapter we'll explore values in depth. Right now though, understand that just because something is true does not mean that the way we are responding to it is helpful. This process is not about changing the content of our client's mind. Because in truth, there are very few opportunities for us to truly change our thoughts permanently, and usually it's without our control. But we can add and expand. We can add new perspectives and expand how we react when that initial thought pops up. Let's take a look at some exercises that can help facilitate that process.

Coaching the Team Metaphor

This is a metaphor I often use with clients to talk about the difference between fusion and defusion:

> *When we get really hooked by our thoughts, it's almost like being an athlete on the field. There are other players running around you. A ball being kicked or thrown. You are completely consumed by that experience. You are in the game. And if you aren't expecting something or aren't ready for it, it can feel overwhelming. You might be running here and there without any real plan.*

However, if you're able to get a little bit of space just outside of the game—maybe instead of a player on the field, you're the coach—you can see the play unfolding a little easier. It's still intense. You still don't have control over every player. And yet, that little bit of space gives you the chance to come up with a different play and guide the team in a different direction.

You've been playing this game for a while now, and it seems pretty exhausting. My goal for today is for us to begin exploring some strategies you can use to get just a little bit of space from those thoughts and feelings on the field so you can intentionally choose what happens next.

Creating Space from Thoughts

There are many exercises out there for establishing a little bit of space from our thoughts. But one that has stood the test of time is an exercise that helps add in the awareness that what we are experiencing is simply a random thought in our head (Hayes et al., 2011).

This exercise is very simple. It begins with a thought:

1. Ask your client to choose a thought they've been struggling with lately. Alternatively, you can select a thought that they have mentioned in session.

2. If you haven't already, take some time to explore with your client what other thoughts, feelings, sensations, or memories are fused with this thought. You want them to have a small reaction to this thought in session to have content to work with.

3. Next, you might add "I am having the thought" so that your client's entire perspective is "I am having the thought [*client thought*]." Have them repeat this full sentence out loud and then debrief what they noticed. There are no wrong answers. This step is usually helpful enough, especially if they are stating it out loud instead of just their head.

4. If you want to take it a step further, you can acknowledge that this thought is coming from the client's mind, which is a thought generation machine. You would have them add "My mind is having the thought" to the beginning of the thought to make the full sentence: "My mind is having the thought [*client thought*]." This can help some clients connect with the idea that the content of our mind is sometimes very arbitrary. Clients with OCD sometimes find it helpful to label that the thought is coming from OCD instead of the mind.

Gray Rock Your Mind Exercise

Narcissistic abuse has been a hot topic lately. Given that as a society, we are starting to talk more about narcissism and behaviors like gaslighting, there are some terms and methods that are more widely known these days. One of them is called the *gray rock method*. This strategy was developed for interacting with people who are abusive, manipulative, or narcissistic. The idea is that you act as interesting as a gray rock. You don't try to argue back with the person, negotiate, or even demonstrate any large emotional response to what they said. In essence, the idea is not to ignore the person, but not really engage with them either. Be utterly boring.

Your client can use the gray rock method for their mind. Instead of getting into arguments or being very reactive to what their mind is saying, you can help them simply acknowledge it in the most boring way possible and then return to what they were doing. Here are some of the phrases my clients and I have come up with for responding to their mind:

- "Cool."
- "Thanks for sharing."
- "Interesting."
- "That's a thought."
- "I'll take that under advisement."
- "Appreciate it."
- "Okay."
- "Sure."

Now, I recognize that depending on the tone, some of these can come across as passive aggressive. But imagine reading them in kind of a playful flippant tone. The goal is to acknowledge that our mind had a thought and respond to it in a way that also highlights that this thought is not going to impact how we are showing up to the world. Some clients may use pop culture references or phrases from their favorite TV show or movie, which adds some additional dimension and fun to the response. And, as always, saying it out loud when possible can make it even more impactful.

Present-Moment Awareness

Many people think of this core ACT process and automatically reduce it to *mindfulness*. While mindfulness can be a way to practice *present-moment awareness*, this is an oversimplification of the process. Or rather, it is an overnarrowing of the process.

The main distinction between present-moment awareness and today's definition of mindfulness is process versus outcome. Present-moment awareness is the process of noticing where your mind is and connecting it to your present experience. Mindfulness practice, as it has been historically used, is very similar. However, as mindfulness has become a cool, edgy, wellness word, it has transformed more into an outcome-based practice. That is, when people talk about mindfulness, they are often focused on what the outcome will be—for example, a "clear mind" or being "peaceful." There are many reasons why this is an incorrect interpretation of mindfulness, but for the sake of this book, let's just say mindfulness is a term like acceptance—it has many meanings and interpretations, not all of which are aligned with our focus in ACT.

All of this is to say that the concept of teaching people to connect with their present experience is not something ACT invented. However, we are hoping to keep its description as clear as possible to avoid the same fate of mindfulness in the commercial world. As the phrase "contact with the present moment" suggests, this core process is action-oriented, not outcome-oriented. We are not focused on changing a person's emotional state. Rather, the goal is to increase a client's skills in noticing where their attention has wandered to and then intentionally focusing their attention on the present moment. Why? Many reasons.

We cannot change patterns we don't know exist. Sometimes clients may be annoyed that we are starting our work with noticing. They want to jump right into the fun, actionable skills that they believe will lead to real change. But we cannot change patterns if we can't see them. Present-moment awareness helps us notice patterns in real time and, with the help of defusion exercises, make different decisions—hopefully values-based decisions.

Our mind is not designed to be constantly present. This is a learned skill. As we discussed in chapter 2, our mind is a threat-detection system. If there is nothing threatening the present moment, its natural default is to jump to the past or the future. Our mind might use this time to reflect on what we said before and point out all the ways we suck. Or it might jump to the future to worry through every what-if scenario we can dream of. Not what I would call helpful or particularly useful. Now, we obviously use this analytical, problem-solving skill at times, and it can be incredibly useful. It is simply not effective as a catch-all default way of operating.

Building the skill of connecting with the present moment can help your client better choose where they want their attention focused. Sometimes they do want to reflect on the past or plan for a future scenario. But this should be their choice. At the end of the day, they can only make decisions and act in the present moment. The present is where we have the most control over our life. Having the ability to engage with the present more often allows us to make intentional choices about how we want to live our life.

In-Session Noticing

Noticing is one of the first foundational skills I introduce to clients. I am a firm believer in the idea that we cannot break patterns we do not see. And if we are operating under the assumption that our clients are coming to therapy because they are stuck in an automatic, default way of responding, it is a fair assumption that they may not be completely aware of what those patterns look like.

In-session noticing comes in two forms. The first is guiding clients through a noticing exercise. This is a more formal way of introducing present-moment awareness. You'll learn how to teach the following practices later in this book:

- Mindful breathing (see chapter 10)
- Body scan (see chapter 10)
- Mindful movement, such as while washing dishes or walking outside (see chapter 10)
- Grounding practice, such as "five senses"
- Being an observer of self, such as noticing the thoughts in their head or physical sensations in their body (see chapter 7)

The other way of introducing noticing in session is through more process-based, in-the-moment opportunities. This may be drawing a client's attention to the fact that their fists are clenched, they have their hand pressed over their heart, or they're playing with their ring. In these moments, you want to lean in with curiosity: "I noticed when we started talking about going home to visit your parents, you started playing with the rings on your finger. Did you notice that?"

In this way, you are able to help your clients pay attention to a cue that may otherwise be invisible to them. You can then dig further, asking them to check in with their body and notice what they are experiencing. Have them drop down into the moment and pause. This can be as simple as asking, "What are you feeling in your body right now in this moment?"

Out-of-Session Noticing

In ACT, we want the work we do in session to continue to change what clients see outside of session. Therefore, you may want to assign homework. Homework can be a more formal practice, like intentionally taking five breaths and counting to 10 with each inhale and exhale. It can be following a mindfulness meditation audio guide. It can be engaging in a stretching routine and noticing how their body feels in these moments. It can also be added on to everyday moments they experience in their life.

Many clients report feeling frustrated that they aren't successful in immediately changing their behavior out of session. As a workaround, I often give the initial task of simply going through their day and noticing when a hook shows up and what they do in response to it. From there, they can come back to therapy and we can discuss what happened, do a functional analysis, and then identify the skills they need to learn in order to interrupt this pattern in the future. Clients also find it helpful when I explain that noticing usually happens in three phases:

1. Engaging in a default behavior, and *after the fact,* realizing that behavior was not helpful
2. Catching the behavior *as it happens* but not having the skills to interrupt the behavior or pivot to something else (this can often be the most frustrating phase)
3. Having the awareness to notice what they usually do and *pause and then pivot* toward a values-based behavior

This explanation can help ease the frustration when they don't make contact with the present moment "correctly" the first few times.

Self-as-Context

Self-as-context is most easily described as the *observer self.* It is a recognition that there is a "you" behind your eyes observing your experience both internally (thoughts, feelings, sensations) and externally (how you interact with the world). In contrast to self-as-content, which focuses on a fixed version of the self that is bound and narrowed by how you identify or describe yourself, self-as-context is not rigid; it is flexible and responsive to the "here and now."

One way we engage with this core process is through perspective changing. Deictic frames focus on the perspective of the person speaking in relation to others, time, and space. Common deictic frames are me/you, here/there, then/now. We can create a number of different perspectives from these frames:

- The client trying to take the perspective of a person in their lives: switch from me to you
- The client talking to their younger self or older self: switch from now to then
- The client noticing how rules may impact them differently in various context: exploring here versus there

Not only does perspective taking help to increase empathy, it also serves as an opportunity to explore function. With self-as-context, we take the perspective of the observer self, increasing our awareness of our own perspective and using deictic frames to explore other perspectives across space and time. For example, we can notice ourselves at home versus at work versus alone versus with family. Perhaps we notice how we are showing up in this moment and how we have shown up in the past. The purpose of this is to loosen the rigidity we have around rules, labels, and roles and instead practice showing up to each moment as a constant self who is witness to what is happening internally and externally. The goal is to use our noticing to develop a sense of self that transcends or exists across various domains of life. The hope is that it leads to feeling more settled in who you are as a person, your values, and a confidence that you can continue to show up to life as yourself even as identities change.

So how do we bring this into session?

Perspective Taking

When we are talking about perspective taking, we mean both looking at the world through another person's perspective as well as connecting with our perspectives across our own timeline. This may include:

- **Talking to our younger self:** Sometimes it is easier to feel compassion for a younger, more innocent version of ourselves. Clients who have lifelong trauma or who struggle with feeling different or unloved in their life may benefit from practicing perspective taking with their younger self. You may ask them about when they first had this experience and how old they were. You might ask them what they would say to their younger self if they had the opportunity to talk with them.

- **Talking to our older self:** You can ask your client, "What do you think your older self [*number*] years from now would be like if you engaged in your values or continued engaging in the patterns you have been?" This can be helpful to look at the long-term impact of something or how their perspective might change if they were in a different phase of life.

- **Exploring how others see us:** When doing values work, I sometimes ask the client, "If I were to ask your loved ones to describe you, what would you want them to say about you?" This can be a great question to get at what qualities and characteristics the client wants to embody in their lives.

This can also be an assignment for them to do; they can ask the people they care about to describe how they think of them.

- **Understanding others' behaviors:** This sometimes gets combined with a functional analysis of another person's behavior. However, it can be helpful for clients to put themselves in someone else's shoes, describe what they know about that person, and then explore why they think the person is behaving the way they are. It is important when using the strategy that you highlight that there is a difference between understanding someone's behavior and saying that their behavior is acceptable. Sometimes highly empathetic people fall into the trap of allowing inappropriate behaviors to slide because they understand the historical context that led to the other person's behavior. We can understand someone's behavior without condoning it or saying that it is acceptable.

Roles and Labels

The other way that we can bring self-as-context into session is through exploring roles and labels that clients are attached to. As we go through life, we take on certain identities and roles. We may have personal titles, such as mother or brother. We may have career-related titles, such as manager or CEO. We also may have labels that we have associated with ourselves, such as hard-working, good, or anxious. Helping clients begin to understand the way those rigid identities might be constricting their life can be useful. Begin to explore those rules and labels, eventually shifting to identify the values associated with those labels. This may include values related to the type of relationships we want, the value we associate our career with, or the qualities and characteristics we want to embody. We can explore how those values show up in many areas of our life and allow for more flexibility than tightly-held rules about how to operate in certain domains of our life.

Values

Values represent what we have chosen to give our life meaning. What we want to be continuously moving toward as a guiding force for living our life. Values are not meant to be checked off. There will be no point in time when we've achieved our values. It is the constant process of choosing and pivoting toward them.

Values can be tricky at times. When society has been constantly geared toward outcomes, goals, and symptom reduction, it can be difficult to figure out what is and is not a value. The easiest way I've found to differentiate the two is that *values are the who and what that matter to us.* They are the qualities and characteristics we want to embody. In comparison, a goal is a concrete, quantifiable objective that can be reached or checked off a list. If we think of values as our north star compass on a lifelong journey, then goals are the mile markers along the way. We can continue to move toward our values even if the roads change.

Values Are Not Goals

Many people who start with goals can get stuck if that goal is no longer attainable. For example, let's say someone can no longer do their job due to their chronic pain. Their goals related to promotion, salary, or financial stability may be out of reach for the moment. Yet their values of supporting their family are still there. Maybe it is something direct such as providing emotional support or helping around the house. Or maybe it is more indirect, like undergoing treatment or attending physical therapy even though they hate it in the service of their family.

Values Are Not Feelings

Sometimes clients will say that their value is peace. And I completely understand the yearning for life to be stable and easy when it has been so hard for so long. But peace is a feeling. Like all feelings, it is fleeting. Temporary. Now, this doesn't mean that how you live your life won't create the by-product of more moments of peace. But chasing a feeling is difficult because it is not something we can always feel on demand. Otherwise, everyone would just choose to feel happy. So what do we do when clients say their value is to never have another nightmare or only feel happy? My go-to response is to first validate and then explore. The following dialogue includes an example of a client who feels this way:

THERAPIST: I imagine after struggling with so much for so long the idea of feeling happy all the time is important to you. If you were to never have another nightmare and be at peace, what would you spend your time doing? What would you be focusing on? [*clarifies values by asking the client to take a feeling and describe it through behaviors*]

CLIENT: So many things. Getting a new job I actually like. Moving out on my own, and honestly, probably moving out of my hometown. I'd travel. Take up random hobbies. Live life.

THERAPIST: That sounds wonderful. You mentioned a couple of different things here. Is it okay if I ask you some questions about them?

CLIENT: Sure.

THERAPIST: You mentioned getting a new job. When you think about the type of career you want to have, what comes to mind? Some people work to get a paycheck and fund the life they want. Other people find a lot of value in their career itself. Maybe it's helping people, being creative, or even being challenged. [*takes a behavior the client mentioned and sees what values are connected with it*]

CLIENT: I mean, I obviously need money to survive. But I really like learning new things and being challenged.

THERAPIST: Okay, great. And what makes you consider moving out of your hometown? If you were looking for a new place to live, what are some of the qualities you would look for in that?

CLIENT: It's not even so much something specific—it's that I've never been anywhere else. I also don't think I'm a big city person. It's very overstimulating even without PTSD. I think I would really enjoy living somewhere with a slower pace of life, or somewhere I wasn't working 60 hours a week. I could actually build community and know my neighbors, and that sort of thing.

THERAPIST: That sounds really beautiful. So working toward creating community where you live and feeling like your environment supports a slower-paced life. Gotcha. When you think of travel, what is enticing about that?

CLIENT: Learning about different cultures, trying different foods, and seeing places I've never been. I think you become a better person when you see all the wonderful ways people live.

THERAPIST: I completely agree with that. So traveling for the purpose of cultural growth, expanding your awareness, and eating amazing food.

CLIENT: Exactly.

THERAPIST: We started this conversation with you talking about wanting to be happy, which I totally get. The issue is if we start off with that as our goal, it can sometimes lead us astray. Because I can't guarantee you'll always be happy. In fact, even if therapy is super successful, I can almost guarantee that you will *not* be happy one hundred percent of the time. Because emotions fluctuate a million times during the day. Not to mention there are a lot of things that make you really happy in the short term, like eating a delicious dessert, that might not help support your goals if you were to always lean into that. [*sets up creative hopelessness*]

CLIENT: Wouldn't it be awesome if it did though?

THERAPIST: Yes, that would be pretty amazing. But I also think all of our emotions tell us things. I know yours have been screaming at you for a really long time, and that's not fun. But even looking at some of the things that are really important to you, I can guess it wouldn't lead to 24/7 happiness. I imagine if you traveled to a place that's very different from where you grew up and you support the culture and the locals and eat delicious food there would be times where you were happy, but there would also be times where you were incredibly uncomfortable or exhausted from jetlag. [*presents unworkability of chasing happiness through client's own examples of what a happy life looks like*]

CLIENT: Yeah, I guess maybe I was exaggerating a little bit when I said I wanted to be happy all the time. I recognize that's not possible.

THERAPIST: What if we turned our attention away from trying to feel a certain way and instead work on developing skills that can help you build this beautiful life you described? Where you have a stimulating and challenging career, you get to move out on your own and build a community in the town you live, and you get to go on awesome adventures. You may still have a range of emotions that show up, but maybe you'd feel more in control of choosing how you showed up to the world. [*provides buy-in to a non-symptom-reduction agenda*]

CLIENT: That works for me. I'm a little nervous about what that looks like, but I'm willing to try.

You may notice some frustration as we move through our work with ACT. Our society puts emphasis on outcomes often. And ACT is largely process-based. Sure, we want our clients to feel better and live fulfilling lives, but ACT clinicians are more concerned with the process of how our clients show up to the world. This may feel different or wrong compared to what you've focused on in therapy previously. That's totally fair. If you're willing, notice that, and let the inquisitive part of yourself explore this new therapy through the lens of an experiment. After all, if you decide another therapy is a better fit for you and your clients, then this book will simply be a way to affirm that for you.

Values Don't Compete

Many times you will encounter situations with clients where they feel conflicted. It feels as if their values are in competition. For example, a parent wants to support their child and provide a stable and safe home for them, but struggles financially and decides to pick up more shifts at work. They may question which of these values to choose, as working more creates financial stability but means being away from their children more often.

As humans, we tend to look at the immediate short-term results of a behavior as opposed to the long-term impact. In this case, taking on extra shifts is the way this client can be a caring and loving parent who supports their child. There is a real need for increased income to provide for them. They are working more in service of their family.

In contrast, consider a parent who takes on extra shifts because being at home is chaotic and difficult, and they like the quiet of the office. They may not be engaging with their values and working toward being the kind of parent they want to be. Keep in mind that this only counts if it's a stated value of the parent. After all, each client gets to choose their own values.

Values Generally Describe What Is Important

An object or person is not a value. Rather, values lie in how we show up to that object or person. For example, if a client said that their partner is important to them, we might ask about the qualities or characteristics they believe make up a healthy, romantic relationship. Their answer might be trust, honesty, connection, adventure, collaboration, and teamwork; *these* are their values, or what truly matters to them. If another client said that nature was really important to them, we would still write this down, but we would then follow up with a question of what is important to them about nature. This might be spending time outside, having moments of silence, or being conscious of our impact on nature; these are values because they describe how they would show up to it.

There are also times when someone has a value that might feel too broad. The one that comes up most in my practice is "health." Health can absolutely be a value, but it is almost like an umbrella term for a series of values. It is worth further explanation. So I may ask a client what about their health they want to be moving toward right now. They might want to focus on being physically strong. You may even find after asking more questions that being strong actually serves their more important value of independence because if they can maintain their strength, then they can live on their own, for example.

With the value of health, some people also talk about what they don't want—"I don't want diabetes like my dad," or "I don't want high blood pressure like my mom." We can't move toward what we want to avoid, so instead, we would want to invert that. Focus on what the client *does* want to be moving toward. This could be balanced eating or having good cardiovascular fitness.

If your client is having trouble narrowing down values, I recommend starting with domains of life that people generally have values in.* These might be one of the following:

- Career
- Relationships: romantic, social, familial
- Personal growth
- Health
- Leisure or passions
- Spirituality

And remember, there is no values police that is going to come into your practice and tell you that the values you are writing down for your client are wrong. The main rules of thumb are to be curious; understand that emotions are not values but can lead us to values; and highlight what someone is moving toward or wants to move toward rather than something they don't want to experience.

Committed Actions

If we continue to think of our values as a north star compass on a lifelong journey and our goals as the mile markers along the way, then committed actions are the intentional ways we steer the "car" that is aligned with our values. Sometimes clients can view committed actions as huge life-altering decisions. However, in reality, every small decision can be a committed action.

For example, on a daily basis I debate with myself whether I *really* need to finish my notes tonight. It's usually the end of my workday. I've seen five to six clients and my stomach is rumbling. I've been staring at a computer screen for more hours than is probably recommended, and my mind says, "You can wake up early tomorrow and finish them before you start work." Except past experience would prove this a lie. I will not wake up early. Instead, tomorrow will come and I will have two days' worth of notes to contemplate avoiding. So when that thought inevitably comes up, I pause. I remind myself that my work is important to me. And that work includes paperwork. Maybe I stretch in my chair first and then write my notes. If my phone dings or my dog comes into the room, the process starts over. I pause. I remind myself that the type of therapist I want to be is one that is reliable and responsible, and I write.

This concept of intentional actions is quite common among behavioral therapies. The distinction is starting with our values and then identifying actions. This can be done with SMART goals (goals that are

---

* For a full downloadable list of common values, visit https://www.theacttherapist.com/ACTskillsmanual.

specific, measurable, achievable, relevant, and time-bound) and behavioral activation. To reiterate, begin with a connection to what is important and then find the smallest step forward in that direction. You likely have a lot of really wonderful skills, exercises, and practices that fit under this term. Just remember that the purpose of these actions is not simply movement, it is movement toward creating a meaningful life for your client.

Exercise: Flex Your Hexaflex Knowledge

Now that you are well versed in the six common ways our clients struggle and the six core ACT processes that serve as antidotes, let's test your knowledge. Please read the following client summary and then fill out the blank inflexahex model of psychological inflexibility to pinpoint what he is struggling with. Then use the blank hexaflex model of psychological flexibility to highlight what core processes he may want to engage.

Elijah is a 26-year-old man. He immigrated to the United States in his early twenties for college and has stayed to work for a large consulting firm. He is coming to therapy to figure out whether he should leave his job, and to help with burnout. He has worked for the last few years to get to his current position, and yet, he feels overworked, is exhausted, and does not find value in his work. He is starting to have thoughts about whether he made the right decision to take this job. He feels that he doesn't know who he is or what he wants to do with his life.

Elijah mentions that assimilating to the US has been a confusing process because there are some things he really loves about the American mindset and some he doesn't like, as they are very different from what he experienced growing up. He states that his work is very challenging and cutthroat, and it doesn't create a lot of opportunities for connection. As a result, he does a lot of networking but doesn't feel that he has a life outside of his work.

He shares that he struggles falling asleep because he is thinking through what-if scenarios for his job and career, and then, when he does fall asleep, he experiences what he calls "stress dreams" and wakes up feeling not rested. Elijah has begun to experience physical manifestations of stress in the form of heart palpitations. Recently, he experienced his first panic attack the morning he had to leave on a flight for a work trip. Elijah has had a recent physical check-up with his doctor and, outside of slightly elevated blood pressure, his health and blood work are within normal range. He comments that he has spent so long trying to become a consultant that he doesn't know who he would be if he gave that up, as it a large part of his identity.

The Inflexahex Model

The Hexaflex Model

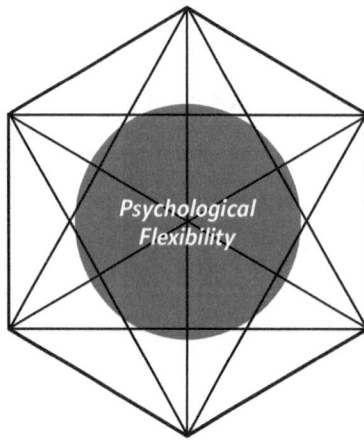

Chapter Takeaways

- Psychological flexibility helps us come in contact with our full experience in order to interrupt patterns that aren't helpful and to engage with our values in the present moment.

- Acceptance in ACT does not mean we have to like our experience or "suck it up." It represents a willingness to come in contact with something painful in the service of our values.

- Self-as-context involves the observer self and the ability to shift deictic frames. The observer self represents the perspective that there is a person behind our eyes who is the witness of both our internal (thoughts, feelings, memories, physical sensations) and external (things we interact with in the world) experiences. Deictic frames help us shift various perspectives in time and space.

- Defusion strategies help us look at our thoughts as merely content of our mind. Doing so creates space between thought and reaction so we can choose how we want to show up to the moment.

- Our values represent what we are constantly choosing to move toward, while our committed actions are the specific and achievable steps along the way, also known as values-based behaviors. This can include cognitive and observable behaviors.

PART II
Getting Started with Your Client

CHAPTER 4
THE ROLE OF DIAGNOSIS IN ACT

Now that we've gone over the basics of ACT, we're going to turn our focus to getting started with your client. Please don't skip these chapters! Even if you have been a therapist for some time, the ways to approach diagnosing (see later in this chapter), intake assessment (see chapter 5), and treatment planning (see chapter 6) from an ACT perspective may be fundamentally different from what you are used to or what you learned in training. We will also examine some of the more challenging aspects of our work, including the ACT approach for suicidal ideation (see chapter 5) to common rebuttals you may encounter as you begin to set up creative hopelessness (see chapter 6). These chapters explore the overall ACT approach and stance toward therapy from the very first interaction with a client.

For many therapists, the *DSM-5* and the concept of diagnosing clients is a love-hate relationship. This gets amplified when we work from a framework that is not a symptom-reduction agenda. How do we navigate our aim in ACT while operating within a medical model that relies on symptoms and diagnostic codes? Not to mention, some clients can't access services without a diagnosis. This chapter will walk you through the traditional uses for diagnoses, the complicated insurance process of expanding access, and the role of diagnoses within a transdiagnostic model.

Before we begin, take some time to consider your training on diagnosing clients and the role of diagnosis in your practice. This will help guide how you approach this topic from an ACT perspective. After all, therapists encompass a variety of licensed professionals in a wide range of settings.

While diagnosis has become a less universally agreed upon topic, I believe its initial purpose makes sense. The goal, in simple terms, was to find common overlap in experiences to better determine how to help others. In order to legitimize mental health services, we integrated with the medical model, which focuses on symptom clusters to diagnose and treat problems. Someone has a symptom, such as a fever and a rash, and their doctor's goal was to identify what those symptoms meant in order to diagnose and treat. It would follow that mental health operates the same way. If someone has panic attacks, fear of having another panic attack, and avoidance of potential triggers for panic attacks, then they might have panic disorder.

And if a group of people has similar symptoms, you could deduce how to help them based on what has helped people similar to them. Scales were developed to measure symptom severity. Research explored how to reduce those symptoms overall—the belief being that reducing those symptoms automatically meant that person's life was improved. Similar to how reducing the fever and the rash meant the person was no longer sick.

We have already covered in chapter 2 how ACT does not follow a symptom-reduction model. So from the onset, ACT can appear at times to be in conflict with diagnosing if the purpose is to identify symptoms to then reduce them.

When we look at symptoms, what we often find is high overlap between symptoms among various diagnoses, huge variability in presentation within a single diagnosis, and comorbidities that pile on multiple diagnoses without a clear way to navigate treatment. For example, people with autism are 50–70 percent more likely to also have attention-deficit hyperactivity disorder (ADHD) and 2 to 4 times more likely to be diagnosed with OCD (Hours et al., 2022; Meier et al., 2015). Meanwhile, three adults with depression who meet diagnostic criteria for major depressive disorder (MDD) could present in completely different ways. That is why in ACT, we begin with looking at the function of clients' behavior. If we focus too much on the symptoms of a diagnosis, we may miss how they are showing up in this specific individual. We want to focus instead on personalizing our approach to each client.

To be clear, I am not saying diagnoses are all terrible and should be done away with. As always, everything has a function in ACT. But we want to have a clear understanding of their role in therapy—in our interactions with clients, treatment planning, and the business side of our work.

ACT as a Transdiagnostic Model

ACT is a transdiagnostic model. This means that it was not developed for a specific diagnosis. Many other therapies, such as dialectical behavioral therapy (DBT), were developed with a specific subset in mind; for DBT, that was borderline personality disorder (BPD). And while it has been generalized out to help clients outside of BPD diagnosis, its initial intention was to help that specific group.

ACT, on the other hand, was created not with a collection of symptoms in mind, but rather as an approach to both our internal and external experience. I tell clients that one of the cool parts of ACT is that while they may be learning it to apply to their current struggles, the same principles can be used for anything that comes up for them in the future. It is highly adaptive. It doesn't focus on the specific content of our internal experience, but rather how those thoughts, feelings, memories, sensations, and urges function within ourselves and between us and the world.

Because ACT is a transdiagnostic model, it can be applied to a variety of difficulties people face. And it has been. ACT has been shown to be effective for a broad range of populations and struggles, which makes diagnosing clients less important from a treatment perspective. Obviously, it is your responsibility as a therapist to ensure you have proper training in working with a specific population and can provide a rationale based on experience and evidence for why you'd recommend ACT as a treatment. Assuming that those criteria have been met, diagnosis from a treatment perspective is not as relevant. At the end of the day, we are training up skills that can be used across symptoms. So why diagnose at all?

Ways Diagnosis Can Help

Some clients come into therapy assuming that they are simply "lazy" or "being dramatic" and that the struggles they are experiencing are minor. They may make comparisons to what others experience. I see this often with trauma clients. They will downplay their own trauma by comparing it to another trauma that they deem worse. Many people have a specific idea of what struggling or dealing with mental health concerns looks like, and they assume if they don't meet that criteria that they "should" be fine.

A diagnosis in this context can be a life-changing experience for some. A validation of everything they've been struggling with. It can help them engage in self-compassion, set boundaries, and start therapy, medication, or both. It can give clients a label that is helpful for navigating their own experience. It's true that labels can be problematic in ACT. After all, the self-as-context core process is all about not narrowing ourselves based on labels. However, labels are not *inherently* bad, and sometimes clients can use a label to help them better understand their own experience. For example, in the Name Your Mind defusion exercise introduced in chapter 2, a client might identify when their "trauma" is saying something.

There are also more practical reasons that a diagnosis can be helpful. If you live in a country like the United States, where treatment coverage for therapy services is tied to diagnosis, then a diagnosis means access to care. There are many instances in which a diagnosis is necessary to access programs, community mental health services, or other types of assistance.

And finally, diagnostic labels give both professionals and society as a whole a common language to talk about problems. We'll talk about the downside of common language in the next section. However, in many instances, being able to clearly communicate what's going on in a few words or one sentence can make a big difference. It is not always comfortable to discuss vulnerabilities. When working in interdisciplinary settings or collaborating with a client's primary care or specialist doctor, using a diagnostic label can help your client access other care within the medical system.

While ACT may be transdiagnostic, many treatments aren't. It's important to know which treatments have significant research with specific populations and conditions. In addition to DBT as a treatment for BPD, exposure response prevention is a gold standard for obsessive-compulsive disorder, and interoceptive exposure can be great for clients struggling with panic disorder. So, even if you are using ACT with every client, you may incorporate other skills, tools, and protocols that show a strong evidence base. We will cover this more in chapter 11.

What are the presenting problems that you primarily work with?

_____

_____

_____

_____

_____

What treatment protocols, skills, and tools have a strong evidence base for these concerns?

_____

_____

_____

_____

_____

Ways Diagnosis Can Hurt

A client once came to session with a curious story. She had received a diagnosis of MDD the session prior. During our session, I checked in with her regarding how she was feeling about this new label. She described a moment during the past week when she was enjoying a movie with her sister and had the thought *You can't laugh. You have depression. Depressed people can't laugh.*

My client immediately fused with the label "depressed," and it activated a whole network in her mind of what a depressed person is. And what they could and couldn't do. Thankfully, we discussed it in session and developed a more nuanced understanding of depression. But it made me realize that every person's experience and relationship with their diagnosis is different.

Labels matter. This is especially true when a label can impact how someone treats us. I've had numerous clients struggle to have their health concerns taken seriously by a doctor due to "anxiety" being in their medical chart. In fact, I often talk with my clients about how to discuss medical issues with doctors when the clients have been dismissed in the past or fear they will be written off as anxious. Many of my young female clients with chronic health conditions and Black clients have trauma from being ignored and gaslit by the medical community. Understanding how a diagnosis can impact your client's experience in various areas of their life is worth exploring. To be clear, I wouldn't encourage them to lie to medical professionals, but understanding how to communicate in a way they can be heard matters.

There are also certain diagnoses that still carry a stigma, as well as certain cultures, generations, and communities where seeking mental healthcare at all is frowned upon. In ACT, we may explore when, where, and to what extent a client chooses to self-disclose either their diagnosis or treatment options. It can be easy to fall into the trap of viewing avoidance as "bad," and yet, it may be congruent with a client's values to avoid talking with family about their mental health or sharing they are in therapy. It may align with their values to lie about it. That is not for you to decide. You can simply create a safe space for clients to process and decide for themselves.

Sometimes we hold onto labels and diagnoses because of what they represent. A few years ago, I was struggling with PTSD and MDD. It was one of the darkest times in my life. And yet, there was a tension inside me holding tight to the labels. I was afraid. Afraid that if I got better, it meant that what I experienced wasn't really that bad. Despite everything PTSD and depression took from me, I was scared that if I got better and moved on with my life that there wouldn't be any proof of the harm I experienced. My wounds were a walking billboard of my trauma. And while I wanted to move forward, I didn't want my pain to be insignificant, because it wasn't. I didn't want to forget.

At times, our labels can be validation of our experience. And there may be concern that if we no longer meet criteria for the label, that our experience is no longer valid. This is a fallacy, of course. I learned this firsthand. And yet, I would be remiss to not describe the pitfalls of holding on too tightly to a diagnosis. This is self-as-content in action. Holding so tightly to a label or identity that it narrows how we can show up to the world. We don't want to have that diagnosis or journey of a person eclipse their whole experience.

Self-as-Context

In chapter 3, we discussed the core ACT process of self-as-context and how it creates psychological flexibility. If your client is holding on tightly to a label—such as "I am depressed," which is self-as-content—it can set them up for a lot of suffering. My client viewed herself as a "depressed person" and therefore felt the constraints that came from operating under the rules of how she believed a "depressed person" should behave. When it comes to mental health labels, this narrowing of behavioral repertoires often comes from stereotypes about different groups. This narrowing only serves to further harm clients and limit their steps forward.

Whether you're working with someone recently fired from a job or a person with schizophrenia, our aim is to help clients explore how the labels, identities, or stereotypes they hold about themselves are impacting them. This can include processing and coming to a place of acceptance around a change in their identity. It can also be a place to explore what is important to them about that label or identity.

For example, a client experiencing an adjustment disorder as a result of retiring may feel a huge loss because so much of who they are was tied up in their job. Identifying why that role mattered so much to them can give insight into what they want to use as a guiding force as they navigate through new transitions, rough patches, and treatment. Maybe the recently retired client values helping others or contributing to society, and their main avenue for that is now gone. With ACT, we can transform their self-as-content label or role into underlying values and then help the client see they can access those values across roles and experiences. That is self-as-context in action.

What are some rules your clients have created for themselves based on their diagnostic labels?

_____
_____
_____
_____
_____
_____
_____
_____
_____

Practical Applications

A discussion of diagnoses in the context of ACT is all well and good, but if we are not also taking into account the context of the workplace setting, we may run into trouble. It is imperative for you to operate under the rules of your licensing board and your workplace, assuming the two are in agreement. You spend a lot of time looking at the function of client behavior, but this is one time where you can explore the function of your own behavior. Here are some takeaways that you may consider incorporating into how you approach your work:

- Look out for self-as-content following a diagnosis or change in circumstance
- Notice if your communication of a diagnosis involves symptom-reduction language
- Use diagnosis as a jumping-off point for exploring patterns of behavior and function with your client

If you are in a hospital, outpatient clinic, or other interdisciplinary setting, there is one more takeaway that you can incorporate into your work. When communicating with other providers and healthcare staff, challenge yourself to not only discuss diagnosis or symptoms, but also function. Even if you aren't introducing ACT to your colleagues, you can begin to influence how they approach clients, through describing the function of clients' behaviors rather than only their diagnosis.

A diagnosis may help inform treatment options. ACT can often serve as a framework or approach while various skills and exercises from other areas can function well underneath the umbrella of ACT. At the end of the day, remember the goal of functional contextualism. Set functional and observable goals for your clients.

Chapter Takeaways

- ACT is a transdiagnostic model, meaning that it was not designed with a specific population in mind and can be used across a range of diagnoses and symptoms.

- Our main focus in ACT is understanding the function of a client's behavior and what patterns aren't serving them anymore.

- Diagnosis can coexist with ACT, even though we are not focused on symptom reduction.

- Receiving a diagnostic label can function as a validating experience for a client or it can promote rules for how a client with that diagnosis is "allowed" to feel or behave. Assess for the function.

CHAPTER 5

INTAKE ASSESSMENT

The dreaded intake assessment. Intake assessments were always the worst part of therapy for me. Second only to paperwork. It felt like an interview with a million and one random questions. Now, as I approach intake assessments from an ACT and functional contextual model, they are not only more enjoyable, but I feel they also give something back to the client.

If we look at intake assessments from a functional contextual viewpoint, there are three main goals:

1. Understand current patterns of behavior that are impacting the client's life or that they want to change.

2. Identify what they care about and want to move toward.

3. Highlight gaps in skills, perspective, or awareness that they need to develop in order to interrupt unhelpful patterns and engage in more values-based behaviors.

This includes looking at both present-moment and historical information. Depending on your workplace, you may have little to no freedom in how you conduct assessments. Keep that in mind as we go through this chapter. I want you to think through how you may make adjustments to what you are already doing while still complying with your practice setting or license requirements. You may find that you will mix it up from time to time, depending on how an intake unfolds. The goal is flexibility.

How to Set Up Intake

You can start an initial session with a new client with an explanation that today's session is an opportunity to learn more about what matters to them and what's getting in the way. You can mention that this session will be a little different from the rest of your work together. You might say, "There is some information I need to get from you, and questions at times may seem random, but please bear with me." With any session, but especially in the first full-time meeting with the client, the questions you ask at the beginning can set the tone for the intake. It sets expectations for what therapy is like. Your goal is to set a tight stimulus control—meaning your goal is to be more intentional and specific to set a narrow focus for what sessions will look like.

As a result, this would not be the time for vague questions such as "What brings you in today?" These types of questions can lead to a wide array of answers. It also can accidentally set the function of therapy as one where the client simply regurgitates all information about a previous week.

Your objective in the intake is two-fold: You want to gather all the information you need to create a treatment plan and set the intention for the client of what therapy with you will look like. This might sound something like this:

> *Today will be our intake session. It will be a little different from our regular therapy sessions. I'm going to be doing a bit of talking and asking you questions that at times might seem random or all over the place. I promise this has a purpose. Our goal today is to get a real understanding of what patterns have been showing up that are getting in the way of you creating the life you want to have. Most of therapy is spent talking about those patterns and developing skills and practices for interrupting them. However, I always like to start therapy exploring what is important to you. Who are the people or things that matter to you and that you want to incorporate more in your life? So, this might be a big question, but when you think about what is important to you, what comes to mind?*

By explaining the intake process in this way, not only are you setting an expectation for your client, but you are also beginning an intervention as part of the intake process: values clarification. In an intake session, you will begin to clarify your client's values, explore fused content, and identify patterns of avoidance. If your intake session is only one session, then you may also incorporate committed actions as treatment goals at the end.

Most clients come in with the idea that the purpose of therapy is to talk about their problems. Many clients are used to going to doctors and talking about which body part hurts and why. Your goal from the onset is to set a different expectation. Your work together is about reducing suffering and increasing engagement with clients' values to create a meaningful life for them. They get to decide what is meaningful. You get to help them navigate that dream.

Setting Tight Stimulus Control

My internship with the San Diego Veterans Affairs had me running a group for ACT for chronic pain. With every group, I'd run a little experiment: I'd ask each group member to go around and share their name and what was important to them in their lives. The first one or two people would comply with that prompt, but then you'd start to see something interesting. As more people shared, instead of starting with values and maybe ending with their struggles as the first or second person did, the pain each person felt would become the forefront of their introduction. It happened literally every time. Even when I prompted them that this would happen, it still did. Why? We are wired, socialized, and distracted by what hurts. We also rarely have safe spaces to explore that. At the end of introductions, or sometimes in the middle if it got particularly long-winded, I'd share my experiment with the group. It was a great introduction to how our mind often has a different agenda than we do. Our mind is understandably focused on reducing pain and increasing survival rather than toward values-engagement.

This experience taught me how important it was to anchor values as the north star that therapy will use to guide the journey. If you let the therapy session or intake flow naturally, you will end up at suffering. It's a natural default. That is why it is your job as a therapist to set a tight stimulus control. The expectations you start the session with are easier to maintain than to introduce later on.

Another important consideration is to be mindful about assuming the answer to a question. Especially when it comes to values. As therapists, we are often focused on patterns that clients feel stuck in, yet we also tend to get stuck in patterns or engage in avoidance. There is a difference between asking specific questions and pulling for specific answers. This is a good practice for noticing when you are making assumptions. And we all make assumptions. It is how our brains plan and organize information. An assumption is simply a thought. There is nothing wrong with the thought itself, but we should be mindful of how we behave in response to that assumption.

My personal mantra is to lead with curiosity and empathy. Both of these are values of mine. They are also super functional. If I can keep curiosity and empathy at the forefront of my mind, it becomes a cheat code to ensure I create space for the client to share their experience. I am engaging in perspective taking to more easily empathize with their experience.

What values of yours do you like to keep at the forefront of your mind when working with clients?

_____
_____
_____
_____

What patterns of avoidance show up for you that make this difficult?

_____
_____
_____
_____

If you don't know the answer to this, that's okay. Spend time observing yourself or reflecting on your sessions afterward. Are there topics or scenarios you tend to shy away from? Maybe you struggle to sit with long pauses, or you rush through to process big emotions instead of creating space for them to exist. I struggle with both experiences at times. Complete a functional analysis on yourself in the therapy room. You can learn a lot about how you're showing up in session, even in your resistance to complete one.

Functional Contextualism and High-Risk Clients

Many times, we have the best of intentions—until someone mentions suicide. In ACT, our stance is that thoughts are spurious. They don't predict the future or necessarily mean anything of importance. They are simply thoughts. And therapists tend to like and connect with this idea... until high-risk red flags are raised. Then I often see therapists falling back into old patterns. However, if we are going to approach our clients as functional contextualists, that shouldn't change depending on what they say. Our actions might change, but our approach doesn't. So how do we navigate this balance?

ACT clinicians approach suicidal ideation, violent intrusive thoughts, flashbacks, and hallucinations the same as any other experience. We lean into curiosity. Sometimes, without meaning to, we can accidentally punish clients for bringing up difficult topics. We may rush into safety planning. The tone or pace of our voice may change. Even the expression on our face may tell our clients that what they told us is abnormal, alarming, or against social norms, even in therapy. So unless you feel in physical danger, take a moment to pause and explore the function of their experience. The following dialogue shows a client-therapist discussion surrounding suicidal ideation:

CLIENT: Honestly, I just don't want to be here anymore. I wish I could go to sleep and never wake up.

THERAPIST: I imagine you must be really hurting for your mind to suggest escaping like that. [*uses defusion strategy: moving from client saying the thought to adding in that their mind suggested the thought*]

CLIENT: It's just never-ending. I keep thinking things are going to change, but they never do. I'm exhausted.

THERAPIST: You've been through a lot. I think anyone would feel exhausted. [*validates client*]

CLIENT: Like, what's the point? I go to therapy and my job, and I'm still here, but life is just awful.

THERAPIST: What are you feeling right now, in your body, as we talk about this? [*begins present-moment awareness practice*]

CLIENT: Numb. And heavy, like I'm being weighed down.

THERAPIST: Almost like you have little weights in your clothes? [*uses a simile to create a more concrete description of what the client is experiencing; notice the therapist does not use provocative examples*]

CLIENT: Or like a giant weighted blanket, but not in a good way.

THERAPIST: [*laughs a little*] That's fair. Is there any part of your body that has feeling or a different sensation? Or is it all numb? [*enhances noticing and distinction*]

CLIENT: Right now?

THERAPIST: Yeah, sitting in the chair right now.

CLIENT: I mean, I guess I can feel my back in the chair. I've been sitting at a weird angle and it's kind of tight. [*adjusts in their seat*]

THERAPIST: Okay, anything else? Doesn't have to be, I'm just curious.

CLIENT: I mean, I guess I can feel my eyeballs.

THERAPIST: Always a good sign. Okay, so you feel a giant weighted blanket holding your body down when you don't want to be. Some pain or aches in your back. Your eyeballs exist. And your mind is having the thought *What's the point?*

CLIENT: Pretty much.

THERAPIST: Thanks for walking me through that. It helps me understand the ways that depression can show up in the moment for you. Would you be willing to try something with me? No is a perfectly fine answer.

CLIENT: Sure, why not.

THERAPIST: Awesome. [*raises hand for the client to see and begins to tap one finger at a time to her thumb*] Do you see what I'm doing with my hand? How I'm tapping each finger to my thumb? Would you try that with me?

CLIENT: [*holds up hand*] Just do this?

THERAPIST: Yes, except I want you to pay attention to the moment you feel your finger touch your thumb. See if you can really zoom in and notice sooner and sooner.

THERAPIST: [*longer pause as they both practice*] What do you notice?

CLIENT: If I pay attention, I can feel it barely touching. It kind of tickles and itches at the same time.

THERAPIST: Excellent! And what about the numbness and suicidal thoughts? Are they still there? Totally okay if they are.

CLIENT: Yeah, they're there still.

THERAPIST: Cool. So even when you feel heaviness and pain, and your mind is suggesting the ultimate escape, you are able to choose where you focus your attention? [*encourages client for noticing; highlights they can create choice using tapping exercise*]

CLIENT: Yeah?

THERAPIST: Perfect. Now, I'm not suggesting you walk around constantly tapping your fingers. But maybe there are other experiences or people in your life that you can intentionally focus on when the heaviness comes in. For example, I know you've mentioned taking your dog to the dog park and crocheting are important to you. And your friends. [*connects client to values; begins safety plan*]

CLIENT: But they're never available.

THERAPIST: That is frustrating that they aren't always available when you really need them. We can discuss some resources for you to reach out to if they aren't available and you need to talk to someone. But I'm wondering if you could schedule some times to get together with your friends. Even if you have to schedule it further out. Does that sound possible? [*shifts to committed actions; introduces crisis hotline resources*]

CLIENT: Yeah, I usually have to reach out to them like a week in advance, but I always forget.

THERAPIST: Okay, well let's explore some ways to make that a bit easier for you.

This work is not a substitute for identifying crisis resources, safety planning, or even contacting support people. It is an approach to frame those experiences within the context of our values. And it gives us the opportunity to include that type of crisis management work within the framework of therapy instead of stepping outside of therapy to address these concerns.

By approaching high-risk concerns from this perspective, we are able to practice defusion, acceptance, and present-moment awareness skills in real time while being ethically and legally responsible. And just because I think it's worth mentioning twice, while you can implement some of these strategies to navigate a scenario where you feel unsafe, your safety and the safety of your client comes first. At that point, the function changes from therapy to safety.

How to Treat Historical Information

A quick note about treating historical information: Some of it is helpful, and some of it may be required as part of your work setting. Regardless of the incentive, let's look at how we frame historical information according to ACT. The goal is to frame historical information in how it impacts the client today. How what they have experienced informs their beliefs, rules, fused content, and patterns. We gather this information with the function of understanding who and what may impact their life and inform their values.

One strategy I have for collecting historical information without making my intake assessments one long Q&A is offering questionnaire forms prior to session. Even if you see clients in person, explore whether you are able to have clients complete a historical questionnaire prior to showing up for the session. This provides an opportunity to relate, in the moment, the experiences in their past to their current concerns without having to ask every question during the session. It creates a more fluid opportunity to engage in functional analysis as part of the intake process. The following dialogue shows how a therapist might address historical information in session:

CLIENT: I have really low self-esteem. My wife always comments how hard I am on myself, but I just don't know how to stop. There's just this voice in my head telling me I'm worthless and ugly and stupid.

THERAPIST: That's got to be really hard getting anything done when your mind is saying such horrible things. When did that voice first start?

CLIENT: It feels like it's always been there, but probably around third grade.

THERAPIST: That's a long time that your mind has been talking to you like that. I noticed in your intake forms that you mentioned that your parents got divorced around that time. Are those two things connected at all? [*approaches with curiosity while being open to the idea that there isn't anything there*]

CLIENT: Yeah, that's when my mom started making comments about me. I'm a lot like my dad, and she hated it. She hated him. We've always had a rocky relationship, but it got so much worse then. I ended up asking to live with my dad full-time because of it but wasn't able to until high school.

THERAPIST: That's awful. You were a child and had nothing to do with their divorce or marriage. I'm sorry your mom wasn't able to separate the two of you in her mind. It makes sense though why that voice is so loud. I imagine as a young boy it was really hurtful and impactful for your own mom to say things like that.

CLIENT: Yeah, it was. And even though as an adult with my own kids I know she was in the wrong, I can't shake those thoughts.

THERAPIST: It makes sense in a way. Those thoughts have had a long time to grow. And I imagine that even when you don't want to, it's hard not to listen to them. Would it be fair to say that one of our goals for therapy would be not only identifying the type of person you want to be but also learning how to create space from those thoughts so even if they continue to be there, you can show up to your life in the way you want? [*sets goals and expectations for what therapy can help with*]

CLIENT: That would be amazing.

One caveat as a cautionary tale: In ACT, we focus on the function of behaviors both internal and external—cognitive and observable. As a result, we spend way more time on the context of our client's experience than the content of that experience. And yet, it can be very easy to get dragged down the rabbit hole with them. Some of the content that your clients will share will be fascinating to you. And it can be very easy to justify using that curiosity to pull on a thread that isn't relevant at all to what you are working on. So whenever you are digging deeper into a story, please pause to ask yourself what the function of it is.

Sometimes we accidentally pull a thread while rapport building. Other times it's with Socratic questioning or by taking the long, scenic route to get to a certain point. Whatever the impetus, remember that our focus is on helping clients notice how they interact with themselves and the world, identify patterns of behavior that are no longer useful to them, and learn to be present, intentional, and engage with what matters to them.

Kelly Wilson, cofounder of ACT, uses the metaphor that clients are sunsets to appreciate, not math problems to solve. Sometimes I think an accurate metaphor for therapy is that we're riding along with our client in the car on their journey. And sometimes instead of helping them move forward toward the life they want to live, we slow down to more closely gawk at the car wreck on the opposite side of the road.

Considerations for Practice Settings

While our aim in ACT is flexibility and adaptability based on who we are sitting across from in the therapy room, we may encounter some very real barriers. Take a moment to think through the requirements for your practice setting. While keeping those requirements in mind, how would you go about incorporating what we've discussed in this chapter into your intake practice? If a client could come away from the intake with one ACT-specific piece of knowledge or information, what would it be?

Even if your intake restrictions are quite rigid, you may be able to preface your first session with an introduction about why you have to get all of this information, and then highlight how this is different from the therapy work you'll be doing together. Or you can incorporate less symptom-reduction language and more values-based goals for treatment, which we'll discuss in depth in chapter 6.

While intakes can be very content-heavy, you can begin to incorporate follow-up questions that explore workability and function. This can be as simple as asking the client what they've noticed over the short term and long term in regard to their behavior and outcome.

At the end of an intake, aim to meet two objectives:

1. Have a clear picture of the client's current unworkable patterns and an understanding of their values and committed actions
2. Client walks away from intake with a new insight into noticing, understanding, or interrupting their patterns

The first objective is relevant for treatment planning and diagnosis. Patterns of experiential avoidance can help inform diagnostic criteria. If we take a step back to look at hooks and avoidance behaviors, we often find all the symptoms of a diagnosis in those two segments. Let's look at someone with PTSD. Their hooks may include feelings of fear, horror, or anger; memories related to the trauma in the form of flashbacks or nightmares; physical sensations of panic; thoughts related to suicidal ideation; and hopeless beliefs about the world. Add to that avoidance behaviors, such as rumination, drinking, and avoiding places or people that remind them of the trauma, and we have a pretty full picture of PTSD criteria. Meanwhile, a person's values can help inform treatment planning. We can use values-based behaviors, or committed actions, as our treatment goals.

The second objective is more vague but no less important. When a client leaves an intake, you want them to have an insight, something to pay attention to for next time you meet, or the beginning of a clear understanding of what exactly they'll be doing in therapy and how it can help them. This does not mean a client will come away from an intake feeling hopeful, excited, or confident. But rather, they will begin to shift from labeling their symptoms to looking for unworkable patterns. This will nicely set you up for introducing creative hopelessness into your next sessions.

The simplest way to create this insight is through noticing. It may be that you notice their voice picks up speed as they talk about their past. Perhaps they almost seem detached from the narrative of their life. Point that out, interrupt it, or do both! It may be that they become dysregulated during intake and you guide them through a present-moment awareness practice like finger tapping (see script in chapter 10) or mindful breathing. Then help them vaguely understand what just happened, and, for example, have them notice outside of therapy other times that a powerful thought or emotion leads to them shutting down. The following dialogue shows how a therapist might wrap up an intake session:

THERAPIST: We're almost wrapping up on our time here today. I really appreciate your willingness to be open and share with me today. I know it can feel tedious or overwhelming to share everything, but it really helps me understand what you've been going through. I know it's been a lot. I can already tell how compassionate and empathetic you are. It seems like relationships are really important to you. [*reinforces acceptance and willingness and begins identifying values*]

CLIENT: Yeah, they are.

THERAPIST: Oftentimes we can look at the source of our greatest pains and find what really matters to us. I know you mentioned a couple times today that of all the horrible statements and accusations your mom made, the one that's hurt the most and stuck around the longest is the idea that you're unlovable and will be alone forever. It makes sense, given how much you want close, loving relationships with the people in your life, why that statement out of all of them would be the most terrifying. My hope for our work together is that you are able to notice those thoughts without letting them take over and change how you show up to the people who matter to you. To give you back a little more control over how you choose to move through the world—rather than those thoughts holding you hostage. [*shows the relationship between pain and values; transitions into expectations for work together*]

Client: I'd really like that.

Therapist: As I mentioned earlier, our clinic conducts intakes over two days, so in our next meeting, we will dive a bit further into some topics we discussed today, and I'll have a few more questions for you. The goal at the end of that session is to have a clear set of treatment goals and a plan for therapy moving forward. Between now and the next time we meet, I'd love if you can simply notice if there are other situations where a thought or memory pops up and you feel like it drags you down a rabbit hole and out of your life. [*sets up homework that involves noticing hooks and avoidance behaviors*]

Chapter Takeaways

- In ACT, the intake assessment can be an opportunity to begin to explore ACT's core processes.

- Hooks and experiential avoidance provide diagnostic symptoms while also helping clients conceptualize their own patterns of behavior.

- The first part of an intake assessment is a great opportunity to set tight stimulus control so clients know what to expect in therapy with you.

- From a functional contextual perspective, we approach suicidal ideation similar to other hooks. They are just thoughts. Though we still appropriately assess for risk—that is, the client's response to those thoughts—and provide crisis intervention and safety plans as appropriate.

- Historical information is explored based on how it informs the client's behavior in the present.

CHAPTER 6

TREATMENT PLANNING AND RELATIONSHIP BUILDING

Treatment planning when you aren't working from a symptom-reduction agenda can be challenging. The most obvious treatment goal is to reduce whatever the client is struggling with. But from an ACT framework, that's not our aim. And yet, we still want and potentially need to develop specific, actionable goals to aim for. So how do we frame this in a way that is easy for clients to understand, makes sense within our framework, and still meets whatever requirements we face in our practice or insurance relationships?

Treatment Goals Are Committed Actions

Let's take a step back and look at what we are trying to achieve in our work. We can think about our treatment goals through the lens of increasing psychological flexibility by improving awareness of our full experience in order to be present and engaged in our values. We can also use the three pillars of focused acceptance and commitment therapy (fACT): open, aware, and engaged (see chapter 7). *Openness* to our experience encompasses acceptance and defusion processes. *Aware* involves present-moment awareness and self-as-context, and *engaged* highlights our values and committed actions.

At the end of the day, our clients' committed actions are the treatment goals. And those committed actions are not only informed by values, but they can include practices from other processes in the hexaflex. When we think about treatment goals in ACT, we are focused on behaviors, both cognitive and observable. These are actions that the client can engage in that are within their control. One of the pitfalls of a symptom-reduction focus is that treatment goals become largely focused on reducing symptoms such as thoughts, feelings, or sensations, which we don't always have control over. As a result, we're basically setting up our clients to the whims of luck. This can perpetuate a narrative with a client that nothing they do matters, because they may try really hard and still not be able to change those symptoms.

Conversely, behavioral goals are within the client's control. In fact, setting committed actions as treatment goals clearly highlights the skills clients need to develop in order to be better equipped to respond to those symptoms. There are other modalities of therapy that take this approach as well—for example, SMART goals are highly actionable.

Adapting Diagnosis-Based Treatment Plans

When we look at specific diagnoses, there are many tried and true practices and skills that have a large evidence backing. When we explore treatment planning under the context of an ACT approach, our goal is to use ACT as a framework and incorporate these practices under the umbrella.

For example, *behavioral activation* for depression is a standard practice. From a CBT perspective, behavioral activation suggests that engaging in different behaviors can change how we feel. This is not too far off from ACT, although we would look at that change in emotion as a by-product rather than the outcome we are seeking. Behavioral activation might be informed by depressive symptoms: social isolation, anhedonia, and so forth. We might encourage a client to get out of bed and shower every morning, or schedule a time to get together with a friend. The assumption being that social engagement, daily routine, and sleeping closer to an eight-hour schedule can help a person feel more energized and connected. Behavioral activation generally starts with a standard series of behaviors. However, they are not grounded in any deeper purpose outside of "these things usually help people feel better."

But what happens if it doesn't? I've had numerous clients come to me and report that their previous therapy helped while they were in therapy, but they stopped seeing the effects when they terminated treatment. Or they felt compelled to lie to their therapist because they were trying so hard to help them but it wasn't working. One of the great benefits of creating behavioral-based goals is that we can focus on what is within our clients' control. And if they are struggling to engage in that goal? We make it smaller and build up from there.

So where does ACT fit in? Values. When treatment planning, we want to explore what outcomes our clients are looking for, and then tie those outcomes to values. The following dialogue shows one way a therapist might establish treatment goals with a client:

THERAPIST: So let's say we fast-forward to three months from now and you feel like therapy is working. What changes would you see in your life?

CLIENT: I wouldn't be crying all the time and would feel more fulfilled in my life.

THERAPIST: Makes sense. If I could be a fly on the wall watching you live this more fulfilled life—in a non-creepy way of course—what would I see you doing? [*asks for behavioral examples to identify committed actions from their symptom-reduction desire*]

CLIENT: Probably leaving the house, going for more walks, actually going to things I'm invited to.

THERAPIST: That sounds great! Is there anything you'd want to be working toward to feel fulfilled? Does that pertain more to your personal life or professional life as well? There are no wrong answers here.

CLIENT: I guess I want to feel like I'm doing something with my life, not simply existing.

THERAPIST: Do you have any idea what that might be? It's okay if you don't. We can work on that.

CLIENT: It might sound silly, but I used to paint. When I was younger, I used to paint and draw and really loved it.

THERAPIST: That's not silly at all!

CLIENT: I know it's not like some huge career goal, but honestly, work is just work to me. I want to have something that is mine and feels creative and helps me get outside.

THERAPIST: Love that. Okay, so I'm hearing connecting with loved ones, getting outside in nature, and creativity are really important to you. And maybe you're feeling a bit disconnected to those values right now. Does that sounds about right? [*summarizes values*]

CLIENT: That's exactly it. But I can't even get out of bed most days and shower, so painting feels impossible.

THERAPIST: I get that. And we'll build up to it. But knowing where you want to be headed can at least give us an idea of why getting out of bed might be worth it. And that's where our work comes in. Learning how to sit with the heaviness and sadness and fatigue to make small steps toward the life you want to create. [*introduces acceptance process*]

The therapist has an idea of this client's values and what they want to create in their life, as well as the ways in which depression is showing up and taking over. Now let's create a plan. I like to think of treatment planning as a series of questions centering the client:

1. What does the client want?
    - A more fulfilling life
2. What are the behaviors associated with this?
    - Saying yes to social events and attending
    - Painting outside
    - Going on walks; leaving the house
3. What values tie into these behaviors?
    - Connection
    - Creativity
    - Nature

4. What is showing up and making this difficult?
    - Depressed mood
    - Tearfulness
    - Low energy
    - Thoughts: *Nothing will ever change*
5. What strategies would be beneficial for her to develop?
    - Defusion from thoughts
    - Acceptance and present-moment awareness of physical and emotional sensations of depression
    - Increased connection to values
    - Committed action; behavioral activation

You may need to be more descriptive for your workplace setting, but in general, this is what that process would look like. Notice that I have not referenced a decrease in any emotion, thought, or physical sensation. Now, the likely by-product of this treatment plan is that the client feels better. But even if they still have depressive symptoms, they will be living a life connected to what is most important to them.

Focusing on What Is Within Our Control

There are lots of things outside of our control: other people, the past, the future, and at times, our internal experience. Our focus is creating goals that are achievable and within our control. Honestly, a lot of therapy can at times feel like a constant redirection to what is within our control in this moment, instead of the time traveling our mind tends to do when left to its own devices. Our aim then is to focus on increasing behaviors that are working and interrupting patterns that aren't. But behaviors are always at the core of that focus. Remember that in ACT, it's not the thoughts or feelings that are problematic—it is how we engage with them. Think *action verbs*.

And even when we are focused on interrupting unworkable patterns, we are not emphasizing the absence or lack of a behavior. Rather, we look toward what we are building. With unhelpful patterns, we are building pivots. We are practicing defusion exercises. We are accepting. Or we are deciding that we aren't willing and then pivoting again to something we can move toward.

Life can very often feel like choosing a shopping cart at a grocery store. Sometimes it's bumpy, sometimes it's smooth, sometimes it's weirdly sticky and we want to recoil, and often, the wheel gets stuck and we have to pull it back a little to push forward again. But whatever surface we have to traverse, there is a way forward. ACT teaches us how to navigate the moments when it's not as smooth. Not through getting rid of the shopping cart and trying to carry our grocery haul in our hands, but rather through noticing what type of force or skill is needed on any given surface.

Now, depending on your setting, you may need to include symptom-reduction behaviors. Maybe your practice setting has strict protocols for treatment planning, or you use assessments that look at symptom severity as a marker, so your goals must reflect reducing the symptom severity. We can work with that. The important piece to keep in mind is always including it within a context of what you are moving toward. Maybe your treatment goal is to decrease or eliminate the prevalence of panic attacks in your client with panic disorder. And yet, the way you go about doing that may involve exposure work grounded in values—informed by what is important to the client and how it improves their functioning in everyday life (see chapter 11).

If you're struggling with the concept of a non-symptom-reduction agenda, that's okay. Think of it as improving function over reducing symptoms. Consider this: Death is a great way to stop feeling pain (we think), but you'd never suggest a client kill themselves. Because the goal isn't really about a client not feeling a certain way—it's about improving their life. We are conditioned to believe that only comes about through symptom reduction, but there are so many examples where that is not the case.

For example, if you have a client with body dysmorphia, you'd never suggest disordered eating, such as stopping eating or starting an extremely restrictive "eat-one-cookie-a-day" diet, even if it works in the short term for weight loss. Because not only is it not sustainable and harmful (even potentially fatal), but it also doesn't help with body dysmorphia. Many clients who undergo bariatric surgery assume going into it that weight loss will solve all of their insecurities. The truth is that many of them still feel insecure about their body and exhibit distorted thinking related to their appearance following weight loss surgery. The number on the scale may have changed, but how that person relates to themselves and their inner monologue has not.

Feelings, thoughts, physical sensations, urges, and memories exist in the moment. They are fleeting. Even if someone feels constantly anxious or apathetic, their experience still fluctuates moment to moment. Any temporary fix is just that, temporary. By moving away from a focus on reducing symptoms, we are moving from short-term to long-term outcomes. From symptom relief to improved functioning. In ACT, we are focused on what we are moving toward, what we are building up, and what works in the long term. As you are crafting your treatment plans and writing your notes, keep that at the forefront of your mind.

Collaborative Goal Setting and Relationship Building

While we are the therapy experts, clients are the experts on their own experience. Treatment planning and goal setting should be a collaborative process informed by the client's goals. Most clients will frame their goals focused on symptom reduction. Your goal from an ACT model is to identify the values and behavioral changes that are aligned with those goals. A simple way to ask this is "If you were no longer struggling with [*symptoms*], what would I see you spending your time doing?" This question reframes the request for reducing symptoms to reducing the struggle with symptoms—an important distinction in ACT. Then, it digs further into what observable changes clients would like to see.

I don't want this to seem like a magician's sleight of hand. We are not tricking clients into changing their goals. Instead, you might engage in creative hopelessness exercises to highlight what is within their control and what isn't. Or you can simply have a conversation with your client:

> *It sounds like you've really been hurting these last few months. I'm glad you decided to come to therapy. I think we can help you get to a place where you are moving forward with your life toward all those wonderful things you mentioned:* [behavioral goals]. *That being said, I'm not a magician, and therapy isn't magic. I can't promise you that you will never experience* [presenting symptoms] *again. What I can do though is help you develop a new way of responding to everything that's been showing up inside you—all the thoughts and feelings and sensations that are keeping you* [insert client's language here: stuck, down, hostage, in the past].
>
> *A lot of times we begin with the desire to just make the "bad" stuff go away. But usually that doesn't change much. You don't feel as awful temporarily, which is nice, but in the end, nothing really changes in how you approach yourself and your world. My hope is that together we can clearly identify what matters to you, notice what patterns aren't serving you anymore, and develop strategies and skills for interrupting those patterns so you can live life the way you want to no matter what shows up. How does that sound?*

Once you get buy-in from clients, then you walk through the treatment plan and steps. You don't need to use all the jargon or identify each exercise you'll be doing—just a basic overview of what you'll focus on and why it can be helpful. This also includes a discussion about frequency of treatment and how long sessions usually last. For example, I had a client who was experiencing panic attacks, met criteria for panic disorder, and also had a childhood trauma that she wanted to process further. We discussed her goals, and I suggested that we focus on developing strategies for her panic first, as those symptoms might get worse as we delve into her trauma. I wanted her to have tools to navigate that process before we began.

Role of Self-Disclosure in ACT

There are many schools of thought on self-disclosure, and your training may have influenced your personal views on this topic. However, if you are bringing ACT into your work, it's important to look at how ACT views self-disclosure and building the therapeutic relationship.

As always, the first question has to do with function. Whenever you are choosing to self-disclose, it is imperative you ask yourself: *How does this serve my client and therapeutic relationship?* The next question: *Is there another way I can achieve the same aim without self-disclosing or by self-disclosing less?* ACT views self-disclosure as a behavior that can benefit or harm therapy depending on how it functions in the therapy room. However, ACT tends to be more welcoming of self-disclosure.

I always let clients know when we first begin working together that it is okay to be curious and ask questions. I highlight that some clients want to know a little bit about their therapists as it makes them feel more comfortable, and others have bad experiences where therapists have shared too much and it was uncomfortable. I let them know that they are always allowed to ask me a question and I will always give an honest answer, even if that answer is that I do not share that information with my clients. They know no question or conversation is off limits as long as it's asked from a place of genuine curiosity, kindness, and respect. From my own observations, younger clients are more likely to ask me personal questions compared to my older clients—the typical exception being older veterans.

The cool thing about self-disclosure is it's not an on-or-off kind of skill. There is a range of ways we self-disclose for the benefit or detriment of the client. You get to decide how comfortable and at what point along the spectrum you want to be. Self-disclosure doesn't have to be specific details about your life. It can be observations you've noticed about your client or reactions you've had to something they've shared. This can be valuable information to help clients see something from a different perspective. It can also be an opportunity to increase their awareness of themselves.

For example, I might share my observations with my client about their body language (crossed arms, eye contact, shaking legs, holding their breath), speech (rapid speech, changing the subject, talking in tangents all of a sudden, stuttering or having trouble finding words), how they talk about themselves (dismissing their experience, downplaying what happened, blaming themselves, hindsight bias, being highly critical, or name-calling). This can help draw the client's attention to what is happening in the moment and create a pause to notice and perhaps engage in a different behavior. This is a great opportunity to practice ACT core processes in session. Sharing your observations can lead into present-moment awareness exercises or a functional analysis on patterns of behavior.

I will sometimes share seemingly "taboo" examples clients might have mentioned previously in an effort to make a client feel safe to discuss a certain topic with me. This usually comes up around sexual preferences or kinks. This can be a great defusion intervention in session. Hearing a therapist casually mention behaviors that elicit a client's deep shame or embarrassment can help the client pause and create space around these feelings. In this way, you are modeling a different response to a topic that a client has learned to hide from or avoid.

If you stay focused on that initial question about function, check in with your clients, and hold firm to professional boundaries, you'll find what works for you, if you haven't already. And remember, you have a professional responsibility to your clients. You do not have a responsibility to share every part of yourself with them.

Tips for Relationship Building

There is a lot that goes into building a collaborative therapeutic relationship. While you have likely learned all about how to do this in school and other trainings, it is such an important component of ACT that I wanted to briefly share what has worked well in my ACT practice over the years:

- **Create an open environment:** One of the hardest roadblocks to therapy can be getting inaccurate feedback from clients. A client may lie about completing homework because they're embarrassed. They may say they understand an exercise when they don't. They may have felt uncomfortable with what you said or did in session but not bring it up. It is your job to create an environment that lessens these factors. Ask questions that don't pull for a rhetorical answer. I sometimes do this by adding, "And no is a perfectly acceptable response" to the end of my questions. I might also ask, "What questions do you have?" instead of "Do you have any questions?"

- **Welcome feedback and questions:** Tell your clients that you are always open to feedback and criticism. Explain that it's your job to pay attention, and their help is a bonus. In fact, they would be doing you a favor by providing feedback.

- **Set appropriate homework expectations:** For example, if a client states they're going to start writing in their journal every evening when they've never written in a journal before, you may offer the suggestion of *thinking* about writing every day but aiming to write in it twice before the next session. By introducing flexibility and realistic expectations, your client may feel less anxious sharing that they didn't write in it at all.

- **Follow up with homework compassionately:** When you ask a client if they did their homework, it can feel really anxiety-provoking for some clients to say no. So instead, you might summarize what you discussed for homework and then ask, "How did attempting that go?" or "Did you have an opportunity to try?" It may seem like a small difference, but leaving room for a variety of responses creates more honesty.

- **Maintain your boundaries:** What you choose to self-disclose, mentioned earlier in this chapter, is part of this. But so is how to handle certain client behaviors and comments. For example, do you have a plan for how to handle sexist, racist, homophobic, or other demeaning or disrespectful comments? Take time and think about what your boundaries are and how you want to handle them so you don't have to figure it out in the moment.

- **Don't lie to your clients:** You may not always choose to answer your clients' questions, but do not lie to them. Tell them this. It helps me to build trust as they know I will call them out when needed and that they can trust what I tell them.

Assessing a Client's Willingness

At the end of the day, the most important aspect of relationship building with your clients is remembering that willingness is not a rhetorical question. Essentially, we are asking our clients if they are willing to come in contact with their full experience, including painful stuff, in order to move in the direction of their values. This comes up at the very start of therapy through creative hopelessness and setting expectations, and it continues through all the work we do together. You may have the best treatment plan that makes the most sense, given a client's presenting concerns and your knowledge of what helps. None of that matters if a client is not willing to engage with certain content or experiences yet. The right treatment plan is one that meets the needs of the client and includes their willingness to come in contact with some pretty big pain.

This is not only something for you to keep in mind, but also something to communicate with clients. Be mindful of how you phrase questions and conversations around treatment goals and steps. When we ask clients if they are willing to try something new and learn to sit with (accept) their full experience in order to move toward what matters most to them, it sounds like we're setting them up for a trick question. What else can they say other than yes? That's the whole reason they're in therapy. But what we are asking of clients is hard. Processing trauma memories, experiencing panic symptoms, and sitting with loneliness is awful. It's a truly unpleasant, challenging, often frustrating, non-linear experience. It's also wonderful and empowering and inspiring in many ways. But only if someone is freely choosing to try.

If you are asking someone if they are willing to interact with, explore, expose, or otherwise face their pain, please know that "no" is a perfectly fine answer. It is okay to not be ready. It is okay for your client to decide they don't want to face that yet, if ever. Setting up this conversation so that it is not rhetorical not only allows you to meet your client where they are at, but it also helps to avoid harm.

Clients who feel forced into an experience they are not ready for may encounter worsening symptoms from those exercises. It may increase their belief that they are the problem when they continue to avoid homework assignments. And it may even cause them to stop therapy. Your goal is to turn that question into a discussion. A conversation about what they feel ready for, what their fears are, and what fused thoughts are telling them—and then create a plan for moving forward. One that is paced to your client's starting point and willingness. You can also validate or commiserate with your client about how frustrating it is to start small. How mean our mind gets when our progress comes with setbacks.

Continue to remind clients that you are working at their pace and wherever they are and however fast or slow they are moving is the right place to begin. We often want to rush to the finish line in both our own lives and with our clients. Yet finding the right starting point and increasing a willingness to start there, even if it's much further back than you or they would like, can help your client reach their goals so much faster. Remember the shopping cart metaphor: Sometimes in therapy, we may want to push forward despite meeting resistance. Don't keep trying to push ahead. Pause, pull back a little, and then find a new path forward. As long as you have a clear vision of where you are headed, you can get there.

How to Handle Common Rebuttals

In your first sessions with clients—particularly as you are introducing ACT, getting buy-in, establishing treatment goals, and building rapport—you may receive some push back. Clients tend to feel at the end of their rope, hesitant, and even resistant. This is completely understandable. They've come to therapy expecting you to make all their pains go away, and here you are saying pain is actually a part of life, that the problem is just their response to it. I've found some helpful ways to get them to think differently about the ACT framework or to be willing to try a new approach. Finding common ground and moving forward is key.

"So there's no hope?"

Sometimes when I introduce creative hopelessness, the message clients hear is that I can't help them. They are hurting and understandably want the pain to stop. In these instances, it's important to walk through a functional analysis to highlight how their attempts to delete or erase their pain doesn't work. But that doesn't mean there isn't hope. We just have to take a different path. And validate their pain. Here's how that might sound:

> *It can feel like that sometimes, can't it? I hate that feeling. While I cannot guarantee you'll never have a nightmare again or never experience panic, I can help you learn how to respond when that stuff shows up so it doesn't continue to snowball into something so huge it takes over your life. Right now your attempts to escape and avoid this pain are exhausting. I can tell how hard you've been working to try to fix this. But maybe it's not that you're not working hard enough but that what you've been trying only works for a little bit. Would you be willing to try something different with me?*

Buy-in can come in the form of curiosity or a willingness to simply try, even if they are unsure it'll make a difference.

"So I just have to suck it up?"

This is why I have an issue with the term *acceptance*. It draws these types of responses. Understandably so. Many people believe the job of a helping professional is to make clients' pain go away. Therefore, to discuss sitting with that pain suggests to the client that they are a lost cause and they just need to get used to how awful their life is. This is not the message we want to be sending. Instead, we want to highlight how our work together in ACT might look different from work they've done in the past. You can give reassurances for the process of the work, but be careful not to attempt to rescue the client here and make promises you can't keep. Here's how you might do this:

> *No, of course not. That would really suck. There is a lot of work that we can do together to help you create a wonderful, meaningful life. It might not look like how you'd always thought, but if you are willing to give it a shot, I think we can do some pretty great work together. That work involves*

learning to recognize some of these patterns that aren't serving you anymore, develop strategies and skills to interrupt those patterns, and begin to identify what actually matters to you in life and what you want to be working toward. Part of this process does involve coming into contact with the stuff you hate. Not so that I can say, "Well, just be okay with it and suck it up," but so you can learn how to navigate life even when it does show up. Because unfortunately, we can't always control when it pops up or not. But we can develop great tools to respond differently when it does.

"I won't be alive for long, so it doesn't matter."

The short answer to this is "If it didn't matter, we wouldn't be discussing it right now." Everyone gets to choose what they want to explore and process in therapy. Clients must know that their consent is imperative to any work they do with you. Furthermore, highlight that it is okay if they don't want to focus on anything now. The idea of venturing into large pains in a client's life is extremely daunting. It's easy for them to think, "Well I've suffered for this long already—what's a few more years?" Play around with this thought. Regardless of how old a client is or how much time they have left in this world, there is always time to live a meaningful life, break unhelpful patterns, and find some peace through dropping the struggle of avoidance. This may be a series of conversations, and that's okay. You want them to be fully onboard or at least willing to take that first step. You can't force anyone into making changes. Nor would you want to. Hold space to acknowledge that these changes can feel hard and heavy—but they're likely worth it. Here's an example of doing so:

> *But doesn't that make it even more important? If you only have a finite amount of time left—and honestly none of us know when our time will be up—what do you have to lose by trying something different? Yes, what we are talking about is hard, heavy, and objectively not fun. But I could say the same thing about what you've been struggling with these past few decades. If it's going to be hard anyway, it might be worth seeing what happens if you do something different. I think it's worth it. Are you willing to give it a shot?*

"So it's all my fault?"

The difficulty with this question is that, in part, the answer is yes. Obviously, clients may not be responsible for past traumas, injuries, and the like. However, their attempts to try to manage those feelings or experiences may be making it worse. Here's how you might tackle this question:

> *No, this is not your fault. Sometimes life or our very biology seems to be working against us. That is not on you. But the ways we try to avoid and escape these pains can accidentally make things worse. It's actually a pretty natural response to pain. It is very human of you to want to not feel scared, hurt, or ashamed. We all want to feel less suffering in life. I'd be concerned if you didn't. It's just the way we usually go about it only works for a little bit and can sometimes hurt us more in the long term. Just*

like how you've noticed your symptoms worsening over time. That's not your fault—you were doing the best you could with the information and support you had. That's why therapy can be helpful. Our work together will be about understanding how our responses to thoughts, feelings, and sensations serve us in the short term and long term. Then, we'll develop some skills based on what would most help you.

"I don't like that. That doesn't seem fair."

It's not. It is imperative that you are not dismissive when clients bring up these conclusions. You may have a tendency to want to smooth everything over. To highlight how different people have different strengths and weaknesses. How everyone has challenges. This is not helpful in this context. And generally, it gives the message that clients are not allowed to feel upset about it, which is the exact opposite of what we are hoping to achieve. In many instances, it's not fair and it sucks. Here's an example answer for this rebuttal:

I don't like it either, to be honest. It's not fair. There are many things in life we simply cannot control: our past, the future, other people, and the way our mind and body works to a great extent. And it is super frustrating at times when something you struggle with so much or never wanted in life is somehow easy for someone else. I am so sorry that [insert thing outside of their control that sucks, such as "You didn't have the type of parents you deserved."]. *You deserved better than that. I can't go back in time and fix that. I can't even make your parents better today. But what we can do is begin to work on giving you the skills to be more in control of the life you lead moving forward. Regardless of who your parents are. So that even in the absence of their support, you can thrive.*

A client once told me that sometimes it feels as if everyone else is herding sheep and she is herding cats. To this day, it's one of my favorite metaphors. It perfectly highlights the ways that sometimes you are facing different challenges in the world compared to others. It also shows how comparison isn't helpful because circumstances are so different. In ACT, our next step is then saying, "Okay, so you're herding cats. How can we make this more successful for you? Unfortunately, I do not have a magic wand to change them into sheep. But if we can start treating them like the cats they are, maybe we have a shot of changing what your next step is."

Chapter Takeaways

- Treatment goals in ACT are committed actions.
- Instead of creating symptom-reduction treatment goals, we are focused on values-based behaviors that are within the client's control.
- Framing the work we do as practice and attempts make it more likely your clients will share with you when they are struggling.
- Self-disclosure is not simply sharing about your life verbally with a client. It can be what you wear, what you say, and observations you make.
- Willingness is not a rhetorical question. Clients have the right to choose what they are willing to engage with in therapy.

PART III

Filling Your ACT Toolbox

CHAPTER 7

PSYCHOLOGICAL FLEXIBILITY TOOLS

As ACT continues to grow and adapt, there are even more tools available to introduce psychological flexibility to your clients. In this chapter, we will cover the most popular tools and approaches for exploring functional analysis, the six core ACT processes, and psychological flexibility. Not only can these tools be useful for your work with clients, but they also help to conceptualize the work we do in ACT. The more perspectives and angles you can learn from, the better.

These tools provide two really useful components. First, they create structure in an otherwise intangible process. For many clients, ACT can feel too abstract at times. There are many new concepts and shifts in perspective. For a client who is struggling, it may feel like trying to catch smoke. Tools like the ones described in this chapter can often give some form to the function of ACT. Worksheets, diagrams, and acronyms can give clients something concrete to engage with. It provides structure for both client and therapist. This is especially true for a therapist who is learning how to navigate through the core processes without falling into the trap of becoming overly wordy.

Second, these tools involve some type of visual component that many clients benefit from. The ACT matrix and the choice point, for example, are great diagrams for clients to create with you in session, but they can also take a picture of it and reflect on it at any time out of session. The more ways that clients are able to engage with the six core processes, functional analysis, and functional contextualism, the more likely this new framework for understanding their experience is to stick.

The ACT Matrix

The ACT matrix was created by Kevin Polk, Jerold Hambright, and Mark Webster to reconceptualize *away moves* as functionally moving away from painful internal experiences (thoughts, feelings, memories, physical sensations) (Polk et al., 2016). This is different from other tools in ACT that view away moves as moving away from values. This newer definition removes some of the punishing nature of moving away from values.

It also serves to validate the very human behavior of wanting to escape pain. By separating this dichotomy from toward or away from values into two distinct behaviors of toward values or away from pain, it creates space for the acknowledgment that away moves aren't inherently "bad," and they often make sense—they just aren't always super helpful.

The ACT matrix is a simple four-quadrant diagram. The horizontal axis represents our movement: moving away from our pain (on the left) and moving toward our values (on the right). The vertical axis represents our context: our observable behaviors (at the top), and our inner experience (at the bottom).

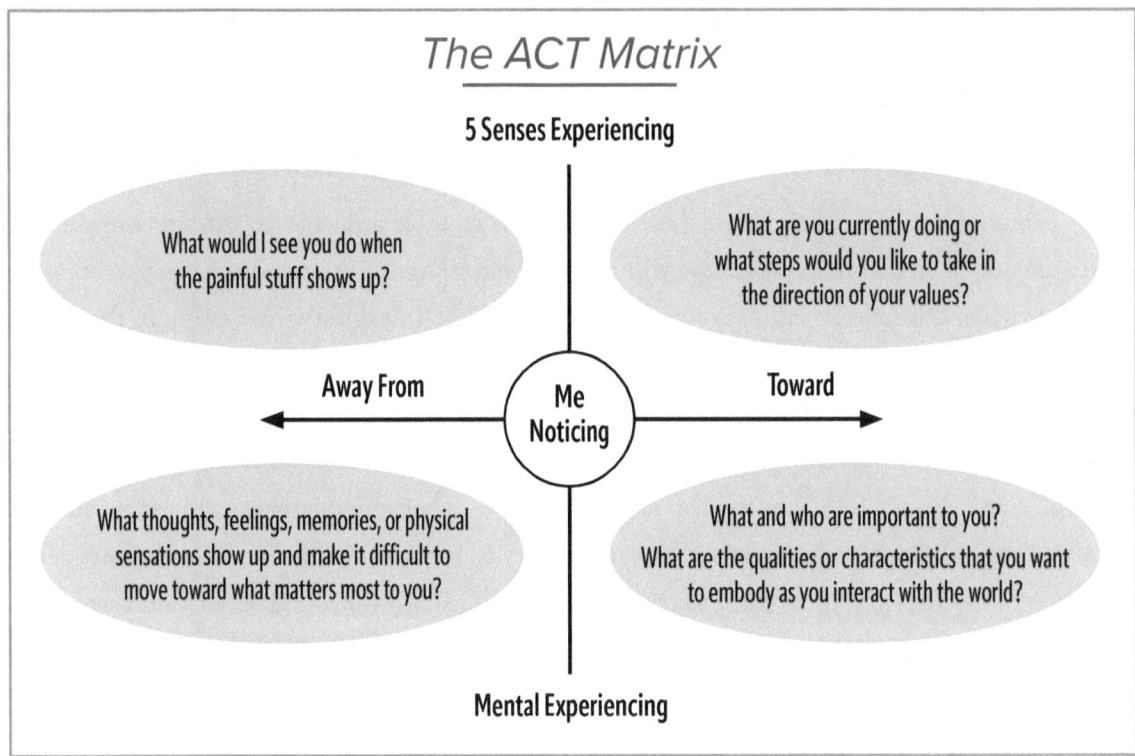

The *bottom right* quadrant represents our values. It answers the questions of "What and who are important to you?" and "What are the qualities or characteristics that you want to embody as you interact with the world?" This quadrant represents our internal experiences—thoughts, feelings, and physical sensations—intersecting with movement toward our values. It is that internal compass that is guiding us toward a meaningful life.

The *bottom left* quadrant represents fusion. It answers the question of "What thoughts, feelings, memories, or physical sensations show up and make it difficult to move toward what matters most to you?" This quadrant represents our internal experiences intersecting with movement away from pain. This is the internal content we are fused with or hooked by that creates pain we don't want to experience.

The *top left* quadrant represents experiential avoidance. It answers the question of "What would I see you do when the painful stuff shows up?" These are the observable behaviors we engage in to try to avoid or escape the internal pain. This quadrant is where all the avoidance actions go.

The *top right* quadrant represents committed actions. It answers the question "What are you currently doing or what steps would you like to take in the direction of your values?" These are the observable behaviors we engage in to move toward our values. These are small steps we can take every day to move toward the life we want to create.

In the center of the diagram, where the two lines meet, is a large circle. This circle represents our noticing or observing self. Sometimes it can feel like life is happening to us. This is a reminder that we are choosing our values, we are taking those steps, and we are witness to our full experience. It also serves to remind us that we get to choose how we show up to the world. And with practice, we can begin to choose more intentionally and more aligned with our values.

Doing a Functional Analysis with the ACT Matrix

We can use the left side of the ACT matrix to do a functional analysis. Using the diagram, you would walk clients through connecting how thoughts, feelings, memories, and physical sensations showing up in the bottom left quadrant lead to a reaction or behavior that shows up in the top left quadrant.

For example, you may start with the thought *What if I made a mistake?* in the bottom left quadrant. Then draw a line to a behavior in the top left quadrant—perhaps something like *Rechecking the document to make sure everything is there.* You can discuss with your client how that works in the short term. You may find this one action alleviates anxiety in the short term, but of course, it always ends up coming back. Or you may find that it's simply the start of a longer pattern. For example, maybe after they recheck the document, they feel "frustrated" or "exhausted" (bottom left) and then maybe they cancel plans with friends (top left). The process of doing a functional analysis doesn't change, but rather, you are using the diagram as a supplement to help clients visualize what this pattern looks like.

One consideration when using the matrix is that by dividing behaviors by observable (top) and internal (bottom), it can be harder to demonstrate a functional analysis with a client in which you show a pattern of antecedent-response. Both hooks—such as the thought *I'm worthless* and cognitive avoidance behaviors, like overthinking, planning, analyzing, and alternate realities—belong in the bottom left quadrant. I like the idea of having all of the avoidance behaviors in one spot because you can distinguish between fused content (the antecedents, which are out of our control) and our response to it (our behaviors, which are within our control). So keep this in mind as you set up the matrix with your clients. You may need to make distinctions when discussing what goes in the bottom left quadrant. Overall, the matrix is an excellent tool for connecting with core processes, exploring functional analysis, and emphasizing the difference between how behaviors operate in the short term and long term.*

---

* For a more in-depth look at the ACT matrix, you can learn directly from the founder, Kevin Polk, at https://www.theactmatrixacademy.com, read *The Essential Guide to The ACT Matrix* (Polk et al., 2016), or check out ways to adapt the matrix from ACT therapist and trainer Jacob Martinez at https://www.theactmatrix.com.

fACT and Three Pillars

Focused acceptance and commitment therapy (fACT) arose from a need for a model of ACT that could be applied in 30-minute sessions. Drs. Patricia Robinson and Kirk Strosahl developed fACT to accommodate various settings, such as with primary care mental health integration, and populations, such as single parents who lack the resources for childcare or access to reliable transportation to attend 60-minute sessions frequently (Strosahl et al., 2012).

fACT approaches the ACT model and psychological flexibility from three pillars: open, aware, and engaged. If you were explaining ACT to a client from this perspective you might say something like this:

> *The focus in ACT is to help you learn how to be **open** to your full experience, including the painful stuff we often want to escape from, in order to be **aware** of how we interact with the world and ourselves in the present moment so that we can become more **engaged** with what matters most to us and break patterns that are no longer serving us.*

As you might be able to surmise by the previous explanation, these three pillars map onto the six core processes and the hexaflex by grouping two like-processes together. The *open* pillar is acceptance and cognitive defusion. The *aware* pillar is present-moment awareness and self-as-context, and the *engaged* pillar is values and committed actions.

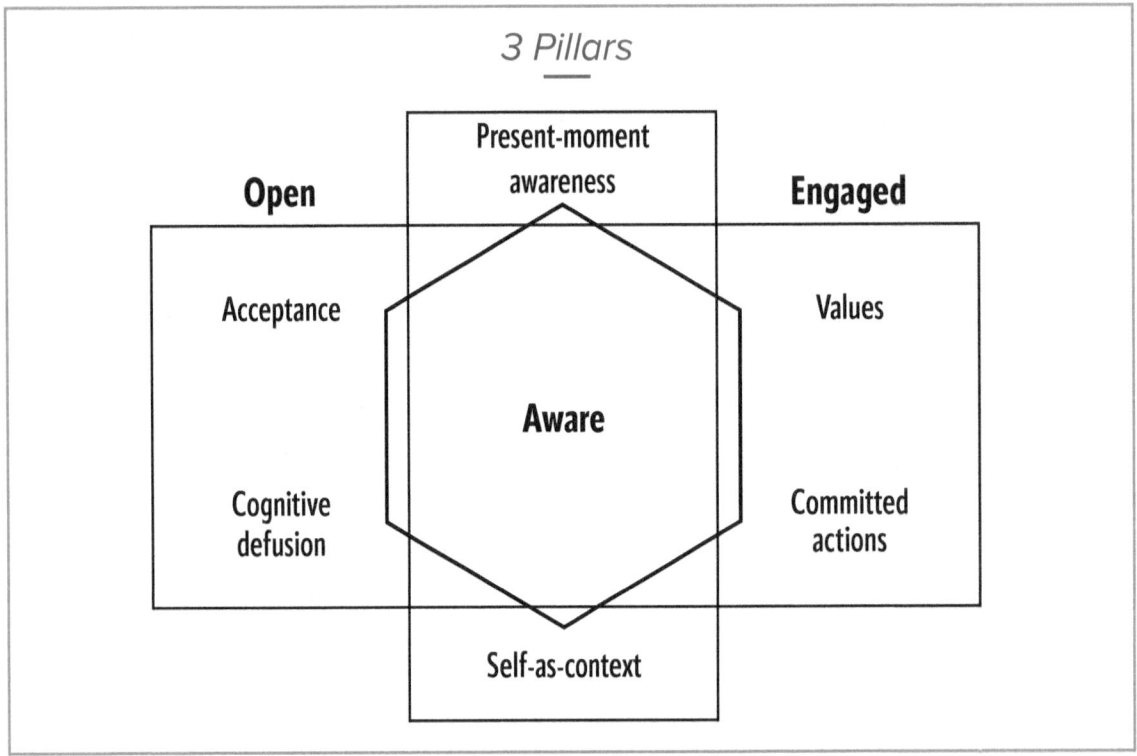

fACT works very well in hospital, primary care, and other outpatient community settings. Because it was designed to be used in brief settings or even one-off meetings, the starting assumption with fACT is that change can begin right now. Instead of the more traditional approach to therapy, where you spend the first session or two information-gathering without any real intervention, fACT maintains that each moment you have with your client or patient is an opportunity for intervention. It forces you to ask, "How would my work change if the next time I see a client is the last chance I have to work with them?"

Let's look at how an initial—or perhaps the only—session might go using a fACT model.

Initial Session Steps

The fACT model uses eight steps for an initial session in order to see meaningful change. It is imperative that you stay on track with the stated problem and goals without getting distracted by "side quests" (interesting threads clients mention that you want to pull). These steps are set up to be completed in a 25–30 minute session:

1. **Setting the stage:** Create expectations around who you are, what therapy will look like, and what your role in therapy is. This is a quick introduction to help set clear guidelines for the work you and the client will be doing together.

2. **Love, work, play, health:** Assess what the client's life looks like in these four domains. *Love* refers to their home life and important relationships, *work* refers to career, education, and job contexts, *play* includes hobbies, leisure activities, and community engagement, such as attending church, and *health* looks at how they are taking care of themselves and what physical and mental health concerns they have.

3. **Time, triggers, trajectory:** Here, you begin to explore when current issues began, what the client has already tried, what makes it worse and better, and the issues' trajectories over time (better, same, or worse).

4. **Problem severity:** This can also be thought of as how much a problem has impacted the client's functioning or disrupted their life. The client rates the severity on a 1–10 scale.

5. **Workability**: Perform a quick functional analysis to explore whether what the client is doing is working in the short term and long term.

6. **Agreement and options:** Get on the same page with the client about what the stated problem is, and offer two potential interventions for addressing the problem. This ensures the client is not overwhelmed with options while also having some say in their treatment.

7. **Intervention:** Provide in-session experiential exercise, skill training, and psychoeducation. End with an actionable step the client can test out in their life after the session.

8. **Confidence and helpfulness:** Check in with the client on how confident they feel in making this change (1–10 scale) and how helpful they found the session (1–10 scale).

Regardless of the setting type in which you are working or the duration of sessions, here are some core competencies from fACT you may want to integrate:*

- Meet the client where they are and walk with them on the journey.
- Imagine that this could be the last time you see this client, and decide what you want them to take away from the meeting.
- Decide which of the six core ACT processes or three fACT pillars the client is struggling with the most, then choose one intervention you could implement for them to work on.
- Always end a session with one actionable item for the client to work on.

The Choice Point

The choice point was first introduced in *The Weight Escape* by Joseph Ciarrochi, Ann Bailey, and Russ Harris (2014)—since then, it has undergone a second revision to be even more helpful (Harris, 2019). It is a simple, client-friendly tool for conducting a functional analysis on patterns of experiential avoidance. This diagram is a great way to visualize where clients have control over their actions.

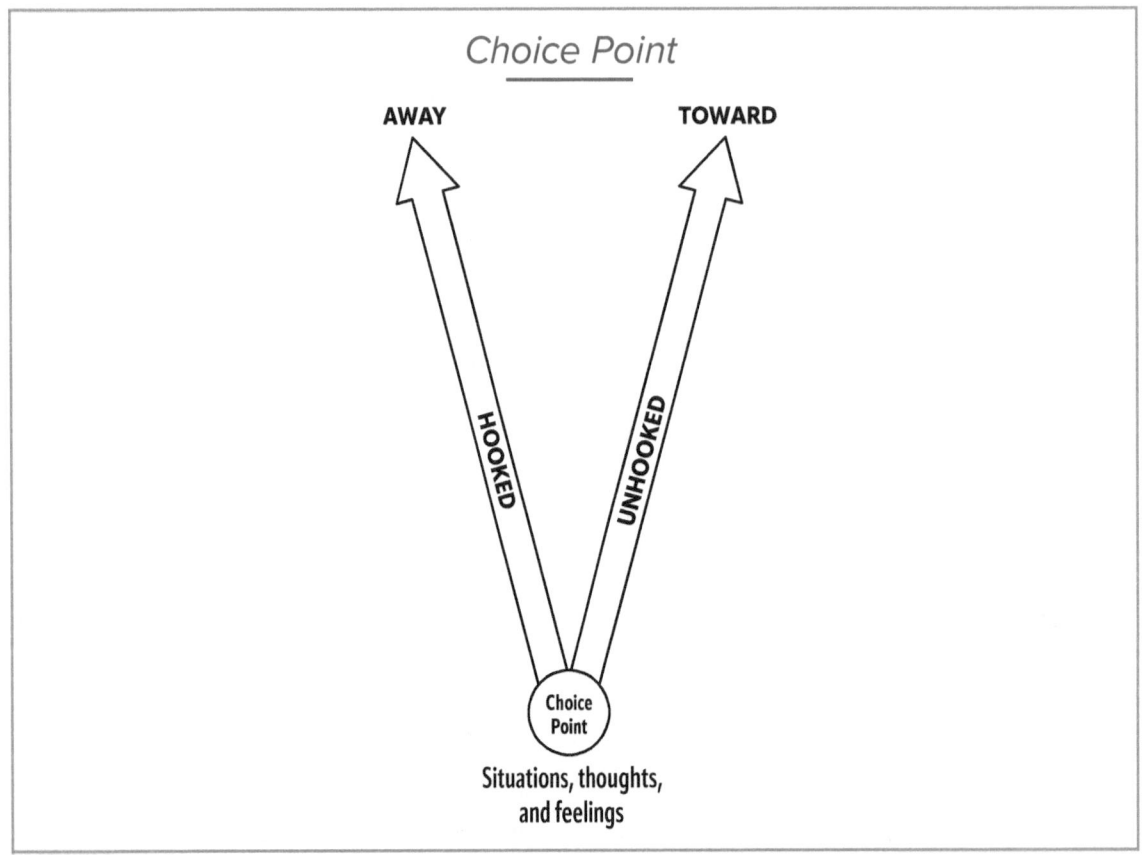

---

* For a more in-depth look at fACT, check out *Brief Interventions for Radical Change* by Kirk Strosahl, Patricia Robinson, and Thomas Gustavsson.

Often when we are stuck in patterns that aren't serving us, it feels as though we have no control. We are simply being dragged along in a very reactive way. Through cognitive defusion exercises, present-moment awareness, and even some self-as-context work, we can begin to notice these patterns as they are happening and create enough space to choose how we want to show up to the moment. If your client is struggling to understand what this looks like, the choice point can be a useful diagram, or even worksheet, for them to use.

The idea behind the choice point is exploring what happens when a client encounters a "challenging situation." When a client encounters a challenging situation or difficult thoughts and feelings, it pushes them to make a choice. They can move *toward* their values, the life they want to live, behaving consistently with the person they want to be and "acting effectively" (Ciarrochi et al., 2014). Or they can choose to move *away* from their values, away from the person they want to be and the long-term outcomes they desire. In these moments, you are either moving *toward* your values or *away* from your values with the actions you are choosing.

The ACT matrix and the choice point have a few differences that are important to note. When it comes to "away moves," the choice point emphasizes moving away from values, while the ACT matrix focuses on moving away from painful internal experiences. Similarly, in the choice point, away moves include both observable and cognitive behaviors, while hooks (painful thoughts, feelings, sensations, memories) are shown separately as the antecedents. The ACT matrix separates cognitive and observable behaviors, where the cognitive behaviors and the hooks (antecedents) are in the same place on the diagram (bottom left quadrant). There is not a right or wrong way to distinguish toward or away moves. However, it is important you understand these distinctions so you can navigate the tools easily.

As with any functional analysis, clients are deciding the function of their own behaviors. You can ask questions or, if they are stuck, share what you think may be happening. You can even offer up examples. But at the end of the day, you are talking about the client's values and their experience of how effective their actions are in moving them toward their values.

What I really love about the choice point is the language around hooks. In the diagram, it shows how getting hooked leads us to move away from our values—whereas if we are able to get *unhooked*, it creates space for us to choose to engage with our values. The imagery of the hook is, in my opinion, an excellent metaphor for fusion and defusion. When we are hooked like a fish on a line, we are no longer in control of what happens next. However, if we are able to get unhooked—or if we can manage not to bite the hook in the first place—then we are free to move how we'd like.

The original choice point also included the acronym *STOP*, with each letter standing for the following ways to assist in making a choice (Ciarrochi et al., 2014):

- **S** is for slowing down, grounding yourself, and mindfully breathing.
- **T** is for taking note of both your internal and external experience.
- **O** is for opening up to make space for difficult internal experiences.
- **P** is for pursuing your values.

Overall, this is a handy tool to talk through scenarios with your clients and help them visualize where in the process they are able to choose how to respond.*

DNA-V

Louise Hayes and Joseph Ciarrochi (2015) developed DNA-V, combining ACT and positive psychology. This model uses different guides and skills that represent various perspectives and ways of interacting with the world to help children and adolescents increase their awareness of patterns and live life more intentionally in accordance with their values. They have also since introduced their model in work with adults (Hayes et al., 2022). DNA-V serves to increase psychological flexibility through contact and intentionality with three categories of behaviors connected with our social and self contexts. The *DNA* portion of DNA-V represents three categories of behaviors we have inside of us:

- **The Discoverer:** The behaviors of the Discoverer move us into action in the real world through exploration, and trial-and-error behaviors. The Discoverer learns through interacting with the world and paying attention to the outcome. Sometimes the Discoverer can get stuck repeating the same patterns over and over without learning from the outcomes. It can also sometimes focus on short-term rewards instead of long-term goals, such as moving toward our values. But any action we take to connect with the world around us as it is happening is the result of the Discoverer, including any time we are paying attention to what is and is not working for us.

- **The Noticer:** The behaviors of the Noticer take in every experience, including all five senses. Similar to the observer self in self-as-context, the Noticer involves behaviors that connect us with the present moment and grounds us in our experience. We can use the Noticer to shift away from the Advisor and connect with the present. The Noticer doesn't judge, suggest, or advise—it simply identifies and notes our experience. This includes thoughts, feelings, memories, physical sensations, and urges happening inside of us, as well as what we can see, hear, taste, touch, and smell in our environment.

- **The Advisor:** The behaviors of the Advisor represent our "inner voice" (Hayes & Ciarrochi, 2015). It is the verbal behaviors that analyze, plan, problem solve, and create rules for reducing risk. The Advisor works hard to try to keep us safe. It is the perfect what-if machine. At times, it can be very useful, such as cautioning us to look both ways before crossing a street or wondering when we need to leave to get to work on time, given traffic and the fact that we need to prepare for a presentation that morning. However, it can also be super unhelpful when it begins to predict

---

* For more resources regarding the choice point, check out Russ Harris's (2022) book *The Happiness Trap,* which includes the choice point 2.0. Harris also has some videos, worksheets, and a choice point 2.0 document on his personal website, which you can visit at https://www.actmindfully.com.au/free-stuff.

future situations, such as worrying what would happen if we got hit by a car or mess up our presentation. The Advisor isn't good or bad. It represents a certain skill our mind has. Our job as humans is to determine when the Advisor is helpful and when it's not.

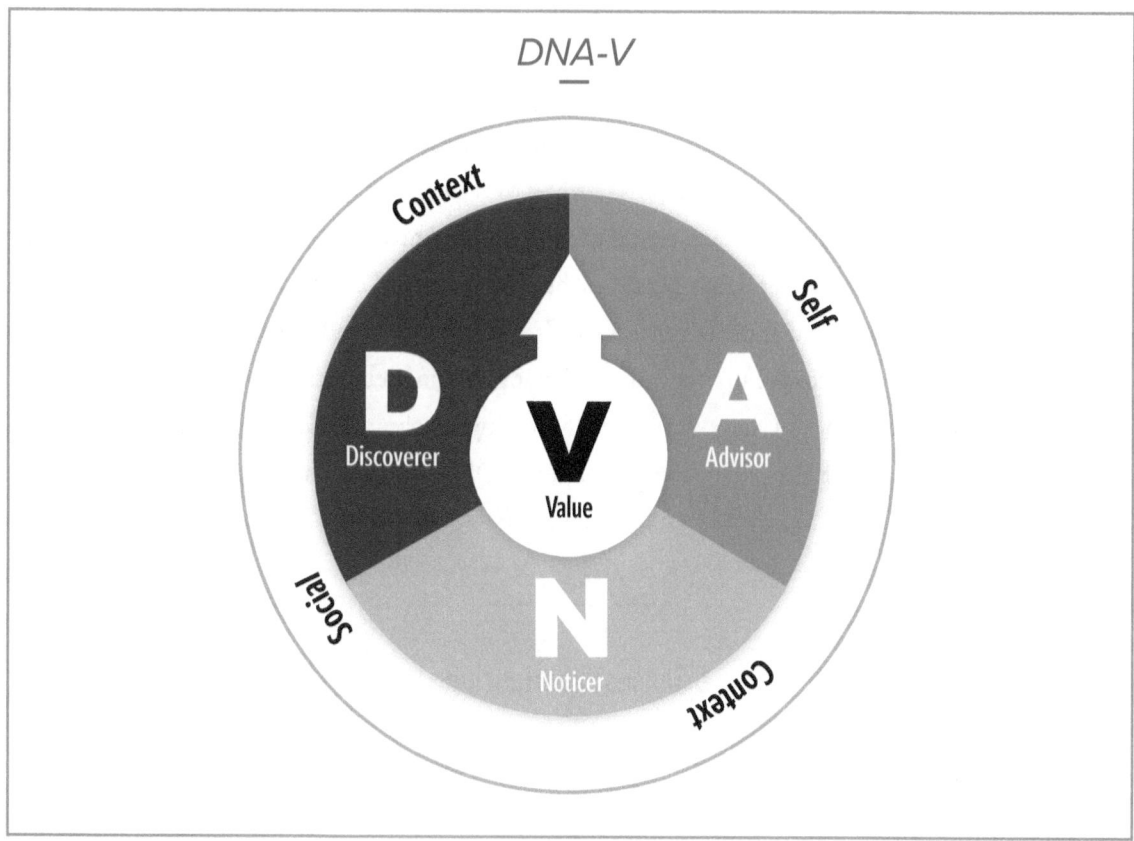

The V in DNA-V represents our *values*. The idea is if we can connect with our values, they can guide us to decide which of the three categories of behaviors should be taking the lead in any given moment. While the Discoverer, the Advisor, and the Noticer represent certain behaviors we all engage in, it can be helpful to view them as three different mentors—similar to the emotions controlling a person's mind in the animated film *Inside Out*. They are there to help us live a values-engaged life.

DNA-V* is particularly useful for clients who appreciate a more concrete approach to their experience. Let's say you have a client with health anxiety, and they are nervous about going to the doctor but know they need to in order to stay on top of their health. They come into session talking about all of the various what-if scenarios that could go wrong. You might interrupt them and ask, "Which mentor is guiding you right now?" This can be a great lead in for a functional analysis: "Is the Advisor who you want guiding you in this moment? What does the Noticer have to say in this moment? If you were listening to the Discoverer right now, what might they encourage you to do in alignment with your values?"

---

* For more information on DNA-V, check out https://dnav.international for great videos and additional materials. For using DNA-V with adults, I suggest *What Makes You Stronger* by Louise Hayes, Joseph Chairrochi, and Ann Bailey; for working with teens, check out *The Thriving Adolescent* by Louise Hayes and Joseph Chairrochi.

Case Study: Oliver

Oliver is a 67-year-old cisgender man. He is married to his wife of 35 years. He came to therapy because he is struggling with the death of his mother. Growing up, Oliver's mother was verbally and physically abusive toward him. She would often belittle him and compare him to his father, who had divorced his mother when Oliver was young. As an adult, Oliver had a strained relationship with his mother, and while they lived near each other, he had limited contact with her and only engaged with her out of a sense of obligation or duty. Oliver's mother died unexpectedly. He now reports feeling overwhelmed, angry, and sad. He says he has been having poor sleep, nightmares, and constant ruminations over how he never got to resolve their relationship. He notes feeling conflicted about her death. At times, he feels relief and almost happiness that a great source of his pain and trauma is gone, and at other times, he feels a deep sense of sadness and grief for the realization that now that she's gone he has to give up hope of ever having a loving relationship with her.

Now that you've learned about Oliver, fill out the following psychological flexibility tools* introduced in this chapter—the ACT matrix, three pillars, choice point, and DNA-V based on his experience and symptoms.

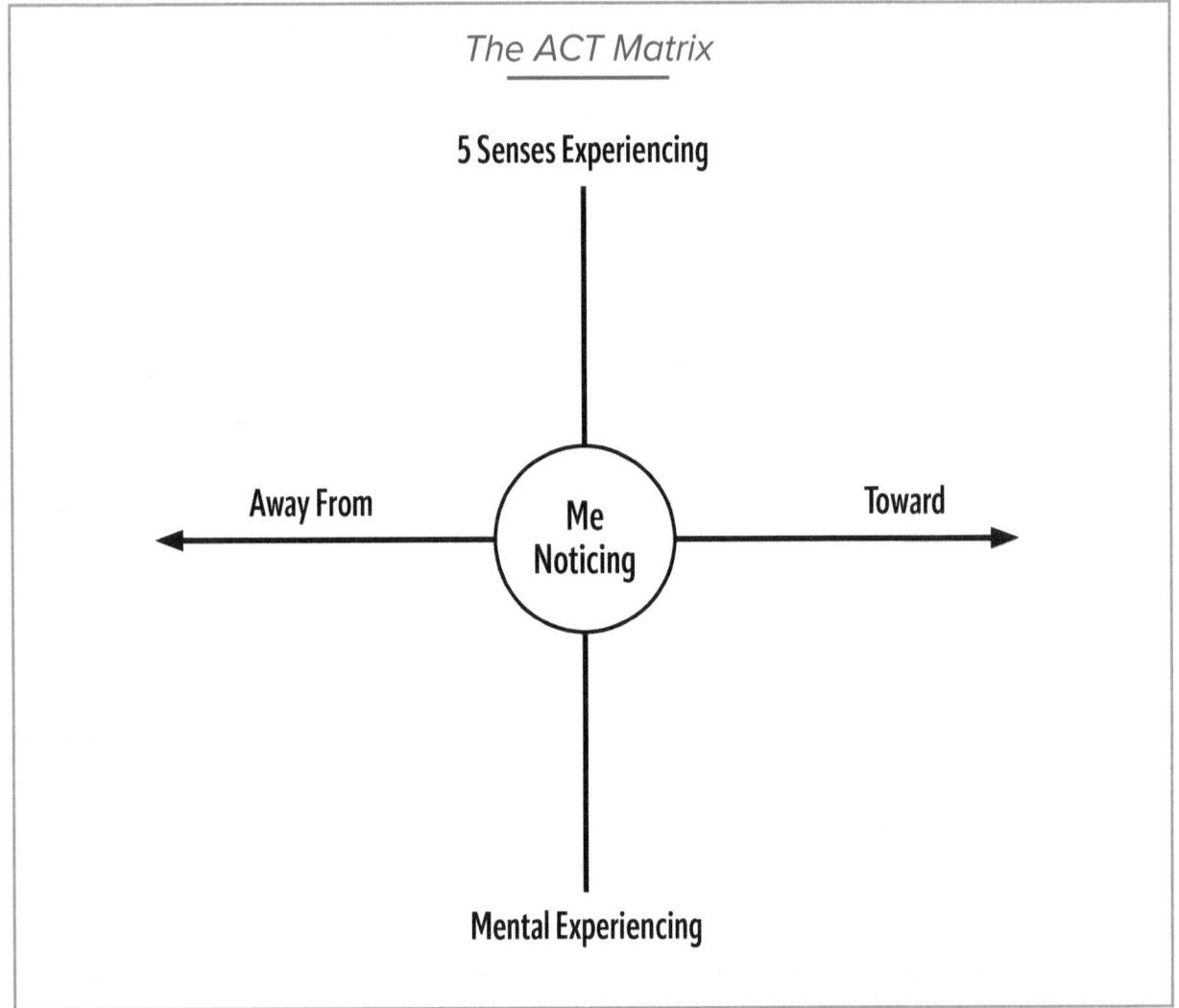

---

* For blank diagrams to download, print, and use in session, visit www.theacttherapist.com/ACTskillsmanual.

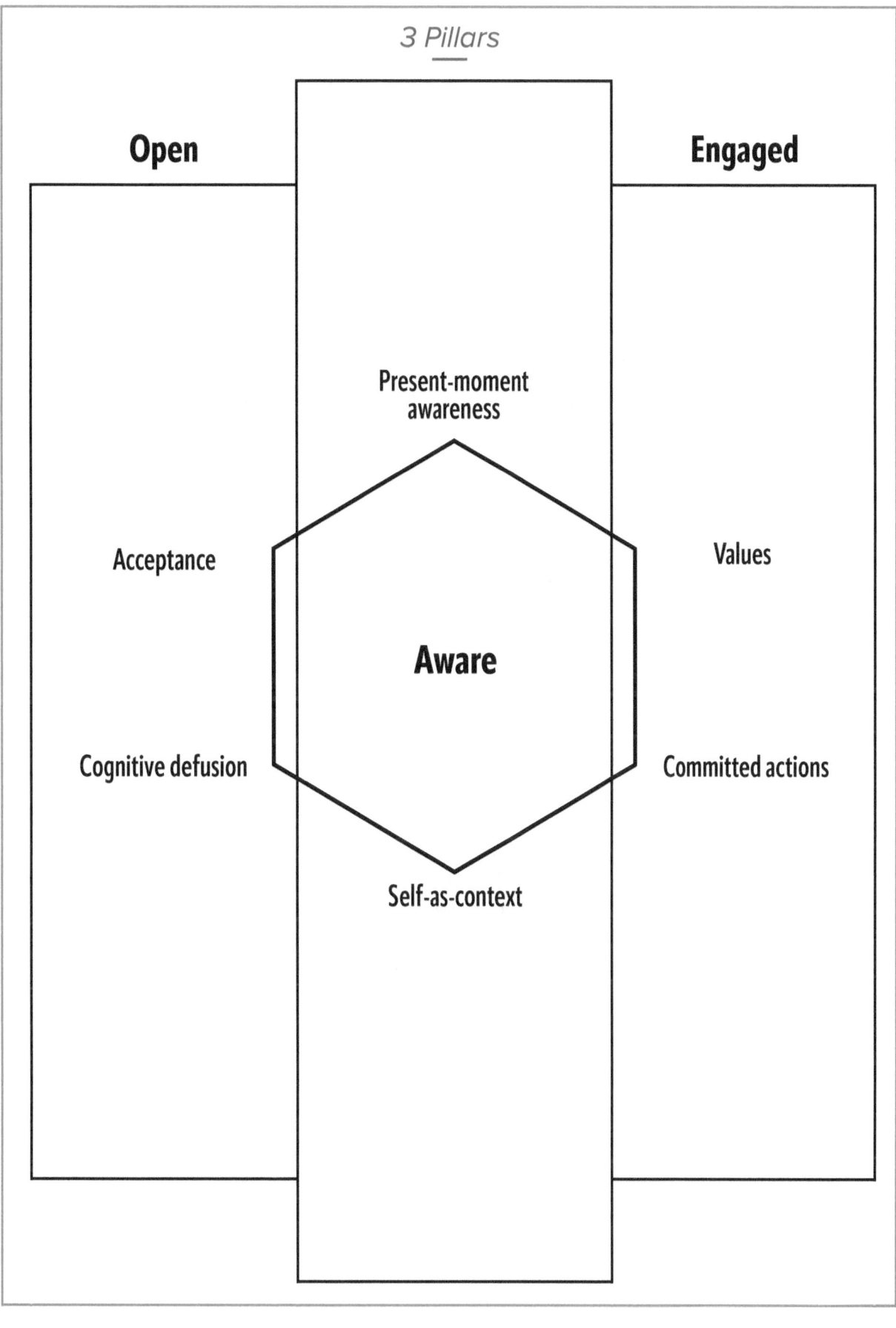

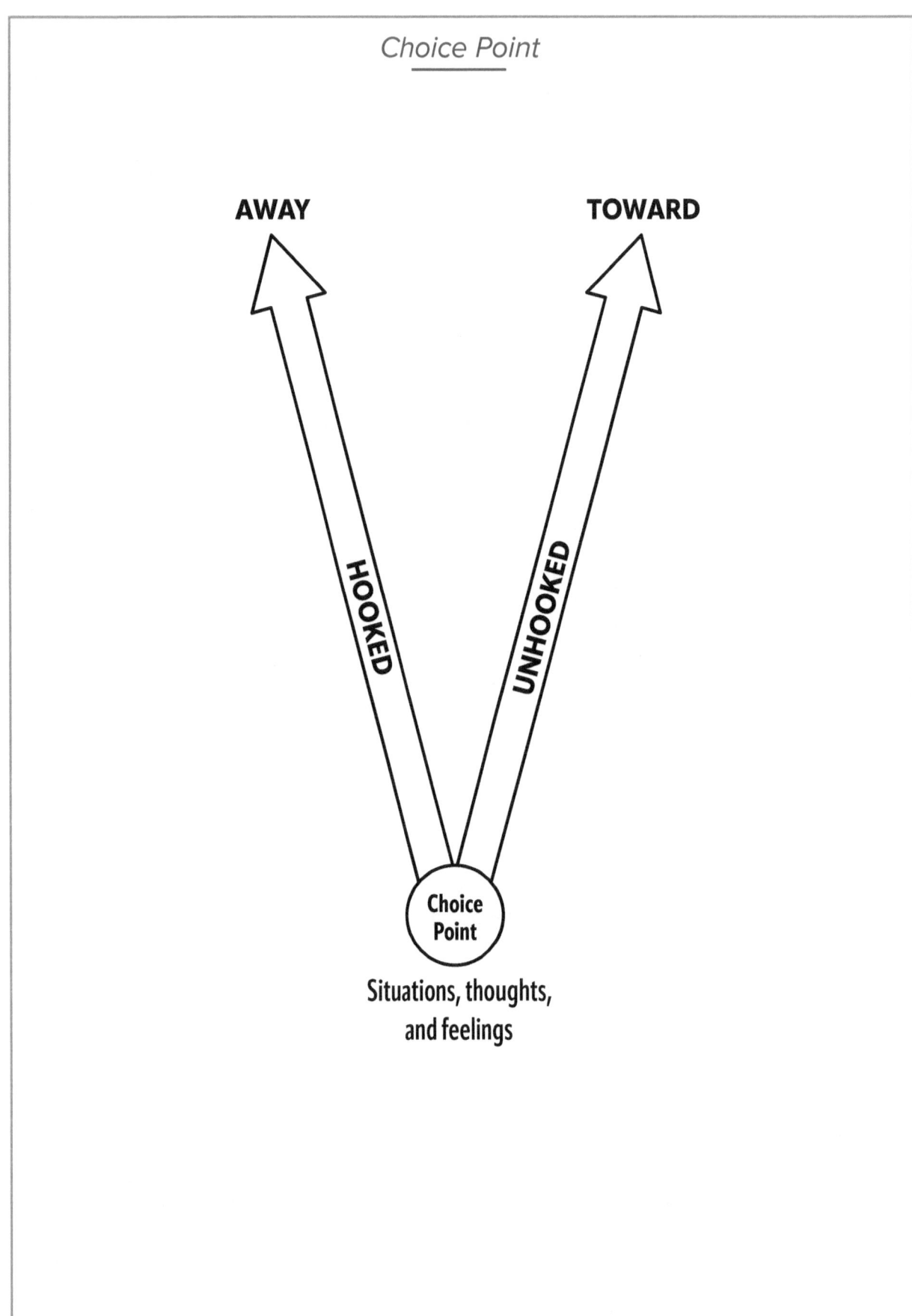

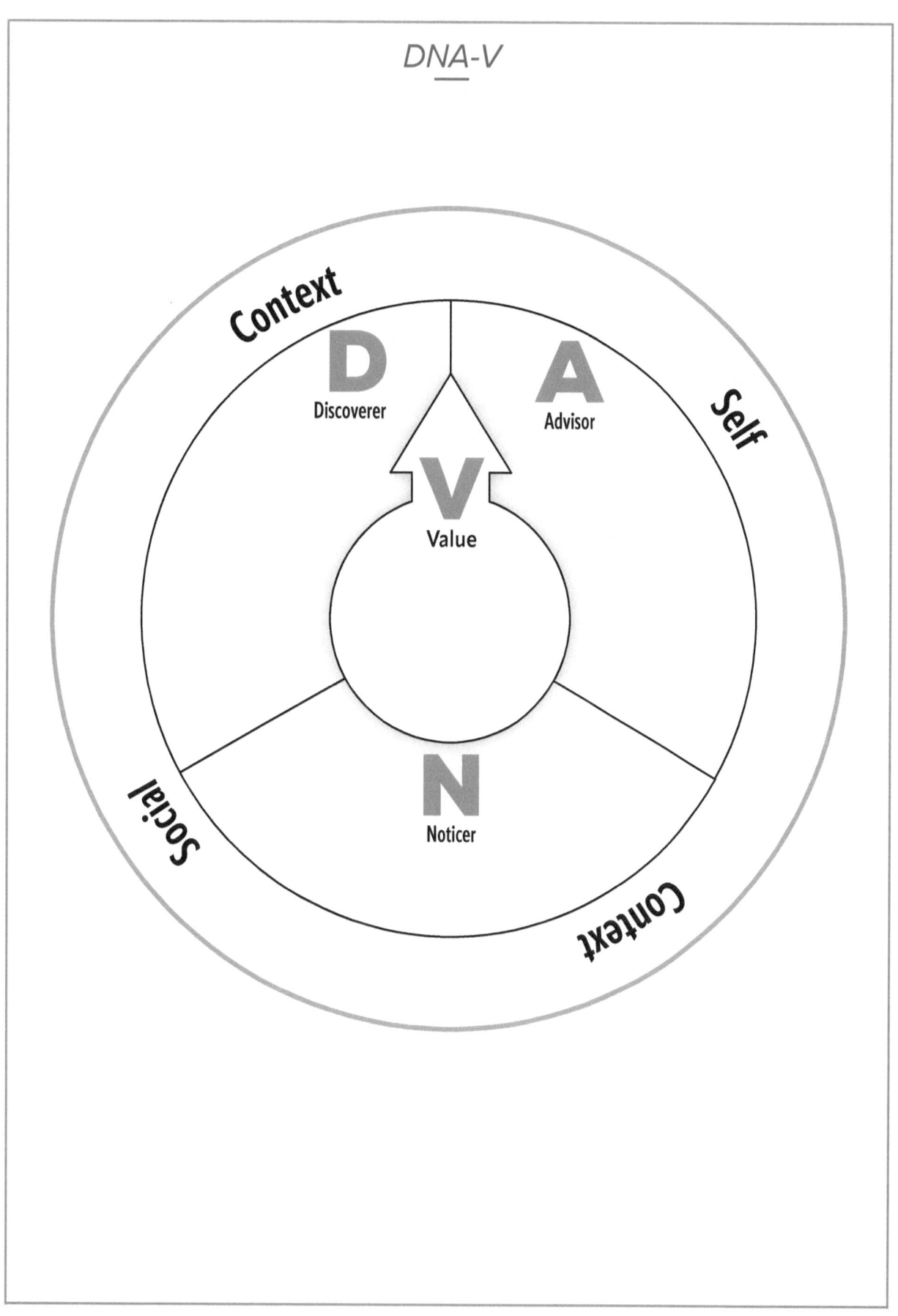

Chapter Takeaways

- The ACT matrix helps clients explore moving toward values and away from pain.
- The choice point is a representation of the decision point where we choose whether to turn toward or away from what matters to us.
- fACT was designed as a brief model of ACT that can be implemented in settings that have shorter sessions (25–30 minutes), as you may only see a client once. fACT emphasizes making impactful change in the initial—and possibly only—session.
- DNA-V includes the Advisor, the Noticer, and the Discoverer, which can be used as metaphors for different types of behaviors your client engages in.

CHAPTER 8
THE PLAYBOOK: A FUNCTIONAL ANALYSIS TOOL

I spent way too much time during the pandemic watching *Ted Lasso*. If you are unfamiliar with the show, I encourage you to go watch it, as it's fantastic. It's a show about an American football coach who goes to England to coach a professional soccer team. As a result of these binges, I developed a whole slew of fun sports metaphors. From this practice, a new way to approach functional analysis was born called the *Playbook*. It was, in part, inspired by the great work of the ACT matrix. However, instead of the two intersecting lines of the matrix, the Playbook diagram is set up similar to a soccer field.

The Playbook Diagram

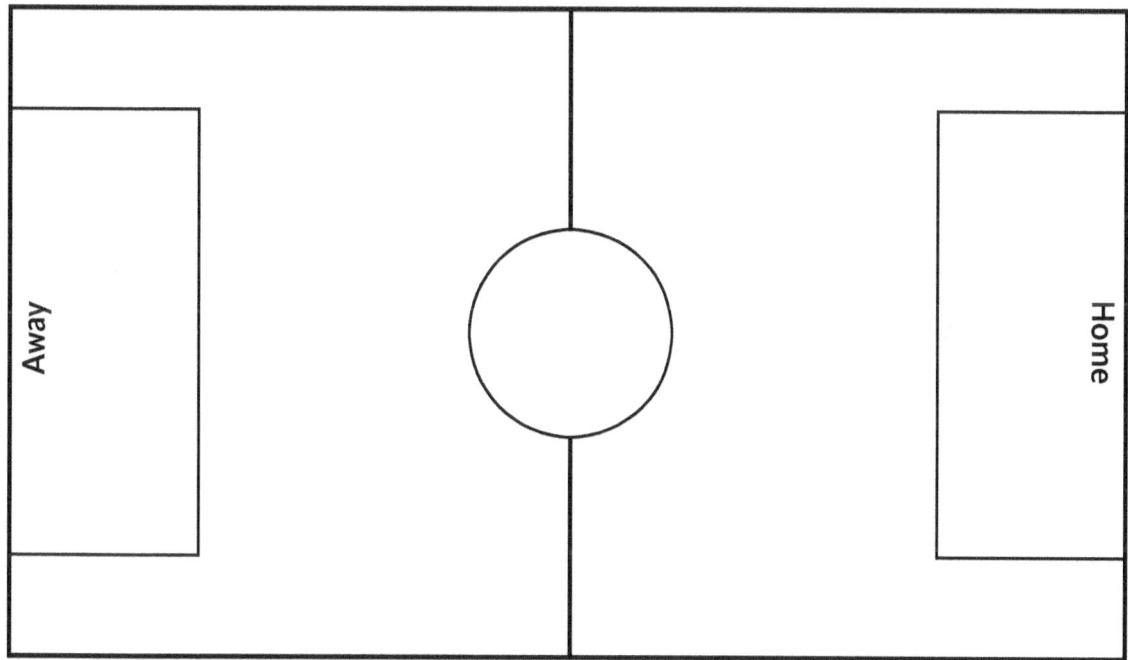

In the game of soccer, there are two objectives: to score goals and to stop the other team from scoring. You're rooting for the home team. They're your team. The players on the home team represent all of the values and experiences and characteristics that you want to embody as you move through the world. The players on the away team represent the thoughts, feelings, memories, sensations, urges, and judgments that make life hard: your hooks.

The away players' signature moves represent your attempts to try to erase, avoid, or control your pain. These moves can be external, such as observable behaviors that someone could see you doing as you interact with the world, like scrolling TikTok, cleaning the pantry, or hitting dismiss on a phone call from a friend. These moves can also be internal or cognitive—things that others can't see you doing, such as planning, analyzing, or running through what-if scenarios.

Unfortunately, the longer the game goes on, the stronger and louder the away players become. In each moment, depending on the contexts and the history that you have with your hooks, you may find the home team not wanting to engage with the other team because of how intense the away team is. Instead, those players run circles around your values.

And then they score. You can conceptualize the away team scoring as successfully avoiding or erasing your pain—in the short term. And every time the away team scores, they seem to get even more confident and cocky with their possession over the ball. They get louder and more aggressive. Consequently, the home team becomes either more reluctant to engage with them, or they put in more time and attention into stopping them. Either way, the home team is too busy playing defense instead of trying to score themselves. You're left wondering how they lost so quickly.

Most people come to therapy because they have gotten into what feels like a losing streak. They're so focused on trying to stop the other team that they forget to move toward what matters to them. Now, the other team isn't evil or bad. Both teams are simply playing a game. Part of the work in ACT is helping our clients notice when they're being forgetful or playing in default mode, and pivot back to the present moment and what's important.

Although not visible on the diagram, there are a lot of other people participating in or watching the game, and they impact the players as well. There may be times when it's helpful to write these other people onto the periphery of the diagram for your client to clarify or visualize the influences in their life. For example, there are referees who come with certain rules about how the game "should" be played. Sometimes these rules are so rigid and abundant that there's no flexibility for the home team to show up to the game in the way that they want. Rules and referees serve to create guidance and stop really atrocious decisions. They are not meant to control the game.

And then there are the coaches. Coaches for the home team might be your support network, family, friends, and mentors in your life. These are people who may influence the players (your values) that you have on the field. At some point, you may realize that some of these people might not be the right fit. At one point in your life they may have been the right people to guide you, but as you've grown or changed, they may be steering you in a direction that doesn't align with your values. As a result, you might want to let them go as coaches.

The away team's coaches represent your threat-detection system. Safety is their top priority. The coaches comprise all of the experiences you have had to date as well as future what-if scenarios that you are afraid of. They use this information to pick players to best represent the pain that is the opposite of your values. They aren't doing this to hurt you, but rather in attempts to protect you (see chapter 2 for a refresher, if needed). Unfortunately, you don't get to fire these coaches. You have less control over them, but you get to choose how you show up to their players (hooks).

And finally, there are the spectators. People who are watching the game unfold but who are often caught up playing their own games. No matter how loud they cheer or how silent they are, you get to choose how you want to show up. It can be easy sometimes to let people on the sidelines influence how the game is played. It's human nature to want to fit in, please others, and be accepted. At the end of the day though, only you can choose what matters to you and how you will work toward creating a home and a life that you love.

So what about that circle in the middle? In the middle, where the two teams meet to begin the game, is your full experience. Your hopes and dreams, values and aspirations, and your pains, hurts, and fears. You need all the players to play the game—even the hooks that you don't like or don't want. They are all there for a reason.

So let's look at how to approach the Playbook diagram and use it as a tool.

Filling Out the Playbook Diagram

Let's put some players on the field! I'll use myself as an example. I'm cheering for the home team, and my team is composed of my values. These players represent how I want to show up to the people and things I care about and what matters most to me in life. The away team's players consist of my hooks—or the thoughts, feelings, memories, and physical sensations that show up and make it difficult to connect with my values. The following image shows a Playbook diagram illustrated with an example of my own experience.

The Playbook Diagram Example

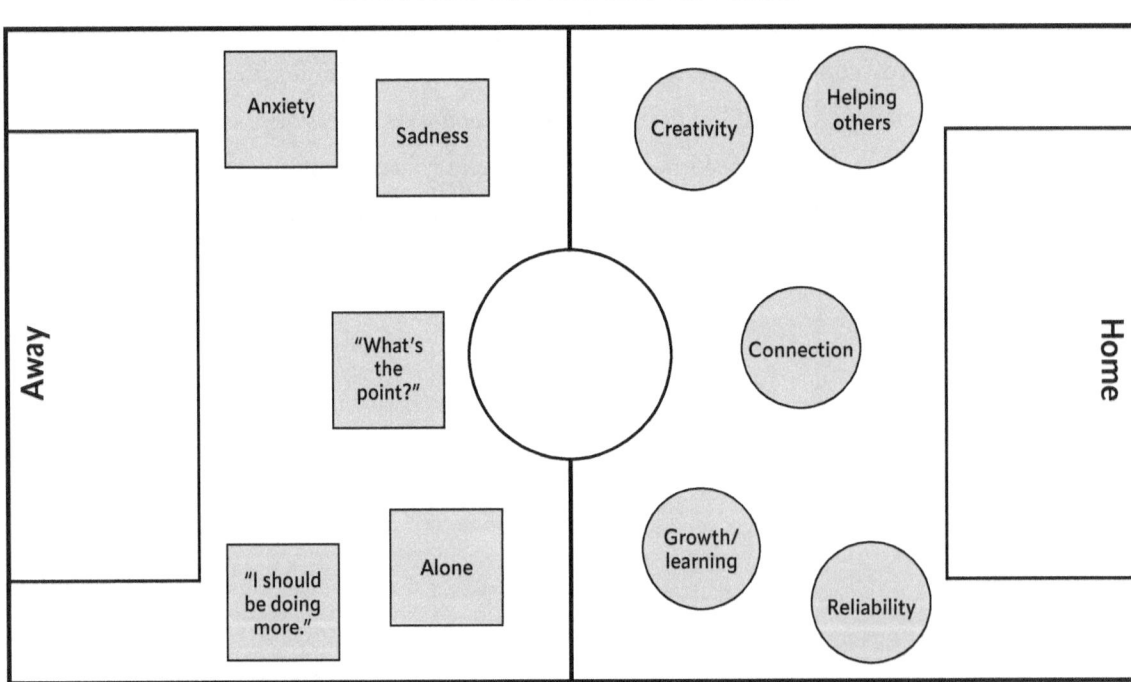

When those hooks on the away team are very loud and strong, it can be easy for them to keep the ball on their side of the field—especially if I am afraid or timid about coming in contact with them. The away players have a number of signature moves they use. Together, they create a pattern where their team always has the ball on their side, and they get better and better with each attempt on the goal. Eventually, my goalkeeper lets a ball through the net. You can conceptualize the away team's goal as me successfully avoiding or erasing pain temporarily in the short term.

Doing a Functional Analysis with the Playbook

This is where a functional analysis comes in. Once you have the away players and their signature moves on the field, you can begin to explore how they create a pattern of play. You can introduce a functional analysis in the exact same way you have seen throughout this book so far. You are essentially looking at hooks (antecedent) and what happens when your client bites those hooks (response and behaviors). Together, you and your client will identify what these observable and cognitive behaviors are, and then write them on the left side of the field. These will be treated as signature moves—the moves that your client makes when they are engaging in experiential avoidance. Let's pretend I am the client in the following dialogue:

Therapist: Okay, so we have a lot of players on the field here, and it looks like we have a lot of moves that they tend to use in the game. Let's take a look at how this all works together. If you think back to a current situation you've struggled with, which player on the field comes to mind?

Client: Honestly, sadness.

Therapist: Okay, so when sadness shows up, what happens next?

Client: I start thinking about how my friends and I used to be really close, but I just feel so distant from them now.

Therapist: Okay, so the first move that sadness makes is kind of reflecting what your friendship used to be. [*draws an arrow from sadness to reflecting*] After that reflecting, what shows up for you?

Client: Then I just start thinking, *Why am I even bothering? They clearly don't want to be my friend.*

Therapist: [*draws line from reflecting to "What's the point?"*] Okay, so you go from feeling sad to reflecting on the past, then kind of thinking *What's even the point?* What happens then?

Client: Then I usually come up with an excuse, cancel plans, and feel utterly alone.

Therapist: So a lot is happening on the field here. Sad to reflecting to thinking *What's the point?* to canceling plans and ending up feeling utterly alone. [*draws the path between these players and moves*] Is there anything else that happens when you feel utterly alone?

Client: I just go to sleep.

Therapist: Okay, so that's the final move. [*draws line from "utterly alone" player to "sleep" move, and then draws an arrow into the net*] So going to sleep is the play for now, but as we both know, it's only temporary.

As the therapist, you would then go into exploring the short-term function compared to the long-term function of that approach. Take a moment to a step back and look at all the back and forth that takes place when the away team has possession of the ball. Breaking it down by pass of the ball can help highlight just how many behaviors the client is engaging in as part of experiential avoidance. This gives many opportunities to interrupt the play and pivot. However, it can feel like a lot, especially when the client is first looking at all the arrows. Take a look at my example diagram below, which now has additional markups to show different moves from each team.

The Playbook Diagram Example

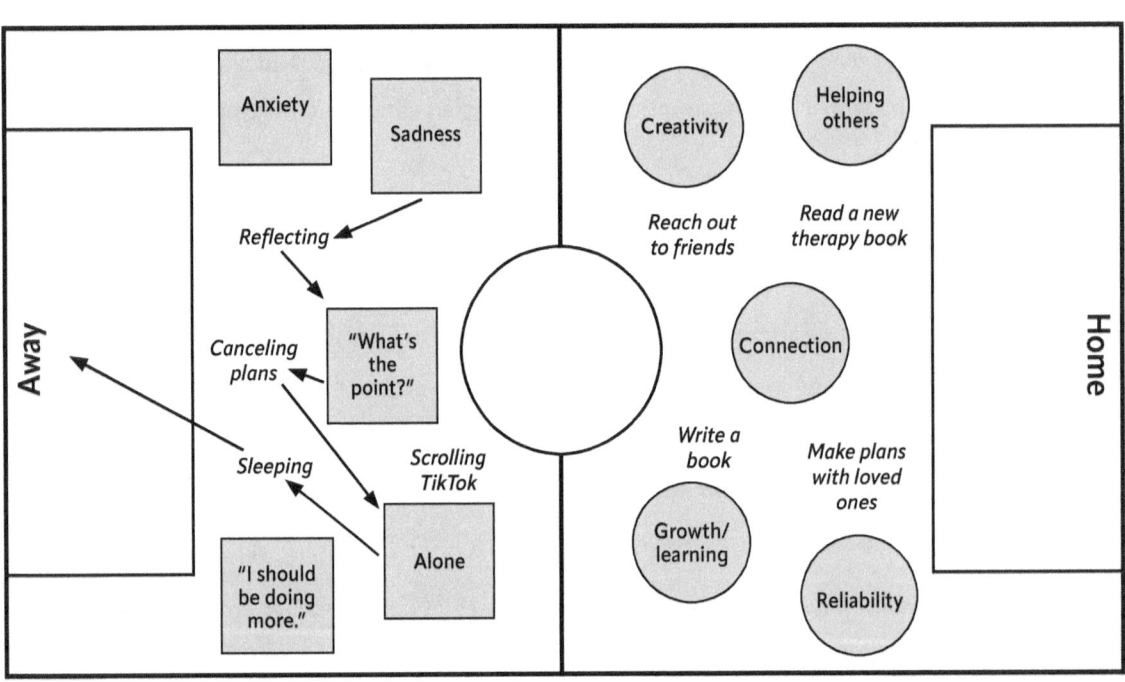

Before we know it, there is absolute chaos on the field. It makes it really hard for the home team to make a move. Thankfully, the home team has some great defensive and offensive moves to work with. Let's start with offensive moves. When the home team has possession of the ball, I can use committed actions. These are the physical actions I am taking to move toward what matters to me—and the goal. These can be skills I already have or ones I'd like to develop or use more often. Notice the skills I wrote down that help me to move toward what matters to me.

Sometimes we forget that our goal on defense isn't just to stop the away team from scoring, but also to pivot the ball toward what matters most to us—the net. As we've seen earlier, if we're just playing keep away, it's exhausting and only works for a little bit. However, if we can notice what the other team's strategy is, we can begin to slow down, intercept it, and move the ball toward the home side of the field. These are the skills your clients will develop in therapy. These are skills of defusion, acceptance, present-moment awareness, and self-as-context. At the beginning, they do not have the ability to even notice what the away players are doing, but with practice, patterns will emerge and clients will begin to feel more confident in their ability to intercept the ball and pivot toward what matters to them.

A very important caveat here: We play for the love of the sport. For the journey of life. Not to win. A very "Ted Lasso" way of approaching life, I know—and one that works in this context. We can't always control what taking steps toward our values will lead to. In other words, we can't guarantee we'll meet our goals—or score one. Just like we can't guarantee that working toward our values means life will be easy or go our way. We do know that the more attempts we take, the higher the likelihood that we live a really meaningful life. But it's not guaranteed. We are focused on the process of the game, not the outcome. So, we stay committed to intentionally showing up to the moment—no matter what team we are playing against or what moves they have. At times, we may need to adapt when we play a particularly difficult team. Maybe we develop some new skills. But all in all, we are always striving to be intentional with our actions and responding to what is happening in this moment.

Hopefully you can begin to see ways that you might incorporate the Playbook into your work with clients. Similar to the ACT matrix, the Playbook creates a visual representation of our values, committed actions, and patterns of experiential avoidance. They both allow for functional analysis of a client's current patterns of behavior. For both the Playbook and the matrix, "away" moves represent "away from pain." The Playbook, however, does not divide the diagram horizontally and does not distinguish between external world and internal world in the same way as the matrix. The main reason for this is that I wanted a way to distinguish between hooks, the automatic internal experiences that pop up without our control, and the client's reactions to those experiences, which are both observable and cognitive behaviors. This way, we can more easily track the hook-response connection.

ACT Core Processes and the Playbook

How does the Playbook map onto the six core processes? Let's take a look! In the diagram below, I've highlighted where we can see the six core processes at play. Let's break it down.

The Playbook Diagram and the Six Core Processes

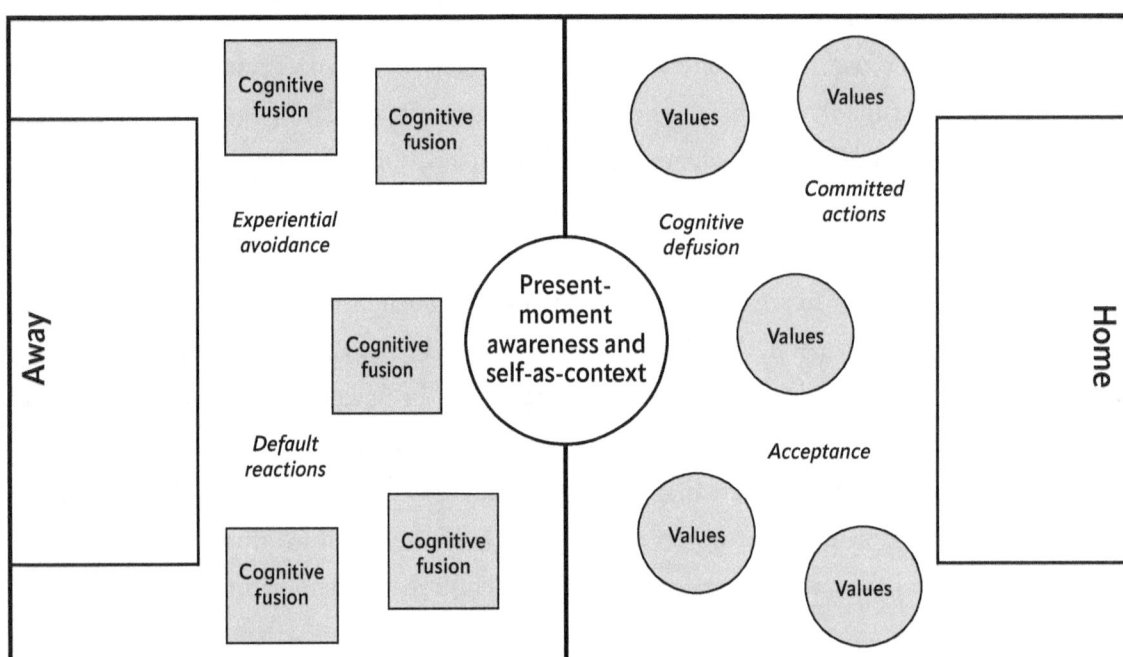

As you know, the home team players on the right represent our values, and their scoring moves represent committed actions. The away players on the left represent our hooks, or cognitive fusion—which is the inverse of defusion. Their scoring moves represent experiential avoidance—our default reactions to attempt to avoid pain—which is the inverse of acceptance. These are both teams' offensive tactics. Every time a home player engages with an away player, the home player is practicing acceptance. And every time a home player stops the away player from making a move, the home player is engaging in a defusion strategy to create space and bring the ball back onto their side of the field, where committed actions take place. And finally, present-moment awareness and self-as-context processes are happening in the moment—in the middle of the field—as we step back and watch the game unfold.

At the end of the day, our goal in therapy is to increase the client's present-moment awareness as the observer of their experience (self-as-context/center of the field). We help them notice their patterns of experiential avoidance (away players and their scoring moves) and use cognitive defusion and acceptance (home players and their defensive moves) to pivot toward what matters to them through committed actions (home players and their scoring moves).

Using the Playbook in Practice

The ACT Playbook can be used at any point during therapy. I like bringing it up in the first or second session. It can be a great tool for mapping out clients' current life and developing treatment goals. What does this look like? Let's look at two case studies to break down how we can use the Playbook to train awareness in clients and identify treatment plan.

Case Study: Simon

Simon comes to therapy because he doesn't quite feel depressed but feels, in his words, "meh." He used to spend a lot of his free time running, crocheting, and learning Spanish, as he loves to travel, but he has lost interest in his hobbies. While he has a couple of friends, he hasn't seen them in a month and feels too embarrassed to respond to their texts because he has nothing going on. Simon has recently been laid off from his engineering job as part of a big cut at his company. While he believes he should be updating his résumé and applying to new jobs, he notes that after spending a month applying and getting constant rejections, he feels hopeless that he will find a job and is worried he will have to move back in with his parents. They are supportive of this option, but he feels that going back to live with them is embarrassing.

Simon explains that he spends most of the day in bed or on the couch watching reruns of his favorite show, "zoning out," and taking naps. He sometimes forgets to eat. While he sleeps about 10 or 11 hours per night, his sleep is fitful and he often wakes up exhausted. He sometimes wakes up in the middle of the night panicked about money. Simon shares that he has worked so hard to build his career and the life he has, and now it feels as if it is all being taken away in one fell swoop. Let's see what Simon's Playbook diagram might look like.

Simon's Playbook Diagram

Away side:
- "I'll never get a job."
- "I should be applying."
- Watch TV
- Ignore text messages
- Embarrassment
- Sleep
- Cancel plans
- Panic
- Ruminate
- Dissociate
- Hopelessness
- Exhaustion, apathy, and anhedonia

Simon (center)

Home side:
- Creativity
- Health
- Go for a run
- Apply for jobs
- Helpful friend
- Travel
- Make plans with friends
- Crochet
- Learning
- Hard work

By filling out the Playbook diagram, we're able to easily identify the following about Simon:

- **Values:** Health (running), creativity (crochet), learning, travel, helpful friend, hard work
- **Hooks:** The thought *I should be applying for a job*, apathy, panic, exhaustion, the thought *I'll never get a job*, anhedonia, hopelessness, embarrassment
- **Avoidance behaviors:** Ruminate on how his life is ruined, cancel plans, ignore text messages, sleep, watch television, dissociate
- **Committed actions:** Apply for jobs, reach out to friends, go for a run

Based on all of this information, we may diagnose Simon with MDD with anxious distress. Given that Simon is engaging with cognitive avoidance behaviors, we may say that one of our treatment goals is to develop defusion skills in order to increase engagement with values.

What other treatment goals might you propose for Simon?

_____
_____
_____
_____
_____
_____

Possible answers: There are a lot of different answers you could have given. Here are a few:

- Increase consistent engagement with committed actions, including applying for jobs and spending time with his friends.
- Use acceptance to process feelings associated with job loss and change in circumstance.
- Increase self-as-context skills for identifying labels related to his career that he is attached to.
- Expand behavioral repertoire in the presence of painful thoughts and feelings.

Case Study: Elodie

Now it's your turn. Get acquainted with Elodie, then fill out the Playbook based on the client summary.

Elodie was diagnosed with multiple sclerosis (MS) at age 29 after years of doctors dismissing her concerns. She is struggling to cope with her diagnosis. She knows she needs to make modifications to her life in order to accommodate her illness, but she often pushes herself too hard. Elodie is frustrated and angry and notes, "It's not fair." She reports feeling lost and unsure how to move forward. Elodie often feels tired throughout the day and has trouble concentrating due to her MS. On top of this, Elodie reports ruminating about the future, feeling irritable and anxious when she hits limits with her body. She notes she has "kind of stopped engaging with life." She comes to therapy at the recommendation of her friend. She explains that she doesn't know if you can help. Use the following diagram to create a Playbook diagram for Elodie.

Elodie's Playbook Diagram

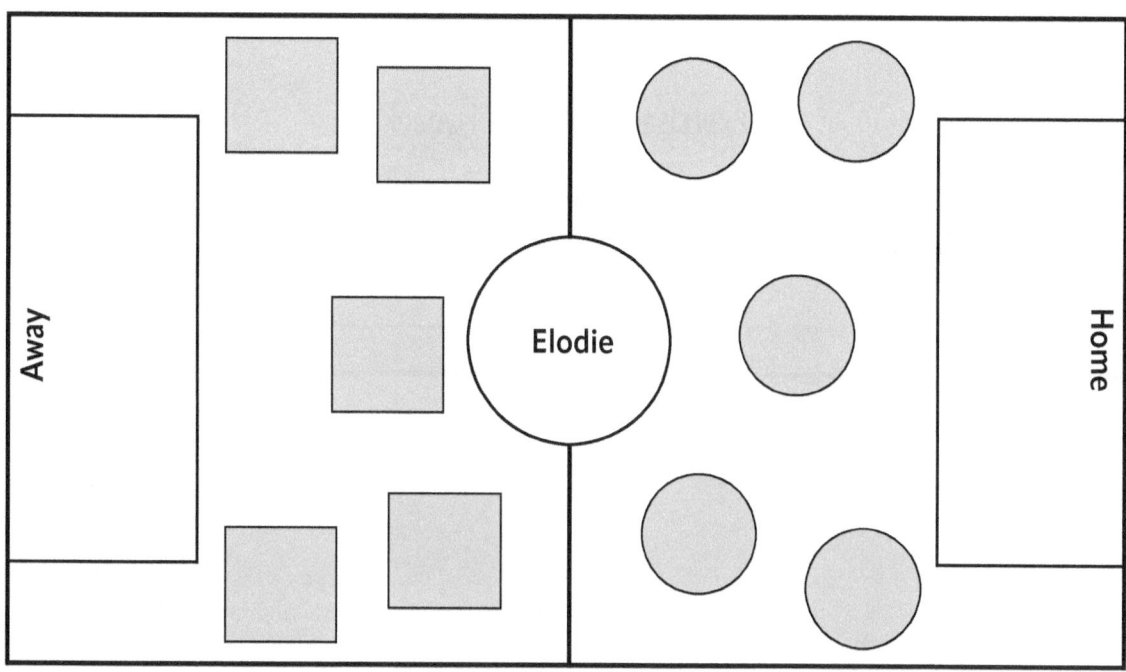

By filling out the Playbook diagram, we're able to identify the following about Elodie:

- Values: _____
- Hooks: _____
- Avoidance behaviors: _____
- Committed actions: _____

What treatment goals might you propose for Elodie? (Reminder: In ACT, we are steering away from using symptom-reduction language for treatment goals.)

- Goal #1: _____
- Goal #2: _____
- Goal #3: _____

Possible answers: There are a lot of different answers you could have given. Here are a few:

- **Values:** Unclear; expressed feeling "lost and unsure how to move forward"
- **Hooks:** MS symptoms, worry about the future, exhaustion, brain fog

- **Avoidance behaviors:** "Stopped engaging in life," "pushes herself too hard"
- **Committed actions:** Unclear; mentioned getting help through going to therapy
- **Goal #1:** Clarify values and what she wants to work toward.
- **Goal #2:** Practice acceptance and defusion to address her diagnosis, limitations, and the future.
- **Goal #3:** Learn to pace activities to better manage her chronic illness.

Exercise: Create the Playbook

Now let's try with one of your clients. Choose one of your own clients. You can list their first name or initials, or you can create a fake name.

Client Name: _____

[Soccer field diagram with "Away" goal on left and "Home" goal on right]

- Values: _____
  _____
  _____

- Hooks: _____
  _____
  _____

- Avoidance behaviors: _____
  _____
  _____

- Committed actions: _____
  _____
  _____

What treatment goals might you propose for this client?

- Goal #1: _____
  _____
  _____

- Goal #2: _____
  _____
  _____

- Goal #3: _____
  _____
  _____

Hopefully this chapter and the previous chapter have shown you just how many ways there are to introduce ACT and functional contextualism to your clients. Please feel free to take the Playbook and adapt it to fit your needs. Who knows, maybe you have a stack of basketball metaphors you've been waiting to use!

At the end of the day, the Playbook is a tool for helping clients take abstract concepts and visualize them in a way that increases their awareness of patterns, their willingness to engage in therapy, and their playfulness. That last one may seem like an odd choice of words. However, a big part of the work we do involves finding new ways for clients to come in contact with difficult, painful stuff. Thinking about their life through a sports metaphor may sound silly, and yet, it can help clients who otherwise struggle to sit with big emotions to be curious and open to trying something new. So with a little therapist magic, maybe they can learn how to play the game differently and create a life they love.

Chapter Takeaways

- The Playbook is an interactive tool you can use with your client to map out the six core processes and their patterns of avoidance in order to create a functional analysis.

- In this activity, neither team is bad or good. The primary objective is playing the game, and each team has a different gameplan in mind: The home team's strategy is to live a meaningful life, and the away team's strategy is to avoid pain.

- The home team's players represent our values, and the away team's players represent cognitive fusion, which we often refer to as *hooks*.

- The home team's signature moves include committed actions, acceptance, and cognitive defusion. The away team's signature moves involve experiential avoidance, or our default reactions to pain.

- The referees can represent self-as-content. These are the strict rules or narratives we may have about ourselves or our life. This is an opportunity to remind clients that they get to choose how to show up to each moment.

- The coaches can represent our support system in life. These people—our family, friends, and mentors—have the ability to influence our values.

CHAPTER 9
LANGUAGE AND METAPHORS

Language is the cornerstone of the work we do as therapists. The ability to communicate is a foundational aspect of our jobs. It is also intrinsic to ACT. We began this book with an understanding of the philosophical underpinning of ACT: functional contextualism (see chapter 1). And yet there is another important theory that has influenced ACT: *relational frame theory* (RFT). Understanding how humans use language symbolically will help inform the language you use in session and how you process the interconnected thoughts clients experience.

In this chapter, we will explore how RFT edifies the work we do in ACT. We will then build on that knowledge with a deeper dive into metaphors. Metaphors are an incredible representation of how symbolic language can enhance a client's learning in therapy. This chapter will cover some commonly used metaphors in ACT and then teach you how to develop your own metaphors based on your clients' interests and experiences. After all, the more common language you and your clients have together, the easier it will be to help them.

Relational Frame Theory

ACT has been fascinated with language since its inception, particularly with relational frame theory. RFT at its core describes how humans use language to create meaning and symbolism beyond the physical properties of an object or experience. It is based on the idea that we create associations or networks between internal and external behaviors. This includes thoughts, feelings, memories, physical sensations, and urges. This process is based on *relational learning,* or *derived relational responding*—the ability to create bidirectional connections between concepts, words, and images. This may seem overcomplicated. However, we do this so often in everyday life that we don't even realize it.

For example, if I show a small child a picture of a dog and say, "dog" and this process is repeated until the child learns the connection, I can later say "dog" and reasonably expect that the child would point to the picture of the dog. The relational frame (or connection) between the image and the sound is bidirectional (goes in both directions). We can also add to this network. We may see different dogs in real life and say "dog" to help the child recognize the various types of dogs that still fit into the category. And if a child's experience with dogs is overall positive, they will add in "good" to their frame of what a dog is. If a child, however, has a scary encounter with a dog, or their parents warn them that dogs are "bad" or "dangerous," they may jump when they hear a dog bark because that bark is connected in a vast network related to "dog" and "bad."

We create these relationships and networks of information so easily that we often forget how unique a skill it is. Relating to different concepts and having shared language allows us to plan for the future and even learn from experiences we've only heard about. Imagine you've never seen a grill before. You're over my house for a BBQ and I say to you, "Be careful, it's hot!" Your mind might bring up a relational network for "hot." Various experiences you've had with "hot" come to mind, and you're able to draw the conclusion that you should not touch the grill without ever having to experience firsthand what touching a grill does or feels like.

Now the cool thing about humans is we not only do this with the physical properties of objects, but we also create arbitrary connections that are not based on the physical properties or an observable experience of something. I know that's a mouthful, but bear with me. This is where the power of symbols comes in. When people are first introduced to Bitcoin, many are perplexed at how something entirely digital could be currency. And yet, most people today have access to online banking, where they can see a number on a screen that they then translate in their mind into physical money. And remember, money is simply a representation of value. In a barter economy, each item has some type of intrinsic, obvious value. Like exchanging a loaf of bread for repairing a broken zipper on a dress. Whereas a dollar bill does not inherently have any worth until we say it does. We're just so used to this symbolic representation that we forget it's arbitrary.

Arbitrary relational responding allows us to use symbols to communicate. This serves as shortcuts for discussing complex topics. For example, if I say, "Life is like a box of chocolates" with no other context, and you have experience with boxes of chocolates, you can come to a few conclusions. If you're familiar with the movie *Forrest Gump*, you may deduce "You never know what you're going to get" because your mind is showing you the rest of the quote from the movie. If you're like my dad and love chocolate, you may conclude that life is wonderful. If you get sick when you eat too much chocolate at once, you may surmise that life is sweet but needs to be savored and enjoyed slowly.

Because of our ability to create these relationships and networks in our mind of various pieces of information and memories, we can learn from others' experiences without going through them ourselves. We can engage in perspective taking by putting ourselves in someone else's shoes based on what we know or imagine about them. We can plan for future scenarios. We can use imagery, metaphors, and stories to communicate. Throughout all of this, we also imbue emotion into these experiences. And sometimes, due to these networks, those emotions get attached to what feels like random objects or behaviors.

What happens when we have traumatic events, life-altering changes, or disappointments in our life? We begin to form default, automatic responses to certain stimuli and derive assumptions based on our past experiences. When those experiences come with a lot of pain, we may also begin to engage in a lot of avoidance and fusion.

The more we understand our own relationships to various concepts and the people we're communicating with, the more accurate we are in getting our meaning across.* It's why, while I think there are some phenomenal common ACT metaphors, some of which we'll cover in this book, I always prefer creating my own based on what I know about the client. The more specific to the person, the more likely we are to find a really impactful and memorable metaphor.

Exercise: Deriving Meaning from Our Relational Frames

Now it's time to practice! To really highlight our ability to arbitrarily assign meaning, complete the following exercise. Read the similes and metaphors related to the completely made-up words. Write down a few examples of what that word could mean and how you came to that conclusion. In creating definitions to made-up words using context clues from metaphors and similes, you are practicing the skills you will build upon to create your own metaphors later on. Notice what memories or examples you draw on to create your definitions.

Crunkleton is like a rain shower on a sunny day.

_____
_____
_____
_____

Dup is a faucet that leaks but never quite enough to fix it.

_____
_____
_____
_____

Luxert feels like a vintage dining set.

_____
_____
_____
_____

These are intentionally vague so you can infer your own meaning based on your relational frames.

---

* If you'd like a more in-depth overview of RFT, I'd recommend *Learning RFT* by Niklas Törneke or *Understanding and Applying Relational Frame Theory* by Siri Ming, Evelyn Gould, and Julia H. Fiebig.

We can also use our experiences and shared understanding of concepts to create symbolic ways of discussing complex topics. Look at the following common mental health words and create at least one symbolic description. For example, *Depression is like riding a bike with flat tires*.

Anxiety is . . .

_____
_____
_____
_____

Grief is . . .

_____
_____
_____
_____

Anger is . . .

_____
_____
_____
_____

As you begin to explore how you want to show up to this work, keep in mind the relational frames that you have and begin to explore the ones that show up for your clients. We just touched the surface of RFT here. If you are able to visualize or conceptualize the ways in which humans can uniquely create relationships, draw inferences, and connect symbols in their lives, you can help your clients notice those patterns and interrupt them when they aren't serving them.

Figurative Language

RFT teaches us how we use symbolism in our lives. Metaphors represent some of the best examples of this process. Facts can be great for changing attitudes but they struggle to make an impact when it comes to behavioral changes. It is rare that education alone will make a tremendous impact on someone's beliefs, let alone behaviors. This makes sense. There's a reason that therapy isn't only psychoeducation. In fact, if facts could change behavior consistently, we wouldn't need therapy—just educational courses.

Stories, on the other hand, can make an enormous impact on how we move through the world. While anecdotes are not grounded in any absolute "Truth," we carry them with us throughout our days, weeks, or even life. The best example of this are politicians: Despite ample evidence to support various positions and stances, politicians often use stories of a certain person or family to illustrate their point. They may even show a picture or trot out the people themselves during a speech to further highlight their position. And it works. Because people relate to people. It is how our brain is wired.

Figurative language, such as similes and metaphors, provides a nice shortcut for jargon-filled language. Instead of giving a lengthy description, you can simply say *X is like Y*, and suddenly the other person knows exactly what you mean. This is one reason that ACT encourages metaphors as a tool.

In a world filled with info dumping and a constant stream of information, it can often be a struggle to remember exact statistics. I sometimes find myself frustrated in session because I want to convey information I think is important and I can't remember the exact data point, so I give an approximation instead or skip sharing altogether. Or maybe I remember the stat but it doesn't hold the same impact as, say, a simile.

For example, if I say one researcher has estimated people born with intersex traits make up approximately 1.7 percent of the general population, you may think that is extremely rare and shrug off the statistic (Fausto-Sterling, 2000). However, if I say people born with intersex traits are as common as people with red hair in the general population, your mind is suddenly filled with all the people you've met in your life who have naturally red hair (Harvey, 2015). It's likely not a massive amount, but each data point now comes with the weight of knowing a whole individual. Suddenly that 1.7 percent feels impactful. You may begin to ask yourself questions related to people born with intersex traits but substitute people with red hair, and suddenly, your perspective on the impact of a bill or social discussion becomes more real. Figurative language can expand understanding and provide an additional context for topics important to your clients.

It also allows you to connect information to emotion. Emotion-charged information is more likely to be encoded into long-term memory and more easily recalled (Tyng et al., 2017). Plus, it's fun! While introducing more figurative language into your sessions may seem daunting at first, it opens up everything in your client's environment to learning. And it keeps you engaged in the therapeutic process instead of defaulting to a rigid protocol.

Popular ACT Metaphors that Work

There are a number of ACT metaphors that are canon at this point—ones that are so common we can reference them by name.* Ideally, as an ACT practitioner, you will develop your own metaphors. For now, though, it is useful to explore some of these popular metaphors to understand why they might be so powerful and what makes them work.

Quicksand

The quicksand metaphor highlights the paradoxical nature of pain and acceptance (Hayes, 2005; Stoddard & Afari, 2014). It demonstrates that attempts to fight or struggle with unwanted experiences only further keep us fused with them, whereas coming in full contact with our experience and allowing it to be there (acceptance) may better help us move through a painful moment.

The brief tips I've learned from watching movies with quicksand suggest that the more you struggle against it, the quicker you get sucked in. If you attempt to increase your surface area contact with the sand and stop struggling, you will remain closer to the surface with a better chance of escape. The following dialogue shows how a therapist might introduce the quicksand metaphor:

CLIENT: I hate feeling this way. I just want it to stop.

THERAPIST: I get that. And I know you've tried really hard to stop hurting.

CLIENT: Well clearly I'm not doing the right thing because it's still here.

THERAPIST: Or maybe the point isn't to get rid of it? You're a great problem solver, so it makes sense your mind is trying to fix this. But what if trying not to feel a certain way only makes it worse? When I was a kid I used to watch these movies where the hero is trying to escape a situation and inevitably ends up stepping in quicksand. He freaks out and starts thrashing around, which only makes him sink faster. He's really strong and quick and used to using those two skills to escape, but quicksand is different. The more you struggle, the more stuck you get. I feel like you're a hero in one of those adventure movies and you're stuck in the quicksand.

CLIENT: So, what? I'm just supposed to sink? Be happy I'm stuck?

THERAPIST: No, just like that hero, you're supposed to stop struggling because it's not working. Sometimes we get so used to our default way of operating that we forget to pay attention to whether it's working or not. Is fighting and trying to escape your metaphorical quicksand working?

---

* For a further review on popular ACT metaphors, check out *The Big Book of ACT Metaphors* by Jill A. Stoddard, PhD and Niloofar Afari, PhD.

CLIENT: You know it's not.

THERAPIST: Okay, so what if we tried something different? In the movies, the hero learns that if he spreads his body out to connect as much of it to the quicksand as possible and actually stops struggling that he stays at the surface and has more time to slowly get unstuck. Sometimes we don't have to make the hurt go away. Sometimes we can let it be there and take small steps toward the life we want to have. Would you be open to learning how to do that?

This metaphor is always fun for me because it feels as if I am actually getting to use the useless piece of quicksand survival information I've gathered from childhood. It's also a physical representation of a more abstract internal process. The more concrete and physical you can create your metaphors, the easier they are to play with and experience. While I've yet to encounter anyone in real life who's had an encounter with quicksand, my mind can easily conjure the image of myself or a daring hero caught in its depths.

The quicksand metaphor also highlights the paradox that to gain control is to let go of attempts to control, which brings up another closely related metaphor. Many of my clients feel as though they are doing everything they can just to "stay afloat." What is sometimes difficult to understand is that to find more "solid ground," or gain more control, they might need to get rid of their old "life vest" that has been keeping their head above water—and instead find a different way to get to shore. Both these metaphors help make sense of an experience that otherwise might be a multistep conversation about logic and fear.

Tug-of-War

When clients first come to therapy they often feel as if they are fighting a war with their mind. An unrelenting battle that never ends. And it's exhausting. They're under the misapprehension that if they can only overpower their mind they can win once and for all. Yet it keeps them from living their life.

Tug-of-war is a creative hopelessness exercise that highlights how focusing on the struggle to avoid our pain creates suffering in the long term (Hayes et al., 1999). It's a metaphorical tug-of-war game with you on one end and your opponent at the other. The goal is to pull the other side past an imaginary line to win and demonstrate you're the strongest. When we're fighting with our mind, it can feel like that. The idea is that as you continue to engage with your opponent (your thoughts) and attempt to fight or beat them, you are forever locked in a battle you can't win. Even if you temporarily win, the opponent returns to try to taunt you into picking up the rope for round two. No matter how clever or persistent you are, you never win in the long term, only in short periods of respite. And while you're locked in this battle, you aren't living your life.

Now, this metaphor can work with various opponents on the other side. Traditionally, it was designed to show how we battle our mind. But many different "opponents" can be on the other side of the rope; for example, some people in the ACT for OCD field will use this metaphor with the "OCD monster" on the opposing side.

The idea behind the tug-of-war metaphor is transitioning from a battle to "dropping the rope" and engaging with the rest of the world (Hayes et al., 1999). ACT helps us learn how to drop the rope—how to notice when our mind is trying to suck us into this unwinnable back and forth. Instead, we must learn to drop the rope, acknowledge the monster at our back, and continue moving in a valued direction. The following dialogue shows how a therapist might introduce the tug-of-war metaphor:

CLIENT: OCD is ruining my life. I feel like I can't even trust my mind.

THERAPIST: It seems like your life has gotten smaller and more complicated over time in response to those intrusive thoughts.

CLIENT: It's just never-ending.

THERAPIST: Having OCD can sometimes feel like a never-ending battle. You against your mind, or rather, you versus OCD. It's like a never-ending game of tug-of-war. OCD sends out an intrusive thought [*mimics a tug with their hands*]: TUG! You engage in a compulsion [*mimics a tug with their hands*]: TUG! And just when you think you can finally rest, OCD sends out another intrusive thought [*mimics a tug with their hands*]: TUG! You may be getting some relief for a little bit, but in the long run, as you said, it's ruining your life.

CLIENT: Yeah, I hate it. Why won't it go away?!

THERAPIST: I know it can feel like you need to beat OCD once and for all to be free of it. But OCD is sneaky. It'll just transform into a new type of intrusive thought.

CLIENT: That's definitely happened before. I never used to have any issues with my wife driving. Now she can't go anywhere without me constantly worried she's dead in a ditch somewhere.

THERAPIST: Exactly. OCD can be sneaky. So what if you just dropped the rope? Stopped playing the game.

CLIENT: What do you mean?

THERAPIST: Every time you play this game with OCD, it's causing you distress and taking your focus and energy away from doing the things that matter to you. Like actually enjoying having a night to yourself to read while your wife is out with her friends. You're so locked into this battle that you miss out on everything. What if instead of trying to beat OCD, you dropped the rope and stopped engaging?

CLIENT: I mean, yeah, that'd be great, but it sounds impossible.

THERAPIST: Would you be open to learning how? It might seem a little different from what you've been doing.

By comparing mental exhaustion and anguish to the physical defeat and fatigue of a never-ending game of tug-of-war, this metaphor validates the client's experience of exhaustion, even if they are physically inactive. The metaphorical dropping of the rope is also a great pivot toward values and committed actions. Once established, this metaphor can be brought up often by asking, "Are you holding the rope?" or "What would dropping the rope right now look like?" or "Would you be willing to join me in an exercise to learn how to drop the rope?"

Chess Board

The chess board metaphor is super versatile. The original function of the metaphor is to discuss self-as-context (Hayes et al., 1999; Stoddard & Afari, 2014). In the chess board metaphor, the pieces on the chess board are the client's internal experiences. One side, let's say the black pieces, are every joyful, excited, peaceful, and wonderful thought or feeling the client has had. The other side, the white pieces, are the fears, trauma, panic, and general experiences the client would label as "negative."

Our mind is often an internal battle between "good" things and "bad" things. Based on what we know about the pieces so far, black might be labeled "good" and the white might be labeled "bad." However, on this chess board, neither black nor white can win: Every time one piece knocks another piece off the board, it returns just the same. Nothing changes. This is a great metaphor for demonstrating how staying stuck struggling in your mind feels like an endless, impossible-to-win battle. A continuous struggle that keeps you away from engaging with your life.

So where are you in this metaphor? You are the chess board itself. Instead of feeling as though there are two sides of you battling it out, you are simply where it is all taking place. And regardless of which pieces are winning and what's on the board, you are a constant. This highlights the self-as-context aspect of ACT—the idea that we are an observer of our experience.

Another similar metaphor to this is the sky metaphor, whereby we are the sky and everything in the sky (clouds, birds, thunder) are our internal experiences. The sky is simply the canvas upon which our internal experiences (thoughts, feelings, urges, memories, physical sensations) play out whatever is happening in the moment.

You can also use the chess board metaphor to acknowledge moments of fusion and work toward defusion. For example, you can use the notion of chess pieces as a shortcut when discussing internal experiences: "What piece on the board can you not let go of?"

This metaphor is adaptable because while it has many components to it (black and white chess pieces, the chessboard) it is quite a simple concept. While we might not all know how to play chess, it is reasonable to assume that most of your clients are familiar enough with the game to get the gist of the metaphor. It can be used to explain a complicated topic, such as self-as-context. It can also emphasize how experiential avoidance—staying engaged with the battle—can limit what moves we can make (that is, continue to play the game instead of pivot toward living your life).

Animal Avatar

The purpose of the animal avatar metaphor is to identify an animal that serves as a physical representation of our mind. The cool thing about animals is that even the scary ones are inherently innocent. Heck, even a giant T-Rex is just doing what T-Rexes do. They're not malevolent beings set on intentionally harming others. They just don't always work well with humans. Or overlap peacefully in our environments. With an animal metaphor, we can highlight that even when our mind feels as if it is trying to harm us, it is really looking out for us. It can be a little bit easier to tap into self-compassion from this stance. By anthropomorphizing (attributing human characteristics to an animal or object) our mind, we are suddenly given a plethora of metaphors and a great way to interact with content that keeps us stuck. The following dialogue shows how a therapist might introduce the animal avatar metaphor:

THERAPIST: This might sound like an odd question, but if your mind were an animal, what animal would it be?

CLIENT: Like a real animal?

THERAPIST: I mean, if you have a mythical creature that comes to mind, you can also use that. But yes, if you imagine your mind as this creature that is constantly commenting on your experience, identifying problems, and worrying about the future, what kind of animal would that be?

CLIENT: I don't know, maybe like a parrot or something.

THERAPIST: What about a parrot reminds you of your mind? [*looks for characteristics that client can tie between how their mind behaves and the qualities of a parrot in order to further build out the metaphor*]

CLIENT: I just had this image of those parrots who get taught a lot of bad phrases and no matter what you do or say, they just keep repeating them over and over again.

THERAPIST: I absolutely love that. So what kind of things is your parrot saying over and over again?

CLIENT: That I am bad and a terrible person, and no one will ever love me or want to be my friend.

THERAPIST: Okay, and let's give this parrot a name. We're not going to name him after anyone you know, and we're not going call him "the worst parrot ever" or anything like that. But if you were to give him a human or a pet name, what would you choose?

CLIENT: Frank.

THERAPIST: Okay, awesome. How long has Frank the parrot been in your life? What's your earliest memory or time period where they were there? [*shifts perspective to younger self*]

CLIENT: Probably forever, but my earliest memory is when I was eight and broke something at my grandma's house.

THERAPIST: So he's been in your life a pretty long time.

CLIENT: Yeah, I wish he would fly away and never come back.

THERAPIST: Fair. I think if that were in the cards, he would've already done that by now.

CLIENT: I fear you may be correct.

THERAPIST: So let's operate under the assumption that Frank is going to be hanging out. Maybe sometimes he flies off to go eat some nuts and hang out with other birds, but most of the time he's either flying overhead or sitting on your shoulder saying some not nice stuff. Now, up until this point, you've been spending a lot of time trying to make Frank go away. You've been talking back to him, trying to shoo him away, throwing rocks at him, and trying to clip his wings. And he just keeps coming back. And while you are engaging with him, you're not living your life. So from now on, what I want you to do is simply notice when Frank comes up. And when he sits on your shoulder and starts yammering on, pat him on the head and say, "Thanks Frank, but I'm good." That process will get a little bit easier with some practice, and then we can begin to pivot toward what you want to do when you're not spending all of your time yelling at Frank.

> This process, including anthropomorphizing, represents what we are working toward in building up psychological flexibility.

Over time, this can become a metaphor you come back to over and over again. You can ask your clients questions like "What is Frank saying right now?" or "Frank seems to be showing up a lot lately—why do you think that is?" The important piece is that the client comes up with the animal and names them.

Creating Your Own Metaphors

If there are so many popular, proven metaphors out there, why even bother creating your own? In general, I'm a functional contextualist at heart. Meaning if something works in a given moment, why mess with it? But I've found that sometimes when learning ACT, we can rely too heavily on scripted exercises and established metaphors. This is fine if we are taking steps to learn ACT as an approach and can integrate an exercise into a larger framework and adapt or pivot as needed.

However, I often find that therapists will try out an exercise or metaphor as a stand-alone intervention and it "doesn't work," that is, it doesn't function the way they expected. Because it was simply a tool to test out, they don't know what to do next. When this happens, therapists can easily fall back onto whatever therapeutic background they have that feels safe and conclude that ACT isn't for them. And that's a shame.

What does this have to do with creating our own metaphors? The less actively engaged we and, by extension, our clients are in the figurative language we use to convey important concepts, the easier it is to get lost.

Have you ever been telling a funny story someone had told you and you get halfway through and realize you've lost the thread? The punchline isn't there. It can be an awkward moment. And it discourages you from trying to tell a funny story in the future. That's how I think of standard metaphors. If we're relaying what someone else created, it can be easy to get stuck in the middle. To focus so much on the words or image we are creating that before we know it, we've lost the plot. And because we didn't create the metaphor or start with the function of it first, it's harder for us to adapt. Learning to create your own metaphors can teach you how to flexibly respond in the moment—which helps to enhance all of your therapeutic work.

Another thing to keep in mind when using other people's metaphors is your audience. For example, quicksand, tug-of-war, and chess are fairly well-known to people of a certain age, that is, those who grew up actually playing tug-of-war and chess, and watching movies with dramatic scenes of people sinking into quicksand. You may that find these metaphors lack relatability with younger populations. It's important when choosing metaphors to be aware of your client's contexts, their learning history, and their childhood experiences. For instance, if they grew up in a different country or with a different language and culture than you, it is likely that at least some of the "common" concepts may not be as transferable. Just one of many reasons to learn to create your own metaphors!

When thinking about the metaphors to use with your clients, there are two approaches. The first is to find or create metaphors that you like that can be used with the most clients. This general approach ensures you have some tools you can pull out whenever you need them. If you are a new or busy clinician, wide-appealing metaphors can offer a sense of security and confidence in your ability to work with clients. However, generic doesn't always stick as well as something tailored for a specific client.

The second approach is—you guessed it—specific. Specific metaphors allow you to really connect what you want the client to remember with something important in their life already. A client is more likely to remember and practice a metaphor if it ties in with their interests. It's even better if the client participates in creating the metaphor!

Step-by-Step Guide to Creating Metaphors

It can be intimidating to attempt to create metaphors on your own. It feels like that moment when you know the answer in class and then totally blank when you get called on. We put so much pressure on ourselves to find the "perfect" words to change our clients' lives that we sometimes go completely blank. Your clients don't need perfect. They need help. Even imperfect help. Every time you do it, you'll get a little bit better. Plus, metaphors and other figurative language are so ingrained in your everyday language that you're probably unaware how natural you are at using them. So basically, you're already halfway there. Let's jump right into the steps to create your own authentic metaphor; this step-by-step guide will use an example client:

1. **Determine the takeaway:** Identify the outcome or process you want to highlight. What are you hoping the client learns, recognizes, or becomes aware of? This is called the takeaway. Is the metaphor an easy-to-remember cue for something more complex? Does it aid in noticing?

   You are in session with a 26-year-old client who works in tech and is struggling with feelings of low self-esteem and loneliness. They want to date and create friendships but avoid using dating apps, talking to coworkers, or being in any scenario where they might feel self-conscious or be rejected. Your goal for this session is to introduce creative hopelessness to your client. You want to use a relatable metaphor to help them understand that their attempts to control, delete, or escape their pain has only left them feeling more alone.

Furthermore, highlight that they can take steps toward the life they want even when their mind is bullying them.

2. **Gather data:** Be on the alert for experiences, interests, and places that the client has already mentioned or information based on their occupation, background, and so forth that you might know of. Although you will want to consider their experiences, activities, hobbies, and interests, I'll use the phrase *data point* to refer to all these elements for the purposes of this book.

    So far, you know your client enjoys their work and likes using computers, writing code, and creating apps. Outside of work they like going rock climbing and cooking new recipes.

3. **Make a functional connection:** Link the data point you've selected with the takeaway you want. To do this, create a relational frame between data point and takeaway.

    With the goal of helping your client realize that avoiding and waiting until they "feel ready" to date and make friends is not working for them, you can extrapolate a few similar ideas: Forcing something doesn't work, trying the same thing over and over again and expecting different results doesn't work, and refusing to do something until the conditions are perfect is unlikely to be helpful.

    From the little you know about rock climbing, you're pretty certain that climbing a challenging course with the mindset that you "must" do it one way is a setup for failure. You know that there could be all sorts of conditions and obstacles, such as a big boulder in the way, that require a climber to change course or make split-second decisions. You can deduce that it takes strength, flexibility, and bravery to climb walls or giant rocks.

4. **When in doubt, ask:** If you're not confident in your knowledge about a topic or want more information to bolster your metaphor, ask. Clients are usually very happy to talk about their interests, and you can find really great gems.

    You could ask, "What types of scenarios would make climbing a certain path impossible?" or "What equipment or tools do you use to ensure your safety?"

5. **Piece together the metaphor:** Share it like a story. Get creative and paint a realistic picture as much as possible.

    Here's how a custom metaphor for this client might sound:

    Imagine for a moment that the steps of dating were different paths for climbing a particularly challenging rock. And before every climb you do now, you stand there and look at it, and analyze the steps you might take. But this time, you come to the conclusion that the climb would be really easy if only there wasn't this one challenging point to get through. And so instead of trying to find a way to climb that challenging part or look at ways to approach from a different angle, you stay on the ground and continue to talk about how much easier it would be if that difficult spot was gone. You think about it and start to get angry or maybe sad that the difficult part is there. You talk about it constantly, and even begin to think of ways you could blow it up or chisel it away—which, at the end of the day, would be way more challenging. All that effort and thinking and planning has done is keep you away from climbing—or anything else important in your life. Plus, the difficult section is still there. But what if you took a different approach? What if instead of focusing your attention on the reality you wish existed, you spent time trying out different ways to climb? Sure, the frustrating roadblock would still be there, but you may find there is another path forward.

There are going to be times when you feel stuck, and that's okay. Use it as an opportunity to bring the client along for the process. Ask them if they have examples or ideas in their life that resemble the takeaway you are trying to impart. Or you can explore with them the challenges of one of their data points. Just like our thoughts, if we try to force metaphors to work in a certain way, we sometimes meet resistance and fail. Don't avoid. See if there are opportunities outside of working with clients to practice making metaphors. Maybe you can practice on a friend or colleague, or sit down after a session to think through what metaphor you might have created in the moment and then try to weave it in next session. Sometimes it can help to have a general idea of the takeaway and data point before going into the session as a sort of cheat sheet. However you choose to approach it, I know you are going to create metaphors that touch your clients and stick with them.

Case Study: Quincy

Now let's meet Quincy. After you read the case study, answer the prompts to create a specific metaphor based on her circumstances.

Quincy is a 29-year-old cisgender bisexual woman in medical residency at a well-known hospital to become a cardiologist. She is single and moved to a large city for her residency where she knows no one. Due to her hectic work schedule and introverted nature, she is struggling to make friends. She describes feeling as though she's accomplishing her professional goal at what feels like the expense of every other aspect of her life. She is displaying depressive symptoms, such as apathy, hopelessness, anhedonia, low appetite, trouble falling and staying asleep, feeling distracted, poor concentration, isolation, and according to her, unprompted crying at random times. In her free time, she mostly watches TikTok videos. She says she tries to run in the park regularly when her schedule allows, and she likes to go out to different coffee shops in the city where she'll sit and read her book or people-watch. Quincy wants to feel better but feels convinced that won't happen until she finishes her training in three more years. She adds that by that time, she'll be so behind everyone else her age that she'll likely never have a "normal" life. Quincy shares that she does love her work and enjoys working with patients to help them recover from cardiac events and stay healthy.

Following the step-by-step guide, let's create a metaphor we could introduce to Quincy in session.

1. **Determine the takeaway:** Which outcome or process do you want to highlight? What are you hoping Quincy learns, recognizes, or becomes aware of? Is the metaphor an easy-to-remember cue for something more complex? Does it aid in noticing?

    As her therapist, you are hoping to emphasize and illustrate one of the following takeaways:

    - Pain and values are two sides of the same coin: Our pain helps point us toward what matters to us.

    - Quincy can take steps toward the life she wants even when she's struggling or if it doesn't look like everyone else's life.

    - Not taking any steps to put herself out there in attempting to make friends or dating is completely understandable but not workable in the long term.

    Choose one of these three takeaways to create a metaphor. Circle your choice. You can always go back and repeat the exercise with different takeaways later for more practice.*

2. **Gather data:** Which of Quincy's interests, hobbies, or activities could you choose to be the data point in the metaphor?

    _____

    _____

---

* For more practice with metaphors, download this worksheet at www.theacttherapist.com/ACTskillsmanual to work with different outcomes and objects or concepts.

3. **Make a functional connection:** Link the data point you've selected with the takeaway you want. To do this, create a relational frame between data point and takeaway. What features, associations, and characteristics of the data point could you use for a metaphor?

   _____
   _____
   _____

   Which of the features, associations, or characteristics fit with the takeaway you are trying to emphasize?

   _____
   _____
   _____

4. **When in doubt, ask:** Is there anything you're not clear on that you'd want to ask Quincy before pulling the metaphor together?

   _____
   _____
   _____

5. **Piece together the metaphor:** Share it like a story. Get creative and paint a realistic picture as much as possible.

   Start with a simile: _____ [*takeaway*]

   is like _____ [*data point*].

   Describe in further detail to create a metaphor. You can start with phrases such as "Imagine that…" or "Let's pretend that…"

   _____
   _____
   _____
   _____

You did it! If you're feeling stuck, you can simply start with the simile and then pretend you're the client asking more questions about how X is like Y. Sometimes answering a question instead of explaining a concept can feel easier to get traction with at first.

Exercise: Make a Metaphor

Let's try with one of your clients.

Think of a client you are feeling stuck with. You can list their first name or initials, or you can create a fake name: _____

1. **Determine the takeaway:** What is the takeaway you are trying to help them learn?

   _____
   _____
   _____

2. **Gather data:** What do you know about their experiences, interests, hobbies, favorite things?

   _____
   _____
   _____

   Pick one data point to use for the metaphor: _____

3. **Make a functional connection:** Link the data point you've selected with the takeaway you want. To do this, create a relational frame between data point and takeaway. What properties, characteristics, movement, qualities, and so forth does this data point have?

   _____
   _____
   _____

   In what ways is the data point like the takeaway you want to emphasize with your client?

   _____
   _____
   _____

4. **When in doubt, ask:** Is there anything you want to clarify with your client?

   _____
   _____
   _____

5. **Piece together the metaphor:**

   Start with a simile: _____ [*takeaway*]

   is like _____ [*data point*].

   Now create the metaphor and share it like a story.

   _____

   _____

   _____

   _____

   _____

Repeat this process a couple of times. Some common metaphors you'll use often have to do with:

- Values
- Experiential avoidance
- How our mind is trying to help us but is bad at it
- Creative hopelessness
- Letting go of the struggle with our mind
- Accepting what is outside of our control
- Ways to relate to more abstract concepts, like feelings or physical sensations

If you are feeling frustrated right now, that is completely normal. Take time to think about your life and your actions and practice creating metaphors. You can look for figurative language you already use or review common ACT metaphors you like and see if you can copy the framework but with another data point and takeaway. And remember, it's always okay to create metaphors prior to session and work up to using metaphors on the fly.

Chapter Takeaways

- RFT describes how humans use language to create meaning and symbolism beyond the physical properties of an object or experience.
- Metaphors are a great opportunity to convey complex or abstract concepts in ACT.
- Creating a metaphor in ACT involves using the client's own experience or interests to better describe an ACT principle or takeaway.
- Whether creating your own metaphor or using one that is popular in ACT, metaphors can be introduced once and then referenced through your work with a client as a constant thread or reminder.
- Creating metaphors with your client makes it more likely that they will remember and use that metaphor.

CHAPTER 10

EMBODIED EXPERIENTIAL WORK

A large part of ACT is paying attention to what is happening in the moment. We train clients to notice what their mind does that may be unhelpful: fusion with thoughts, jumping to the past or future, or cognitive avoidance behaviors, to name a few. We also clarify values and help clients take steps toward what matters to them through committed actions.

In this chapter, we focus on the noticing that happens *within* the body. Perhaps you have clients who are so overwhelmed by loud sensations, such as panic symptoms, that they wish they could not feel their body. Or you may have clients with ADHD who struggle with other traditional forms of mindfulness and would benefit from a different way to connect with their experience. You may even work with trauma clients who are completely dissociated from the sensations in their body. This chapter will walk you through *embodied experiential work* from various disciplines that can be incorporated within an ACT framework.

Embodied experiential work involves exercises that happen in the therapy session that help clients connect with their body. These exercises may increase clients' awareness of various sensations, postural changes, or nonverbal ways of communicating (crossed arms, hand pressed to chest). Connecting with the body can create space to practice different ACT core processes. Present-moment awareness is obviously present in all of these practices, since at their core they involve noticing in the present. But we can also pull in acceptance and defusion practices to help with both physical pain in the body and painful emotional sensations related to panic, fear, or anger.

As you move through this chapter, practice the exercises yourself. This can help you understand what clients may experience and how they may struggle.

Body Scan

The body scan exercise is an excellent opportunity to show clients how something can be experienced both in focus and out of focus. It highlights that while we may not always be able to control what internal experiences pop up, we can, with practice, control where we focus our attention. This exercise lasts about five minutes. When in session, the client will likely be sitting in a chair or on a couch, but when they practice at home, they may do so lying down or in any position that works for them. This exercise can be done with eyes open or closed.

Read the following script and notice how attention is drawn to how our focus works, even in the presence of uncomfortable sensations. After completing this exercise in session, invite your client to practice this once per day. If your client has trouble focusing without a voice guiding them, you can offer to have the in-session exercise audio recorded so they can play it back at home.

Body Scan Script

Take a moment to notice how your body is positioned and make any adjustments you want to. There's no right posture to have when doing this exercise. If you feel comfortable, you can close your eyes, otherwise just have a soft gaze on something in front of you. I will have my eyes open during the exercise.

I am going to walk you through noticing different sensations that are showing up in your body. To start with, let's bring your attention to your breath. All you're doing is noticing the rise and fall as you breathe in and out. There's no need to change your breathing—just notice how you normally breathe. And for a couple moments here, simply follow your breath going in and out. Notice the parts of your body that move as you breathe in and out. You may feel your body settling a little bit more into your seat.

[Remain quiet for about 30 seconds.]

Now shift your focus to the top of your head. Imagine for a second I asked you to balance a book on the top of your head. Draw your attention to whatever point at the top you feel that book would go. And then slowly from there, we're going to draw attention forward and down over your face. And simply pay attention to any sensations you notice. Maybe your forehead is tense, or your nose is itchy, or your lips are dry. You may feel a desire to push away from certain sensations or comment on uncomfortable sensations. That's totally normal. Right now we're simply noticing, and describing. So starting with your forehead, begin to scan down over your eyes and across your nose and cheeks all the way until we get to your collarbone.

[Remain quiet for about 30 seconds.]

Your attention is going to split as you follow the sensations down your arms all the way to the tips of your fingers. Maybe you can feel where the edge of your shirt touches your skin, or the temperature difference from your skin exposed to the air to the skin under your clothes. And see for a moment, without moving your hands too much, if you can feel each individual finger.

Then move your attention to your chest and your belly—exploring the trunk of your body. Your mind may briefly reconnect with a sensation of your breathing. Maybe you become a little bit more aware of if you feel hungry or full, or if there is softness or tightness throughout your posture. Simply note that.

[Remain quiet for about 30 seconds.]

Then move down into your seat, and your legs, all the way to the tips of your toes. You may even wiggle your toes to see if you can feel each individual one. Notice that the sensations have always been there. Now that you're drawing attention to them, they get a little bit louder. Recall that you noticed your breath at the beginning of this practice, and as we went through different parts, your attention of your breathing faded to the background. Let's see if you can shift your focus and bring it into the forefront again. Move your attention to your chest and belly.

Sit with your breath for a couple of inhales and exhales.

[Remain quiet for about three full breaths.]

Now move your attention back to your feet, maybe pressing your feet into the ground. Imagine if you painted the bottom of your feet and then pressed it into the soul of your shoe. What imprint would it leave as you lifted up your foot?

We may not always get to control what sensations or experiences show up inside of us, but with practice, we can begin to choose what we pull into focus and what we let fade into the background. This doesn't mean it will go away. But it may be easier to carry with you.

When you're ready, start to bring a little movement into your body. Maybe extend your legs, or reach your arms up to the sky, or wiggle your fingers. And when you're ready, in your own time, lift your gaze and come back to the room.

What did you notice?

Okay, now it's your turn. Practice the body scan on yourself and notice what comes up. Remember that this may take some getting used to—if you're having trouble doing it on your own without guidance (totally fair!), feel free to follow along with an audio recorded script.*

---

* Visit www.theacttherapist.com/ACTskillsmanual for audio recordings of body scan scripts you can follow along with.

Five Senses

One way to help clients connect with the present moment when they are struggling to check in with their body is to engage the five senses in their environment. This is typically taught in a 5-4-3-2-1 sequence, whereby your client notices five things they can see, four things they can touch, three things they can hear, two things they can smell, and one thing they can taste. However, there is no correct way to engage with the five senses. The important piece is that they are noticing and describing what they experience—not making judgments about it. Now, their mind might make judgments, but the goal is to redirect to what they are experiencing.

For this exercise, your clients will have their eyes open. There is no correct amount of time to spend with each sense, but there should be a long enough pause (at least 10 seconds) between senses to truly notice the sensation the client is taking in. Otherwise, your client may default to simply labeling the items without really noticing them. Because some of these senses may not be readily available in your office, you might have some items they can smell (perhaps a candle with a lid on it) and something they can taste (glass of water, coffee, mint).

Five Senses Script

This exercise is about noticing all of the sensations that are showing up in this moment. There might be ones that are really loud and others that are quite quiet. Your goal is simply to check in with your environment and see what you can notice.

To begin, find yourself in a comfortable position—whatever that feels like for you. This will be an eyes-open exercise. First, let's take a couple of breaths to settle into this moment. As you take a breath in, notice how your chest and belly expand.

[Pause for inhale; inhale along with client.]

And as you breath out, notice how your body deflates a little and settles into the chair more.

[Pause for exhale; exhale with client.]

Take two more breaths following the inhale and exhale.

[Model behavior by focusing on breaths as well.]

Now I'm going to walk you through each of the five senses. First, I want you to notice five things around you that you can see. For each item, say out loud what you are looking at, and then take a couple of moments to linger on that visual, taking in its details. This isn't something you need to rush through. I want you to actually see each item.

[Pause as client notices five things they can see. If they are rushing, give them a cue to slow down and notice details of what they see.]

Now I want you to look around you and find four things that you can touch. I want you to actually reach out and touch them, notice the sensations, and then say out loud what you are feeling. This can be the clothing on your body or objects around you in the room.

[Pause as client touches four things.]

Next, I want you to share three things you can hear. These sounds may be a little quieter, so if closing your eyes helps you to isolate each sound, you can do that as well. State three sounds that you notice.

[Pause as client shares three sounds.]

Now see if you can find two things that you smell. This could be the shampoo you used in your hair, your laundry detergent, or even a smell in the air. Really pause and settle into this moment, as scents can take a second to come into focus.

[Pause as client shares two scents. This is one they may struggle with the most, depending on what is around them. It's okay if they can't find two scents.]

And finally, one thing you can taste.

[Pause as they taste.]

And again, let's come back to our breath. Take one inhale and one exhale.

[Pause for breath.]

What was that exercise like for you? What did you notice?

I like to practice with my senses a different way—by pausing to notice the qualities of these items. For example, I wrote this paragraph in an airport lounge while waiting to board a plane to go on vacation. To move into present-moment awareness, I notice my husband's beer on the table: The little bubbles seem to be organized in columns as they float to the top. The glass has condensation on it, and the rim of the glass looks white due to the light shining on it. I'm taking in the glass of beer instead of simply labeling it. As I take a sip from my water bottle, I feel the cold water in my mouth. I notice how my tongue moves to help me swallow. I feel the opening of the water bottle against my bottom lip, and the slight difference in texture against my fingertips from the various stickers on my water bottle.

Ready to try? Look around your space now and see what you can see, hear, touch, smell, and taste. Pause on each sense you notice and describe it. Pretend you're an alien who has never encountered these before, and explore them.

If you are adapting this exercise, please be mindful of what senses your client has access to and to what extent. Those with blindness may still have some sight or awareness of light in their eyes. Those who are deaf may feel vibrations. Clients with ringing in their ears may benefit from bringing other sounds in the environment to the forefront of their focus. There are many ways to interact with the environment around you. Find what works with your client instead of feeling stuck to a specific script. The sensations you encounter do not have to be exciting or even pleasant to explore.

Mindful Movement

A great opportunity to practice present-moment awareness is in everyday movements that we often engage in perfunctorily or automatically. Showering, for example, is typically a time when people space out. This is not a bad thing. There are benefits to daydreaming, planning for the future, and reflecting on the past. These exercises are simply opportunities to practice intentionally focusing your attention during moments when you often aren't present. And who knows, maybe you'll notice something you never have before.

Your clients can practice mindfulness with any behavior they do. Maybe they have a moment in their lives when they are trying to be more present: the commute home, dinner, work meetings, or any number of things. The prompt is simple: Pick an activity, and pay attention to the details of the moment.

Mindful Movement Activities

Taking a shower: Pay attention to the sensation of the water. See if you can follow different streams of water along your body. Notice when they fall off. Feel the way you wash your hair. Do you massage the shampoo in or rub it over your head? How does that differ from washing your body? Notice where you wash your body. Do you have a certain routine for getting every part clean? The goal here isn't to take a longer shower—it's to pay attention while you are showering.

Washing the dishes: Notice the process for each item you wash as well as the entire event from start to finish. Feel the sponge in your hands—how you move it along a plate compared to a bowl or coffee mug. How do your hands hold onto dishes when they are soapy? Watch how your hands move around a dish to clean it and then rinse it. As you wash, you may notice different textures from food particles that are still attached. Or maybe the dish soap you use has a particular scent. The goal is not to change how you wash dishes, but simply to check in more deeply to the steps you take while washing.

Going for a walk: Take a walk around your neighborhood, somewhere you feel safe, or maybe somewhere you go often. Notice the different sounds you hear. Take a breath in and notice the scents. Feel the way your feet strike the ground, or if you are using any assistance devices, notice how your weight shifts in your body or how your arms tense to move you forward. What do you see? Examine each house or street as if you are seeing it for the first time. Pay attention to colors, textures, and small details. You'd be surprised what you notice when you are really looking.

Doing it differently: Another way to practice dropping into the moment is to perform a behavior in a different manner than usual so you are forced to focus more. The best example I have of this is to brush your teeth with your opposite hand. Using your other hand forces your brain to focus on the movements your hand makes instead of nearly operating on autopilot. It also can help you realize the areas of your mouth that need more attention. How are you holding the toothbrush? What do your muscles feel like making the movements to brush your teeth? Pay attention to whether you are favoring one side. Try visualizing the end of the toothbrush on your teeth.

Some other examples of doing it differently might be walking your dog holding the leash with your nondominant hand, switching your hand that holds the fork or knife while eating, getting dressed in a different order, or tying your shoes differently (for example, two bunny ears versus one).

Troubleshooting Mindful Movement

Clients may share that they intended to do a mindful movement exercise but got distracted; this is an excellent opportunity to talk about defaults—how our mind defaults to not being present. From a survival perspective, there is little incentive to be present when there isn't an immediate threat. It makes sense for our mind to wander. When they share this, be sure to validate their frustration. Remind them that this is the purpose of the practice—to notice they are distracted and then return to the present moment—over and over again. Over time, it'll get easier, but they will still practice returning to the present. The following dialogue shows how this conversation might go:

THERAPIST: Last week we talked about practicing mindful activities in everyday life. Were you able to practice?

CLIENT: I thought about it. Does that count?

THERAPIST: It does! That's usually the first step. What happened after you thought about it?

CLIENT: I always thought about the activity during the times I couldn't do it. We had talked about me paying attention when I take a shower and when I walk my dog. However, I'd only remember it when I was getting ready for bed in the evening or right when I got back inside from a walk.

THERAPIST: That sounds frustrating.

CLIENT: It was! My mind is always doing that—giving me helpful information at the worst possible time.

THERAPIST: Yeah, our mind is good at that. When we first started working together, I mentioned how our mind is kind of like a threat-detection system. When there is nothing of note going on in the present moment, it defaults to time traveling to the past or the future in order to better prepare. We specifically chose walking your dog and taking a shower because those tend to be mindless, daydreaming moments for you. So it makes sense that it's going to be a little challenging to redirect your attention to the present in those moments.

CLIENT: I guess that makes sense. I just hate it.

THERAPIST: Totally fair. Let's discuss some ways we can increase the likelihood you get to practice these exercises over the next week.

Reminders, implementation intentions (if-then statements), and visual cues can be used to increase the likelihood that clients will engage in homework on their own. These can be alerts on their phone that they set up during the session. It can also be something as simple as a sticky note stuck to their mirror in their bathroom. One of the positives of telehealth is a client can set a reminder like this up during a session, so it's ready for when they need it.

Finally, it's important to emphasize that any moment can be an opportunity to be present. Maybe a client set the intention to be mindful when walking their dog, but if they remember while washing their face in the evening, remind them that they can pay attention to that moment instead.

Finger Tapping

This is something I naturally do as a stimming behavior and hadn't realized there is history and science behind it. For this exercise, your clients must have fingers, mobility in their fingers, and sensation in their fingers. The main benefits of this exercise are that it is unobtrusive and can be done in the moment. It is designed to help us focus our attention on a sensation—one that is so small that we must intentionally narrow our focus to feel it. Once our focus is narrowed to this one sensation, it can then be slowly expanded out to various sensations, both within our body and in the space around us.

Finger Tapping Script

Lift your hand up with your palm facing you. Begin by tapping the pad of your index finger to the pad of your thumb. Next, tap your middle finger to your thumb, then your ring finger, and pinky finger. Repeat.

Pay attention to the moment you can feel your finger and thumb meet. See if with each finger you can tap lighter and lighter.

If this feels difficult to do because you are looking at your fingers you can always close your eyes or place your hand out of view, such as in your lap or to your side.

Your mind will want to wander after doing this one or two times. That's completely normal. But each time that happens, try to catch where your mind has gone off to, notice it, and then return your attention to your tapping fingers.

One of my criticisms with many exercises designed to connect someone to their experience in the moment is that it often takes people *out* of the moment. Eyes-closed exercises, for instance, cannot be done in many settings. If we're in the middle of an argument, driving, or walking, we cannot easily or safely close our eyes to connect with our experience and be more present. Finger tapping, however, helps us connect without leaving the moment. It can be done subtly in our lap or with our hands to our sides.

This exercise can also be a starting point for other practices. For example, your client can begin with finger tapping and then expand to other sensations they notice in their body. From there, they could transition into defusion and acceptance practices. Other times, they may expand outward from finger tapping into the world around them by engaging in five senses. Or they could simply connect with the moment through conversation or actions.

Some people, like myself, may note that finger tapping may make their fingers feel tingly or itchy after a little while. Advise them to simply rub their fingertips against their legs or arms to dispel the sensation.

Feet Mapping

Most often, when clients are experiencing intense physical sensations due to emotional distress, the symptoms they feel in their body generally lie between their neck and their navel, or in the trunk of their bodies. For this general tendency, I like exercises that focus on moving attention to the extremities. Being able to zoom in to fingers or toes helps to give your client's mind something specific to focus on that isn't associated with intense symptoms. This practice gives the client the chance to ground themselves before attempting to accept or defuse from more intense sensations, like a racing heart or tightening throat.

Some of the following script is included in the body scan exercise, but here, we spend more time on just one body part. Clients must have functional use and sensation in their feet. This exercise is best done with feet flat on the ground (no need to take off shoes).

Feet Mapping Script

Take a moment and notice the sensations in your feet. Maybe even wiggle your toes. Unlike your fingers, it can be hard to feel each individual toe. See if you can begin to sort out where they are.

[Pause for 20–30 seconds.]

Begin to rock your feet side to side so that one side of your foot is touching the ground and the other side is up. Then switch. Raise your heel. Now plant your heel and raise your toes.

[Pause for 20–30 seconds.]

Imagine you took a big paintbrush and painted the bottom of your feet. Then you pressed your feet into the ground. Can you picture the pattern it would make? Feel the parts of your feet that press into the ground and any gaps you might leave.

I love this exercise because while it is effective, it's also a little silly. And what is a better defusion exercise than laughter?

Defusion of Physical Sensations

What do we do with those large and loud physical sensations—racing heart, hyperventilation, pressure in the chest, knot in the stomach—that seem to take over? If our goal isn't to get rid of them, what is the goal? In ACT, that involves a combination of acceptance and defusion.

First, we acknowledge that the sensation is there, and then we practice getting some space from it so it doesn't feel like it's consuming us. I often use the following metaphor: It's the difference between being inside a really messy room versus standing in the doorway looking in. Inside the room, you can't get a full picture of what you are experiencing. Maybe you trip over a toy or have to step over a pile of books on the ground. It's hard to get a clear picture of where to begin because you can't take it all in at once. Standing in the doorway can better help you visualize what needs attention now and what steps you can take next. So how do we get space from such a messy room?

The following dialogue follows a client with physical symptoms of panic:

THERAPIST: Even just talking about this seems to be impacting you. You're talking more rapidly and tapping your foot. What are you feeling right now? [*Shares observation and connects to present moment*]

CLIENT: Kind of panicky, to be honest.

THERAPIST: That's okay. If you're open to it, this could be a good opportunity to practice some of the skills we've been talking about. We can stop at any time if it's too much. Would you be open to trying? No is an okay response as well.

CLIENT: Sure, why not?

THERAPIST: Okay, first, let's just notice what sensations you are feeling. Your mind is going to want to jump to the loudest ones, so let's start there. What is the most intense sensation you're feeling?

CLIENT: [*rubs their chest*] I feel this pressure on my chest. It's awful. Feels like I can't breathe.

THERAPIST: Does it feel like there's a heavy weight on your chest pressing down?

CLIENT: Yeah, exactly like that, and kind of squeezing a little too.

THERAPIST: Okay, great description. Would you say it's like having a fat cat sitting on your chest or a giant lion? [*introduces metaphor that may add some playfulness into the moment*]

CLIENT: Definitely a giant lion.

THERAPIST: It's just laying across your chest taking a bit of a nap. [*creates imagery (this time something that is benign and passive)*]

CLIENT: Yeah, I wish it'd go away.

THERAPIST: Fair. But it seems to be taking a longer nap, so for right now, can you notice where their body is pressing into you and where the parts of your chest begin to let up a little?

CLIENT: [*places hand in middle of chest, above sternum*] Right here is the worst.

THERAPIST: Okay, great noticing. Can you keep your hand there for a second? Just notice that even though your mind is saying you can't breathe, you're able to bring air in and expel air out. Your mind might want you to take giant breaths, but you actually just need sips of air to breathe. [*begins present-moment noticing exercise*]

CLIENT: I still don't like it.

THERAPIST: Oh no one does! However, we want to make a distinction between uncomfortable and dangerous. Your mind is labeling everything as dangerous right now and it's not super helpful.

CLIENT: That's for sure.

THERAPIST: Let's move on to other sensations. What else are you feeling in your body?

CLIENT: I don't know if this counts, but I feel kind of hot and sweaty all over.

THERAPIST: That totally counts and is normal when you're feeling panicky. Now, for this one, you can either close your eyes or keep them open, but I want you to imagine a heat map. Like the ones they use in those spy films—where the people in the buildings light up bright red and things that are cold are more blue. Anything neutral is kind of yellow. Do you know what I mean? [*offers the space to notice without labels of good or bad*]

CLIENT: Yeah, I think so. What am I imagining?

THERAPIST: Scan your body and notice which areas are really hot and sweaty. Picture those bright red. Then notice areas where your body feels neutral, maybe make those yellow or purple. And then, the areas that feel cold, if any, make blue. By the end, you'll have a color map of your body.

CLIENT: Okay, I can do that.

THERAPIST: Great! If it's helpful, you can describe it out loud, or I can guide you through.

CLIENT: Can you guide me? I get distracted.

THERAPIST: No problem. Thanks for asking. It's totally normal to get distracted. Okay, where is it the hottest?

CLIENT: My head, neck, thighs, and palms.

THERAPIST: Okay great, so your head, neck, thighs, and palms are bright red. Which areas are kind of neutral or lighter red? Like you have to think about it to notice them?

CLIENT: I guess my arms and shins and ears.

THERAPIST: Perfect! Okay, so your arms and shins and ears are kind of yellow or maybe even purple.

CLIENT: I like purple.

THERAPIST: Purple it is then! And what about blue areas? Anywhere feel kind of cool or clammy?

CLIENT: I didn't think anywhere, but now that I think about it, maybe my nose and lips, and my toes.

THERAPIST: Awesome. So your nose, lips, and toes are blue. Can you begin to see the color map of your body?

CLIENT: Yes, though the lion is still napping on my chest.

THERAPIST: That's okay, he can hang out there. He's a friendly lion. Uncomfortable, but not dangerous. Anywhere else sticking out to you? [*continues to reinforce a distinction between uncomfortable and dangerous so client can later make the distinction on their own*]

CLIENT: I just feel like there's a pit in my stomach.

THERAPIST: Great noticing. Okay, if you could picture that pit—is it hard like a rock? What shape is it? Does it have a smooth or jagged surface?

CLIENT: It's kind of like a hard ball.

THERAPIST: What size is it?

CLIENT: Maybe the size of my fist?

THERAPIST: Okay, a hard ball the size of your fist. Does it have a color?

CLIENT: Black.

THERAPIST: Gotcha, an emo ball. I imagine the ball is not super comfortable?

CLIENT: [*laughs*] That's correct.

THERAPIST: Fair enough. Not dangerous, but uncomfortable. I wonder if we can practice breathing around it. Sometimes when we feel a heavy ball like that, our muscles tend to tense around it or instinctively try to push it away, which makes everything feel worse. Could you try softening around it? Like a deflated balloon? Just slump a bit in your chair.

CLIENT: [*client slumps*]

THERAPIST: Now, with your next exhale, just sigh out so you're elongating that exhale. Be as dramatic as my dog. [*Side note: My dog dramatically sighs during therapy sessions sometimes, so that's a helpful cue to my clients. You may use something else.*]

CLIENT: [*laughs and then sighs through an open mouth*]

THERAPIST: What are you noticing now?

CLIENT: I feel kind of exhausted but better.

THERAPIST: When your body is ramping up into panic, it can be really exhausting. The next time it starts to show up, do you think you'd be able to practice one of the things we talked about today? [*The therapist is careful not to reinforce that the goal is to "feel better." Instead, they focus on validating the client's experience and switch to committed actions.*]

CLIENT: Yeah, I still feel like garbage, but they helped.

THERAPIST: I'll take that as a win.

Troubleshooting Issues

Many times we introduce an exercise with an assumption for the outcome. This is normal and understandable. However, in ACT, we focus on the process. Not the outcome. This approach can make it easier to pivot when an exercise elicits a different result than what you were assuming. Let's look at some of the common concerns or issues that arise when introducing new practices, especially ones that emphasize awareness of present moment and physical sensations.

Unwillingness to Engage with an Exercise

When I worked at a veterans affairs hospital during my internship, I had many older veterans give me skeptical looks throughout most of therapy. Some had little experience talking about their feelings and felt uncomfortable with the more "touchy-feely" parts of our work. Others had zero interest in closing their eyes (totally fair!). It's important to recognize where your client is coming from. In this case, their generation, faith, culture, or family upbringing may have large biases, judgments, or beliefs that make it harder for them to engage with the more abstract or emotion-heavy aspects of therapy. A client who has been taught their whole lives to "suck it up" or "don't share family business" will understandably have a hard time describing their experiences, especially if it paints their family or community in a poor light. In these cases, focusing on the therapeutic relationship is a must.

It may take longer for someone who is hesitant with information to trust you. This can be a situation where self-disclosure, especially around feelings or thoughts or experiences, can be useful. It not only builds trust but models behavior. These clients may just not have the language to express their feelings. I've found feelings wheels or charts to be helpful in expanding a client's vocabulary around how they're feeling. Or you can use your own experience to model various feelings you think they may be experiencing.

And please, be mindful of how you talk about your client's community, faith, family, and culture. A client may default to defending their community if you come in too hard with condemning actions they have experienced. This can be an excellent opportunity to explore rules or beliefs that they have related to therapy, their experiences, or even their own feelings. Taking the time to understand and practice perspective taking can help you empathize with both your client and their history. Remember, you can understand why someone behaved the way they did without saying their behavior is acceptable to you. That distinction can be useful for clients and yourself as you navigate working with a large range of people.

At the end of the day, if a client tells you no, listen. Acceptance at its core is a willingness to acknowledge and engage with your full experience. And sometimes clients are not willing. That is okay, and it is their right. If a client is not willing to engage with certain exercises or discuss certain topics, respect that. Not only is that the ethical response, but it helps to build the therapeutic relationship. Clients may share things with you that they've never told another soul. It is understandable, therefore, that it may take some time. You are free to revisit the topic later on in therapy. They may be more open to discussing it, or they may not be. It may be useful to highlight how avoiding a topic will not make it magically go away and may impede therapy progress, but that is their right. However, not every single aspect of a person needs to be uncovered, excavated, and examined in order for healing to occur.

Determining the Exercise Was "Not Helpful"

Sometimes we try an exercise and a client states that it was "not helpful." It is useful to hear directly from them what they meant by "not helpful," but in general, this often happens for one of two reasons.

A client may be under the impression that an exercise would make the thought, feeling, or sensation go away. They may say it is still present, or they "don't feel any different." This can be a great opportunity to return to creative hopelessness (see chapter 2). Some clients really struggle with the concept that they can't just make certain thoughts, feelings, or experiences go away. Or maybe they misunderstood the purpose of the exercise. Highlighting the process you are looking to build can help them move away from the outcome they were trying to force.

Sometimes this may be a sign that you were doing a lot of "talking at" instead of "exploring with" your client. It happens to the best of us! In this case, walk them through a functional analysis. Talk through what shows up for them, how they typically respond, and how that response is working so far. Investigate how long they've struggled with these patterns of responding. Highlight the efforts they've made on their own across time to create the change they are looking for. Sit with those feelings. The frustration and heaviness can be functional in these moments. It is hard to let go of the hope that you have a secret pill or magic wand that fixes everything.

Alternatively, a client may have struggled to engage with an exercise. This can show up if your client struggles with imaginative exercises. Some people are not able to picture anything in their minds, which can make some of the metaphors and defusion exercises harder to connect with. If that's the case, you might find your client understandably frustrated. Some clients may be finding out for the first time that their mind can't do something that other minds can. Or this may be a skill they've struggled with for a long time, and this frustration is a sucky reminder. Whatever the reason, reassure them that it's okay—it's why we try out different exercises and then switch to an exercise that is a little more concrete. This may involve talking through an experience or focusing on physical sensations instead of thoughts.

For exercises like mindfulness, these skills can be developed. So if a client is frustrated, validate that, then back up, working on either a different exercise—or a shorter or simpler one. When it comes to mindful breathing, for example, many people need some type of audio guide to practice at home. They also tend to get distracted when starting out, so shorter exercises (think two to five minutes) at the beginning can build up self-efficacy. This can also be the case for clients who generally have trouble regulating their attention: those with a traumatic brain injury or ADHD. These clients may "zone out" the minute you start the exercise or have trouble following complex, multistep instructions. Keep it simple.

Not every exercise is going to connect with every person. Framing the exercises as something you are going to "try out" or "test" like an experiment can help set up appropriate expectations. If an exercise or metaphor doesn't land, that's okay! Explore why it may not have connected with your client and pivot. Pivoting may look like trying a different exercise or jumping to a different core process.

Dissociation

We dissociate or "check out" from the present moment in a number of ways. Some, like flashbacks, can be jarring and distressing. Others, like rumination, can provoke anxiety or panic. Distractibility (such as with clients with ADHD) can also be frustrating—for both you and the client. So how do you help clients stay engaged? What do you do when they dissociate?

For attention span issues, the goal is to increase engagement with the present moment and intentionally shift focus from whatever the client is focused on to what is happening in the present. This can literally be a 30-second noticing exercise. Many therapists start off with exercises that may be too long for their clients. Short, engaging present-moment practices may be best to start with—especially anything that connects to physical sensations (which are easier to notice) or movement. Create space to acknowledge the frustration your client has. Remember, this is an opportunity to practice. If they were experts already, you wouldn't be focused on this.

If you work with clients who have flashbacks, violent intrusive images and thoughts, or hallucinations, you'll want to discuss beforehand what they'd like you to do or what has helped in the past. For example, never touch or lean close to a client having a flashback unless they have specifically asked you to. And obviously, regardless of their ask, please keep in mind your ethical and professional boundaries.

Before beginning any exercise designed to connect with a client's internal experience, know what to expect. What do their flashbacks typically look like? What level of awareness do they have? Are their hallucinations visual, auditory, or both? This can give you some clues to notice when they are beginning to struggle, as they may not always be able to say, "Hey, I'm having a flashback right now." Now, this doesn't have to be an intense or scary conversation. You don't want to give your client the impression that you are afraid of their experience or that this is something super scary you have to prepare for. All you're doing is learning about their experience so you can best support them. Keep it casual and supportive.

If you notice their body posture or attention change during the exercise, simply acknowledge what you're noticing and draw them into noticing. You might say, "You look really tense all of a sudden. What are you experiencing?" or "Your eyes seem a little out of focus to me. What is your mind doing?" Be mindful of the tone and pace of your voice. You don't need to treat your client like a wounded animal. A stern voice, rapid speech, or any tapping, snapping, or clapping noises may not be conducive to a safe environment. Your role is to guide your client back to the present moment through describing, noticing, and defusing. The following dialogue shows a situation where a client is dissociating:

THERAPIST: It seems like you're having a big reaction. Can you share what you're experiencing?

CLIENT: I just can't stop thinking about that kid. I can see him in my mind.

THERAPIST: That must be really hard. Is your mind taking you back to the scene?

CLIENT: Yeah, I can see him. It's like in high definition.

THERAPIST: I know you said that happens sometimes. Can I help you through this?

CLIENT: He was so young. I swear for a moment I thought it was my own son.

THERAPIST: [takes an audible breath in and out to model for client] I noticed your hands are fisted really tightly together. Could you try opening your hands for me?

CLIENT: My whole body is so tense.

THERAPIST: It's reacting to your flashback. That's pretty common. We're going to slowly start bringing your mind back to this moment, okay? Can you open your hands for me?

CLIENT: [unclenches fists]

THERAPIST: Great job. Now, can you feel your feet? I want you to try to wiggle your toes.

CLIENT: My toes? Uh, yeah, I guess I can do that.

THERAPIST: Can you feel each individual toe? Sometimes if you wiggle them you can separate them a little.

CLIENT: I can notice my big toe and pinky toe. The rest are all stuck together.

THERAPIST: That sounds like a good place to start.

CLIENT: My mind keeps going back there. I can't stop it.

THERAPIST: Of course it does. It's loud and distressing. Your mind wants to keep an eye on it. But you are safe in this moment. Can you look around here and tell me what you see?

CLIENT: [*takes a shaky breath and lifts head then looks around*] We're in your office.

THERAPIST: Does anything specific stand out that you can see in this room?

CLIENT: [*rubs his hands on his thighs and shifts in his seat*] Your coffee mug has dinosaurs on it.

THERAPIST: I know. Isn't it awesome?

This can be a slow process. Don't rush it. Help them connect to the present, describe their experience, and then talk through what happened. Summarize the skills you used so that they can practice replicating it on their own. The goal is for them to identify the skills that helped them the most and then practice those daily when they are not distressed. It's easier to pull up a skill during a flashback that they've practiced over and over again under boring circumstances than trying to use a skill for the first time when they're overwhelmed and struggling. I often use the metaphor of a professional athlete: they practice their signature move over and over before using it in the big game.

Panic Attacks

Clients with a history of panic attacks can be afraid of having one in session. That's an understandable fear. Many clients describe panic attacks as feeling as if they are dying or having a heart attack. I state this not because I think you don't know, but rather because our knowledge that panic attacks aren't dangerous—simply scary and uncomfortable—can make us dismissive of these fears at times. It makes sense that your client would be worried about having a panic attack when asked to come in contact with feelings, thoughts, and physical sensations. After all, there is probably a pretty good reason why they have been avoiding doing so.

If your client has a history of panic attacks or has commented that breathing exercises make them feel anxious, discuss it before jumping into the exercise. You may begin with coming in contact with less anxiety-provoking physical sensations. For example, maybe you begin with a finger tapping exercise instead of mindful breathing. Talk through their fears. Use your previous work together to highlight the difference between uncomfortable and dangerous.

Many of my clients fear that they will faint. We discuss how we sometimes accidentally induce hyperventilation. In response to feeling like we can't breathe, we rapidly suck in more air, which can lead to an increase in CO_2 levels and feelings of dizziness or lightheadedness. I often jokingly say that if they do faint, their body will automatically take over breathing and they'll wake up. A little psychoeducation can go a long way in helping client understand what exactly is happening within their body.

When clients express concern over having a panic attack, after validating and exploring their concerns, I tend to light-heartedly suggest, "If you do have a panic attack, then we'll have a great opportunity to practice in session!" Hearing my lack of concern can be grounding. Plus, it gives me an opportunity to expand their behavioral repertoire. The thought of having a panic attack doesn't always have to lead to fear and avoidance. It can lead to the thought *This is an opportunity to practice.*

What happens if they do have a panic attack? First off, this is very unlikely to happen. I've done exposure work with countless clients with panic disorder, PTSD, OCD, and illness-anxiety disorder. They may experience panic symptoms, but that doesn't mean it'll lead to a full-fledged panic attack—usually because they aren't getting in their own way during the session.

If you are doing an experiential exercise and a client requests wanting to stop, shares a physical sensation they are experiencing, or presents distress in any way, pause the exercise. Use this as a chance to stay in the moment without leaving it. Ask them to describe what they are experiencing. Maybe walk them through a functional analysis of what they would generally do next. Help them distinguish between what they are experiencing and what the environment is telling them. The following dialogue shows a therapist reacting to a client in the throes of panic:

CLIENT: I don't like this.

THERAPIST: Okay, let's pause here for a second. What are you feeling? [*slows down voice to help control pace of client*]

CLIENT: I'm feeling really flushed and hot and just sweaty. I think I'm going to pass out.

THERAPIST: Is that how panic attacks usually start for you?

> The therapist remains neutral and calm. The client is safe sitting in the chair. Continue to talk and explore in order to interrupt the client's "Oh no, it's a panic attack" process.

CLIENT: Yes. I hate this.

THERAPIST: Okay, would you let me guide you through this?

CLIENT: As long as I don't have to stand up or anything. I don't think I can.

THERAPIST: No standing involved. In fact, can you feel the chair underneath you? Feel where your legs and back press into the chair. Take a second and notice how you're sitting in the chair. Sometimes we get kind of tense when that hot or flushed feeling shows up. See if you can soften into the chair. [*begins grounding practice*]

CLIENT: I don't think I can. I feel like there's so much energy running through my body.

THERAPIST: Great noticing. It makes sense that your body wants to tense up in response to a feeling you don't like. Can you exhale for me? It looks like you're holding your breath. [*shifts to a different practice the moment client does not feel able to participate*]

CLIENT: [*sighs out*] I think I was. I told you I do that sometimes.

THERAPIST: I remember. When we feel discomfort, our natural instinct is to tense against it. But while you may feel all sweaty and like bolts of energy are shooting through you, there is nothing dangerous inside you. See with your next exhale if you can soften your body a little bit.

CLIENT: [*pauses for a moment and exhales*]

THERAPIST: There you go. See if you can let your shoulders droop down and back... Great job... Notice how your body kind of curled into itself. Could you try uncrossing your arms and just letting them rest in your lap?

CLIENT: [*shifts in seat and adjusts arms*] I hate feeling this way.

THERAPIST: That's because it really sucks. But you're doing an excellent job moving through it. What other areas of tension in your body do you notice that you can try creating space for?

While unpleasant for the client and potentially distressing for you, having panic symptoms in a session can be an excellent opportunity to observe. Many times clients aren't aware of the initial signs of panic attacks. Not only can you help walk them through the experience, but you can also point out body posture, breathing patterns, speech rate, and other signs you notice. This can help them begin to increase awareness of their body before the symptoms become more severe.

Client Not Practicing

It can be frustrating for both client and therapist when a client consistently comes back and reports that they are not completing their homework for the week. The therapist is confused because the client seemed motivated during the session. The client may feel shame, embarrassment, or anger that they once again didn't follow through. In this instance, therapy can very much be a reflection of the problems the client faces in their life. Patterns that exist in their life are often mirrored in therapy—which is great! It gives us an opportunity to work through it in real time.

The simplest reason a client does not complete homework or exercises outside of session is that what you are asking of them is too big of a step. Clients and therapists set goals based on what seems doable. This may be based on the client's past performance or their own stated goals. The most important data point for progress, however, is where the client is starting. If someone wants to exercise three days per week or practice mindfulness for 10 minutes every morning, that seems reasonable. And yet, if a client is starting from zero, it may be asking too much.

If a stated practice is not working, then start with 10 percent of it. This is also an excellent opportunity to practice intentionality. I once had a client who valued strength and their health but avoided the gym. They loved weightlifting. However, they had gained some weight since the last time they were at the gym and struggled with fears that others would judge them or make fun of them for exercising. They were so fused with this fear that they stayed away from something they loved.

So where did we start? Putting on exercise clothes when they came home from work. And going nowhere. Then putting on exercise clothes and leaving the house, but not to the gym. Then driving to the gym. Then walking into the gym. It was such a slow process that they became frustrated that I wouldn't let them go into the gym. By the time it came to actually exercise, we had built up enough practice of approaching, setting intentions, changing habits, and doing defusion exercises that the transition back to exercise was a lot smoother.

Many people are resistant to starting so far behind the finish line. It feels embarrassing. It may lead to thoughts that they are lazy or a failure. And yet, starting small is the key when they are resisting or avoiding practice outside of session. Talk through this process with your client. Acknowledge and validate all the thoughts about what they "should" be able to do. Explore those fused thoughts.

Where your client starts is exactly the right place for them to be. If you or they try to rush things, it will simply reinforce the pattern of short-term success followed by a swift return to their old patterns. You don't want them to practice old behaviors they've already proven don't work; rather, you want them to practice behaviors that will lead to long-term change. You are working toward a radical shift to how they approach their mind and world. That takes time. Relay these points to your client. And if it turns out they aren't quite ready to tackle their stated goals, that's okay. Meet them where they are.

Co-Opted for Control Agenda

Most of my clients, like myself, are problem solvers. They have highly analytical minds. Those minds tend to default to fixing. And when it comes to uncomfortable feelings or difficult thoughts, fixing usually means "making it go away." This is a useful skill in some situations. But when it becomes the default, clients tend to view all skills and scenarios as opportunities to control or change an experience. That's why setting an expectation at the beginning of therapy and the beginning of certain practices is helpful (see chapter 2). As you now know, ACT is a non-symptom-reduction approach. And yet, sometimes our work gets co-opted as part of that same control agenda.

You'll notice this when clients tell you that an exercise "didn't work," as we discussed earlier in this section. Inquire further. They'll usually comment that they "still felt anxious" or that the "thoughts were still there." It just goes to show how ingrained this belief is. Clients may default to the expectation that if they do the right things, they never have to encounter pain. When clients share this type of feedback, use this as an opportunity to further explore their struggle with the idea that they can't always delete, erase, or control their internal experience. Circle back around to creative hopelessness (see chapter 2). Then you can explain the process that you are building. The process of noticing, interrupting, and intentionally focusing.

This can be particularly true if clients are using apps or other sources of media to practice. For example, if your client likes or wants to try eyes-closed mindfulness exercises or breathing exercises, that's great! But sometimes the recorded exercises clients find online have a control agenda message: *Do this and then you'll feel calm*. Remind them that their goal with the exercise is to practice intentionally connecting to their present moment. And then to reconnect with the message of the skill they are trying to build. In this case, repetition is their friend.

Chapter Takeaways

- Embodied experiential work involves any exercise that help clients connect with their body or senses in the present moment.

- There are many practices that already exist that you can add to an ACT framework to aid clients in practicing present-moment awareness.

- When using an exercise in ACT, we want to make sure we are not suggesting that the exercise will make a person feel calm, experience less anxiety, or stick to any other symptom-reduction agenda. That may be a by-product, but it is not the purpose of the practice.

- The goal is to practice these exercises in session with the client so you can process the experience and roadblocks with them in the moment. Then have them go home and practice on their own.

- Embodied experiential work is process-based (noticing or focusing attention in the moment) rather than outcome-focused (aiming to feel a certain way after).

Hopefully this chapter has given you insights into how you can use a client's sensory experience to increase present-moment awareness. In this next chapter, we will further explore how to adapt exercises and interventions that you already use within an ACT framework.

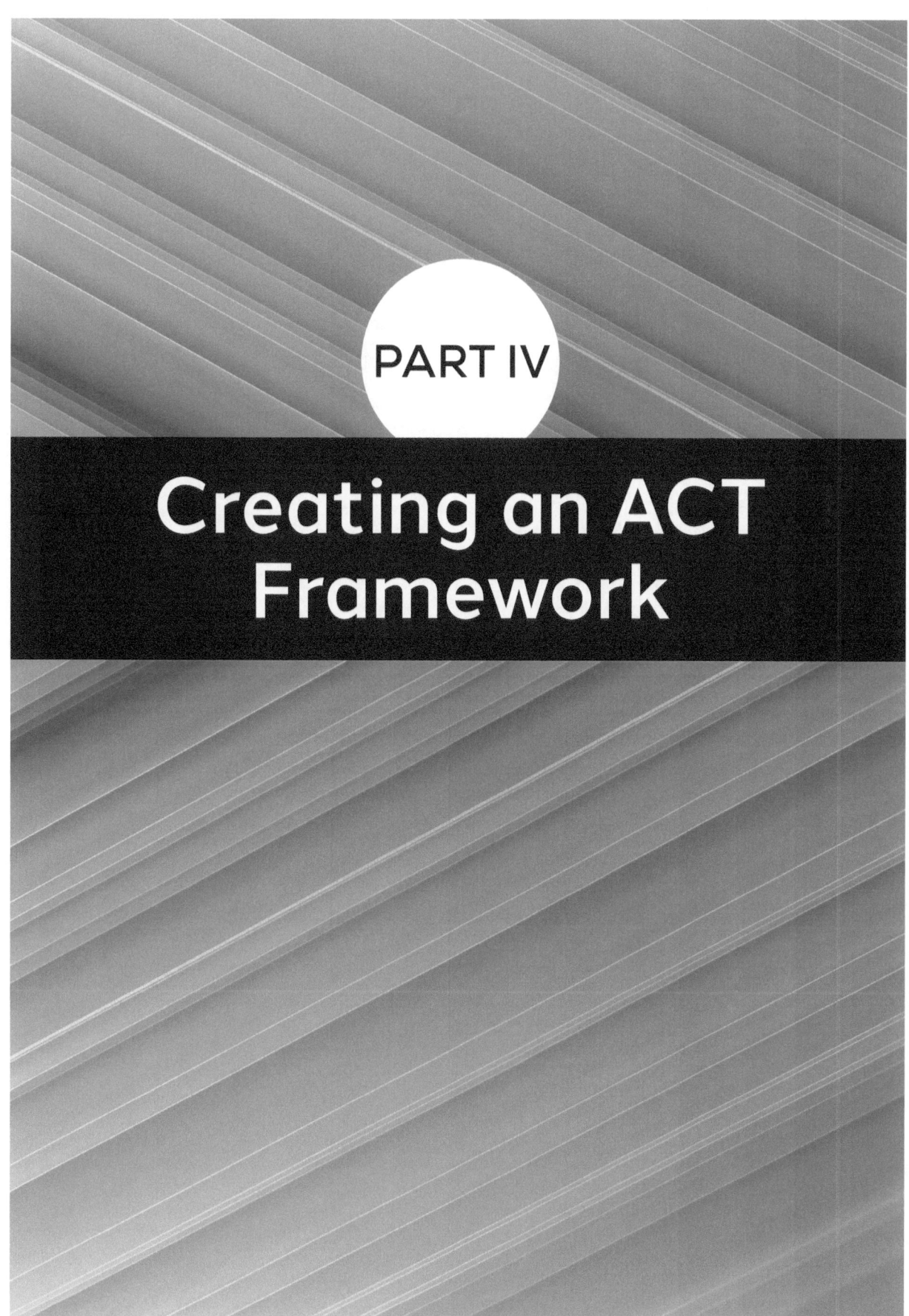

PART IV
Creating an ACT Framework

CHAPTER 11

INCORPORATING OTHER SKILLS INTO ACT

Learning ACT doesn't mean throwing out everything you've learned to date. There are many evidence-based skills, techniques, and protocols from other disciplines that have value and help people. In other words, you can implement a potentially new ACT framework to approach your work with your clients while still maintaining the other great work you are already doing.

So how do you begin to combine these skills into a cohesive and theoretically consistent practice? In this chapter, I will walk you through my strategy for navigating therapy work from an ACT framework. We will discuss a couple prominent therapy practices and how they might be modified to be consistent with ACT. By the end of this chapter, you'll have clear guidelines for combining the work you currently use, as well as any other continuing education you hope to take, with ACT.

As you go through this chapter, consider the skills, techniques, and tools you currently incorporate in your work with clients. List the skills or tools you currently use with your clients that you find most effective and are most consistently used. They could include a specific metaphor, worksheet, technique, or even something as broad as exposure work.

_____

_____

_____

_____

_____

_____

_____

_____

Please keep these handy as you read and begin to think how these concepts could fit in with ACT.

Navigating Therapy from an ACT Framework

Let's review the main steps of the ACT framework. By this point, these should be very familiar to you, but they are vital to keep as consistent and fixed parts of any work in ACT. Therefore, keep them at the forefront of your mind as you consider integrating other practices into the framework. They provide a great starting point for making your work more consistent with ACT.

Principle #1: Start from a Functional Contextual Framework

Functional contextualism focuses on how something functions in a given context. This ensures you move away from labeling behaviors as "good" or "bad" or "right" or "wrong" and instead look at their function. Most people default to behaviors that lead to short-term rewards but are not helpful in the long term. In ACT, we are helping clients notice these behavioral patterns, build skills to interrupt them, and pivot to engaging with behaviors that are aligned with their long-term values.

Principle #2: Remove Any Symptom-Reduction Language or Promises

ACT operates from a non-symptom-reduction agenda. Essentially, we aren't trying to reduce feelings, thoughts, or sensations. Those are by-products of how we interact with the world. Instead, we are working to increase a client's ability to intentionally choose how they want to show up to life. Sometimes that leads to a decrease in symptoms, but it is not the goal. ACT is additive, not subtractive. Your aim is to expand your client's behavioral repertoire and increase engagement with values.

Principle #3: Make Treatment Plans Based on Values

Most treatment plans generally identify goals or outcomes for therapy. These outcomes often include reducing symptoms, learning new skills, and identifying specific behaviors or actions a client will engage in. In ACT, we want our values to guide how we show up to the world. Our clients' goals, skills, and responses to internal experiences (thoughts, feelings, memories, sensations, urges) would ideally be guided by what matters to them. Use your client's self-identified values as a guiding force for informing treatment protocols.

If you use these three principles as guides for conceptualizing your work with clients, you will be able to adapt almost any skill to fit within an ACT framework. Next, I'll walk you through the most common skills I get asked about.

Behavior Change Strategies

Behavioral activation, goal setting, habit change, SMART goals: All of these behavioral change strategies are great, actionable ways to set and measure observable behaviors your client wants to increase. These strategies can definitely be implemented into an ACT framework. As with any goal we set in ACT, any behavior change strategy begins with values. We want to highlight with the client how this small step connects back to their larger values. Adding this extra layer of meaning to their goals not only increases their motivation to engage with the goal, but it also creates a narrative that even small decisions can serve their values.

Speaking of motivation, my clients often use the excuse that they aren't motivated to do something, and that stops them from making change. Here's what I explain:

> *When we approach motivation as a feeling, it leaves us completely at its mercy. On a whim, it can decide to show up and energize us or swiftly dissipate, usually when we are halfway through a project. While there are strategies to increase the likelihood this feeling will show up, it is, at the end of the day, not in our control. If the ability to live the life we want to live depends on a certain feeling or experience coming and going, that can be pretty terrifying and disappointing. But when we think of motivation as an action, and we have a clear idea of what we want to do and the values attached to that action, it is far easier to make that choice to move. In other words, can we still direct our body to action without the feeling? Yes! That leads us right to willingness. Are we willing to take this one action in the service of our values when it's hard? Sometimes the answer is yes. Other times the answer is no. Maybe the action needs to be modified or made smaller. But it is still our choice.*

The other piece to consider when developing behavior change strategies with clients is that you are not engaging with this behavior to decrease a symptom, but rather to help them engage with the life they want to create for themselves. Again, this is an additive approach—not a subtractive one.

For example, with behavioral activation it is common to discuss this process as "follow your feet"—the idea being that if we act and engage with the world, our feelings will follow. Within an ACT framework, we would modify this. While behaving in accordance with our values can make us feel happy, it is not a guarantee. We cannot guarantee that a client will feel any specific way, as feelings are fleeting. Instead, you'd use this as an opportunity to discuss how we often behave in a very reactive manner. You might say something like this:

> *We respond to whatever is showing up inside of ourselves and in the world. This can be exhausting and seem as if you are constantly one big emotion-driven machine without control. Practicing small steps you can take in your life, even when you don't feel like it, can be a great way to show yourself that you get to choose how you show up to a moment. You can always take your feelings with you, but you don't have to feel a certain way to behave a certain way. We start small because this is a new practice for most people and we want to have wins (actually doing the action) early on. This isn't*

about looking for perfection. Our goal is to increase how often we are engaging with our values. And again, we can do that through very small steps.

With a more behavior-based goal or any homework assignment, my motto is: *If you didn't do it, you had an opportunity to notice!* Every time a client is unsuccessful at meeting their goal, it tells us something. Ask yourself, "What was happening that made it difficult for them to show up?" This is not a failure—it's a learning opportunity. Sometimes we learn that what we thought was a small step was really a large one, and we need to scale down to start. Other times we learn that more hooks showed up than we expected and we weren't prepared. This creates the chance to develop a new skill connected with the six core processes.

Doing the work on the inside is awesome, but that's only half of the equation. Clients want to make noticeable changes in how they show up to their life. You probably want that for them and yourself as well. In ACT, values guide the actions we take. When in doubt, start with values, and then take the next smallest step in that direction. There are a lot of great behavior-based therapies and techniques out there. Try them out and see how they can fit within an ACT framework.

Grounding Exercises

One question that often gets asked during trainings is whether there is space in ACT for grounding techniques. After all, grounding techniques are meant to reduce whatever the distressing symptom is that is flooding the client—in other words, an agenda to change their current state to one that feels more stable or calm. Now, as we know, ACT has a non-symptom-reduction agenda. However, functional contextualism, which underpins ACT, is focused on what works in a given setting, meaning that even though grounding exercises are based on a symptom-reduction premise, there is room for them in therapy while using ACT. (See chapter 10 for several grounding exercises.) Now, to be clear, I would caution against setting up any exercise with the expectation that a client will feel or not feel a certain emotion or sensation after the exercise—mostly because you really don't know what will happen.

DBT, for example, has many effective distress tolerance and emotion regulation skills, such as holding an ice cube, intensely exercising, or dunking your face in cold water. From an ACT perspective, these skills are excellent at helping a person ground themselves in the present moment. When they are flooded or fused with intense emotions or other internal experiences, these strategies can help them defuse from those feelings or sensations in order to notice their context and choose what to do next rather than what their emotions dictate. Framing it in this way helps clients focus on what they are adding to the experience (noticing or grounding skills) rather than what they may be attempting to remove (big feelings). It helps to build confidence that they can coexist with their big feelings. It shows them that they have emergency brakes they can use to get a little breathing room when needed.

I would also recommend combining grounding skills with imaginal or interoceptive exposure work (see later in this chapter). These should not necessarily happen in the same session. However, if you are teaching clients grounding skills to help them feel anchored in the present moment during a storm—such as paced breathing exercises or progressive muscle relaxation—they may also benefit from exposure work to practice moving through the storm. This way, clients also get practice in session sitting with big emotions and, with your help, learning how to create space for them so the client can choose how they want to show up next.

While we'd love to save our clients from scary experiences, we can't promise them that they will never have another panic attack, flashback, or dissociative episode. What I have seen in practice, though, is that those experiences, while still overwhelming, create less reactivity over time. One of my clients once told me he had his first panic attack in months. When I asked him about it, he responded that it "wasn't fun," but he was able to move through and get on with his day. This is the outcome we hope to see with ACT. He knew that he was capable of feeling that intensity, using skills we've worked on (including grounding exercises), and then continuing to move toward his values. I think that's pretty awesome.

Thought Records

Whether your client is gratitude journaling, breaking down a DBT behavior chain analysis, or a creating a CBT thought record, recording what they are experiencing and bringing that back into session can be extremely helpful. It gives you insight into their patterns in real time. It also gives the client practice in pausing, noticing, and reflecting. These practices may be the easiest to incorporate into an ACT framework because the client's main focus is identifying what they are experiencing in the present moment.

If you'd like your thought records to include some type of analysis or behavior change, focus on identifying if the current actions move them toward their value or away from pain. You can help them identify the main hurt that showed up in that moment and then what value that hurt is the inverse of. From there, they can explore what action would have taken them toward their value. The following dialogue shows what this might look like:

Therapist: Let's go over what happened over the past week. I see here in your record form that you were feeling really hurt and angry about a situation. What about it was so hurtful?

Client: I thought they were my friend. And then I find out that they are gossiping about me behind my back and making fun of me. I just feel so stupid.

Therapist: Why do you feel stupid? There's no way you could've known they were doing this until you found out. I think anyone would feel hurt in that situation.

Client: I guess I'm just embarrassed because I really thought I was making a close friend, and I trusted them and opened up to them. But we really didn't even know each other that long, so I don't know why I am so upset. It sucks, but I should be fine.

THERAPIST: You're allowed to be upset. I know how important trust is to you. And how hard you've been working to create meaningful connections with others. Sometimes pain highlights what we care about most, and it can show up when what we value has been lost, betrayed, or violated in some way. In this case, trust and connection is really important to you; you were open and authentic with this person, and it hurts that they took advantage of that. [*demonstrates how pain is the inverse of values*]

Thought records and journaling can also be a great support for case conceptualization. Instead of relying on recall, clients can write down on paper or in their phone exactly what they were experiencing. You can use this information to inform the next steps or skills that would be most useful for the client. Journaling can also help those who struggle at times to label or identify their internal experiences. The process encourages descriptive language.

I will sometimes "ban" clients from using certain words if that is their default. For example, if a client has a tendency to label everything as "anxiety," I might discuss with them how we can tend to default to certain language—how this default label does not always allow us to connect with our experience in the present. And then every time they use the word "anxiety," I would pause and ask them, "What does anxiety look like right now?" or "What does that mean?" This helps the client build a more robust vocabulary for their internal experience as well as increase their contact with the present moment.

Thought Restructuring

Is there a way for CBT's thought restructuring to be introduced in an ACT framework? Yes—it just looks a little different. The main concept behind cognitive restructuring is that a person has a thought that is exaggerated or not consistent with reality. Through the process of cognitive restructuring, often with the help of worksheets, clients explore the thought and the facts and experiences related to the assumption they are making, and they replace that initial thought with one that is more realistic.

The idea of deleting or replacing a thought makes this practice not consistent with ACT. It is also not consistent with how our brain works. We cannot delete or erase thoughts or ideas on command. While over time, we do lose certain thoughts, memories, and information, it is most often content that we are disengaged from or neutral about. Instead, let's look at the components of cognitive restructuring and see which might be useful within an ACT framework.

Looking for evidence for or against an idea can be a helpful cognitive behavior. Saying a positive mantra to ourselves can be useful in situations when we need to start an activity or perform. Adding another way of thinking about a situation to the context can help us expand our behavioral repertoire. Essentially, instead of deleting or replacing one thought with another, we are acknowledging that initial thought and adding this new perspective about the situation, which can create different outcomes than simply reacting to the initial thought. Think of that initial thought as a hook or antecedent, and these cognitive behaviors as actions that help us defuse from that initial thought and pivot toward values. Throughout this process though, we are highlighting that this is not enacting long-term change in our thoughts or feelings. It is simply an action we are engaging with to move us toward our values.

When I played basketball in high school, I'd do a little skip before games and tell myself, "You got this." I do a similar "shake it off" routine and mantra before giving trainings. I know it's not erasing my insecurities or removing the nervousness that comes from performing. It does, however, make me laugh a little, and the repetition helps me connect with other similar experiences that have turned out well. It's giving my mind something to focus on. And because I know none of these strategies is guaranteed to make me feel a certain way or deliver a certain outcome, I can use it as a short-term tool to get me from point A to point B.

The most important considerations for any type of thought restructuring kind of skill include the following:

- You are not erasing, deleting, or replacing a thought.
- You are adding in a new way of thinking of something to a client's relational network.
- This practice is in the service of moving toward their values—not reducing or changing a feeling or outcome.
- This is not a substitute for feeling their feelings and practicing acceptance.

Meditation

Meditation as the process of noticing is already very consistent with ACT. This can mean focusing on something external, like a flickering candle flame or the scenery around us. Or it can be something internal, such as watching our thoughts and feelings in an observer self role. This may or may not be what your client thinks of when the topic of meditation comes up. Meditation's popularity in Western culture has brought with it a lot of conflicting information. For example, many clients come in with a pre-existing notion that meditation "clears the mind." The idea is that if you meditate, you are at peace and have no thoughts.

Let me be clear: That's not the purpose of meditation, nor is it something we can guarantee. When introducing mindfulness, meditation, or any grounding or noticing exercises to your client, it is important that you highlight what the exercise is, what it looks like, and how it can help. Be sure to validate a client who feels antsy or frustrated by their lack of focus when trying meditation. This is normal. You can explain like this:

> *Our mind is not used to being intentionally directed or stepping back into an observer role. So, of course, when we try to do that, it struggles. In this way, meditation is very much like a muscle. You can't expect to do one crunch and have abs of steel. You can't expect to practice one 10-minute meditation introduction and master engagement with the present moment.*

Clients may try meditation as a formal noticing practice; to ground them at the start, middle, or end of their day to increase their awareness of their thoughts, feelings, and physical sensations; to practice self-as-context; or even to come in contact with their feelings and thoughts as a start to acceptance and defusion practices. Remind them that these practices are process-based, not outcome-driven. We cannot predict how they might feel during or after the experience, but with continued practice, they will develop skills that can translate to other areas of their life.

Imaginative Exposure, Interoceptive Exposure, and In Vivo Exposure

As someone who works with a lot of anxious people, I love exposure work. There are a number of exposure-based protocols with strong evidence base—and they can absolutely be included in therapy from an ACT framework. The most important point to highlight, which may be different from how you have approached it in the past, is that your focus is not on reducing symptoms but increasing engagement. (I know, I sound like a broken record, but this point is foundational.) From this standpoint, you want to ensure that you are choosing exposures that are consistent with their values. When building an exposure hierarchy, always start with values. Ask yourself, "What is important to the client, and what are the ways in which their attempts to avoid anxiety or fear has limited their life?"

Perhaps you have a client with agoraphobia. They want to spend more time with their family and friends. Yet every time they try to leave their neighborhood, they begin to panic. Typically, you'd create an exposure hierarchy that helps the client take small steps further from their house, likely in combination with interoceptive exposure. From an ACT framework, you would try to tie in the connection and social component into every step they take. While it's important that they can leave the house on their own, they could first start with walking around the neighborhood with their sister, and next time, they could grab coffee with their friend at the coffee shop right next to their neighborhood. By adding in a tie to values in their exposure work, you can increase both connection with what matters to them and the notion that while their response to panic in the short term works, it is taking them further from what matters to them in the long term.

When introducing imaginal or interoceptive exposure work, you may highlight at the beginning that their mind has certain default reactions to sensations or memories. You might say, "While we can't always control when or how those feelings come up, we want to practice responding differently."

For *imaginal exposure*, it's likely that the reaction your client has to their trauma memory is appropriate for the trauma. It was a traumatic experience, after all. The distinction you are making is not that the reaction to the trauma is not helpful or accurate, but rather once that memory comes up in session or in their life, your client is reacting to it as if it is happening in real time—which is not helpful, as the trauma is not occurring in that moment. Through imaginal exposure, you can distinguish between the memory itself, which is traumatic, and the current context they are in, which is safe. Then your client can choose how they want to show up to the moment based on the context they are in, not the memory they are experiencing.

With *interoceptive exposure*, you introduce the concept that your client's mind has started labeling certain sensations as unsafe (rapid heart rate, tightening in chest, shakiness, shortness of breath). Through practicing interoceptive exposure in session, you are able to help the client distinguish between unsafe and simply uncomfortable sensations. By practicing interoceptive exposure in a safe environment (your office or their home via telehealth) they can learn firsthand that the sensations are not unsafe, even if their mind says otherwise. Those sensations might always be uncomfortable to experience, but based on when they are happening, your client can identify that they are not unsafe to experience. Your client can then choose how they want to show up to the moment using their values.

When in doubt, remember that if you are 1) starting from a functional contextualist standpoint, 2) not trying to erase or reduce a specific symptom, and 3) keeping values at the forefront of your work, you're off to a great start.

Exercise: Skills Review

At the beginning of this chapter, you wrote down the exercises and skills that you find really valuable in your practice. Now that we've walked through some examples of how to make different skills ACT-consistent, let's take a look at the skills and exercises you often use.

Skills and exercises:

_____
_____
_____
_____
_____
_____

Are any parts of the skills or exercises inconsistent with ACT? Could a client make an assumption about the purpose or outcome that would be inconsistent with ACT?

_____
_____
_____
_____
_____
_____

How would you frame each skill or exercise within the ACT model? You might need to highlight that it is process-focused, not outcome-focused; understand that the goal is to increase steps toward values, not reduce symptoms; or distinguish between this context and what the mind tells your client the context is.

What could you add to these skills and exercises to highlight ACT core processes?

Chapter Takeaways

- There are many exercises from other disciplines that can fit within an ACT approach. The main focus is ensuring you are not promising to eliminate or reduce symptoms.
- Exposure work can be enhanced by first connecting to a person's values.
- Cognitive restructuring skills can be a great way to expand a client's cognitive behavioral repertoire (available responses) to painful thoughts (antecedents or hooks).
- Meditation is a process-based skill focused on noticing the present moment, training how to direct client's attention, and tapping into the observer self.
- Behavior change strategies influenced by a person's values can help engagement with committed actions.

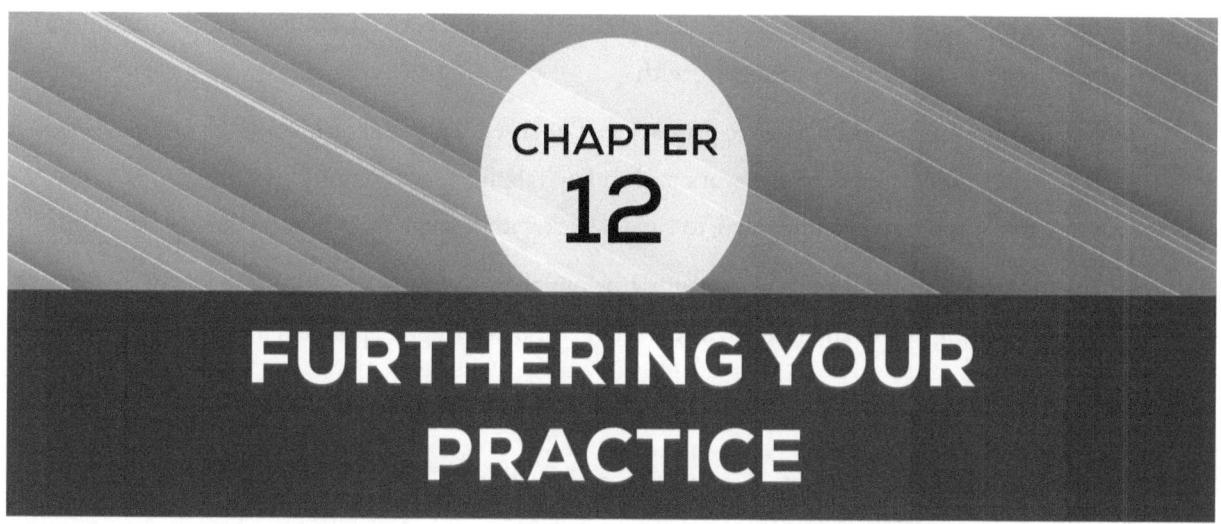

CHAPTER 12

FURTHERING YOUR PRACTICE

Congratulations! You've gained practical know-how for bringing acceptance and commitment therapy into the work you do with your clients! This chapter covers what to do when you get stuck, how to further your practice, and ways to build an ACT community. By the end of this book, my hope is that you come away with a clear next step of how to incorporate an ACT framework into the great work you are doing.

How to Pivot

What happens when things don't go according to plan? It is inevitable when practicing a new way of showing up to your clients that you will find yourself getting stuck. Maybe you went in with a specific plan of how to introduce a topic and your client responded in a different way that totally threw you off your plan. Maybe you tried a new exercise, and as we previously discussed, your client stated that it "didn't work." All of these things will happen at some point.

It might sound silly and definitely redundant at this point, but if you continue falling back on a functional contextual approach and lean into therapy from the perspective of trying to help your client notice what works in a given situation, you usually find your way back. Here are some reminders for entering the therapy room:

- **Focus on what works in a given situation:** Help clients highlight the distinction between what works in the short term and what works in the long term.

- **Stick with a non-symptom-reduction agenda:** Look out for any attempts by yourself or the client to veer back toward a symptom-reduction agenda. It is very easy for any exercise to suddenly become a control strategy. Stay focused on the process, not the outcome.

- **Be flexible with your agenda:** Go into therapy with a loose agenda of what you want to practice, and be willing to adapt to what shows up in the room. This does not mean chasing every interesting bunny down a rabbit hole and getting lost in the content. Rather, stay flexible to the process your client may be struggling with.

- **Fluidly move among the six core processes:** The six core processes lean on each other. It's okay if you start off doing acceptance work and end up talking about committed actions. It is nearly impossible, and not recommended, to rigidly stick with just one core process during a session.

- **Be honest:** Be truthful and transparent with your clients—and yourself. While this might initially refer to getting buy-in and informed consent, it's also just a good approach in general.

Ways to Further the Practice

We've gone through many exercises, scripts, concepts, and tools to use both in and out of sessions. You may have started your practice with ones that felt more accessible or straightforward. As you continue to practice ACT, challenge yourself to weave in and out of the processes with a more fluid approach. If you find yourself stuck in a therapy "rut," such as holding on tightly to a certain way of introducing creative hopelessness or using a single go-to metaphor for cognitive defusion, it is time to take a step back and pivot.

It is just as important that you are sensitive to the context and pay attention to what works in a given setting. Find ways to practice outside of session. This could be creating case conceptualizations using the hexaflex. Perhaps you could join peer consultation groups and discuss your clients from an ACT perspective.

You can also practice ACT in your everyday life. Have fun with deictic frames and practice perspective taking with loved ones, strangers, or even on your own. Have a conversation with a loved one exploring your values and the type of life you want to create for yourself. Try out different present-moment awareness exercises and notice the ones you connect with—and the ones you absolutely hate. Challenge yourself to step outside of your comfort zone and come in contact with your full experience. After some practice, it may also be beneficial to consider a formal assessment to look at the ways you've improved, where your strengths lie, and what areas of ACT would be helpful for you to focus more energy toward.*

There are so many awesome ways to bring this work to your practice and into your life. As you are on this journey, remember that willingness is not a rhetorical question, and it is perfectly okay to say no. You can always introduce less new material at a time. Even increasing contact with one core process has the ability to increase overall psychological flexibility.

---

* One such assessment, the ACT Fidelity Measure (ACT-FM) assessment, can help you notice any gaps in your implementation of ACT with clients (O'Neill et al., 2019). Please visit www.theacttherapist.com/ACTskillsmanual to download and complete the original measure.

Finding Community

When using ACT with your clients, it can feel pretty lonely. It's hard to consult with yourself when you don't know the answer, and we aren't always the best at offering alternative perspectives. Thankfully, there is a robust ACT community that spans cities, countries, and continents. The Association for Contextual Behavioral Science (ACBS)* is a wealth of resources, offering interesting protocols, a phenomenal journal, and interest groups wide enough that you are likely to find a place where you fit. Full disclosure: I am a member of ACBS and have served on various boards within the organization in volunteer positions for years now.

Finding and connecting with a local chapter, affiliate, or peer group can be a great way to continue your practice and, if you need some extra CE, it's a great excuse to travel. ACBS has a conference every year in a different location. Because it is an international organization, the conference is located outside of North America about every other year. Its chapters also sometimes hold smaller conferences and trainings locally. The ACBS community does include a membership fee; however, it is values-based and adjusted for varying socioeconomic statuses in different countries. You don't have to join—I will never know—but it is a resource available to you.

Before we wrap up, I want to commend you for getting to this point. Even if you skimmed over some sections or skipped a chapter entirely, you did something that, in my opinion, is really difficult. You showed up to try to learn something new. The further I've gotten from finishing graduate school and entering the "real world" as a psychologist—almost 10 years now—the more I've realized how difficult it is to carve out time for learning new things. It can be very easy to stick with what you've learned in school. It might even be quite effective. So I think it's pretty awesome that you shared your time and attention with me to see what else is out there. I hope that whatever value connects you to this process, you can hold onto it as you translate what you learned in this book into your life.

Case Study: Sterling

I want to end this book with the story of one of my past clients. When Sterling started therapy with me, he was in his mid-thirties. On paper, his life was great. He owned his own home, had risen to a high-level, high-paying job in his company, and was happily married. He was also working so much that every couple of months his body would just give out. He'd feel weak and dizzy, have heart palpitations, and sleep for a few days straight before jumping right back into the chaos.

He came to therapy because he knew that probably shouldn't be happening. But he didn't know how to get out of it. His job required that he worked long hours, traveled frequently, and it was stressful. So how could he manage his stress, anxiety, and time while also reaching his financial and work goals?

We spent a good bit of time exploring his values. It was difficult because he fell into that category of having a strong sense of what he definitely did not value or did not want to be, but he had never taken

---

* Visit the Association for Contextual Behavioral Science online at https://contextualscience.org.

the time to explore what *did* matter to him. Through that exploration, we identified that having financial security, being authentic, being a loving and present partner, mentoring others, and enjoying cooking were central to his values.

We began looking at his patterns and quickly realized how little connection he had to his values on a regular basis. One thing was clear though: Working the way he did caused a lot of harm to himself and his relationship. He was a client whom I struggled to get buy-in from. He wanted me to tell him a way to better optimize his life so he could work even more. I remember asking him, "What happens to you if you continue to work like this for the next decade?" His answer was immediate: "I become one of those guys who drops dead from a heart attack at 45." So instead of focusing on optimization, we focused on taking more steps toward his values.

When we stopped working together, he had left his job for an even better paying one that required less time and allowed him to have more of a mentorship role. He and his wife started cooking together more. He adopted a cat. And he stopped needing to take two to three days every few months to recover from his life. He still has stress, but he is now in control of how he responds to it.

The most profound part of the work we did together was processing an old hurt that had burrowed itself deep inside of him. Almost a year into our work, he disclosed his childhood trauma to me. Something he had trusted with very few people in his life. What began with burnout led to processing this trauma. I am still to this day so honored that he trusted me with his story. And so proud of him for making some difficult decisions to create a wonderful life.

You never know where therapy will take you or your client. I know with ACT, if I can help people identify what matters to them, give them a framework for understanding their patterns and the skills to break free of ones that no longer serve them, they can create a beautiful life for themselves—no matter what curveballs they face. I hope that you can put this book into practice in a way that works for you—to help even more people let go of the struggle and live beautiful, imperfect lives.

REFERENCES

You can find the downloadable content from this book at
https://www.theacttherapist.com/ACTskillsmanual

Arch, J. J., Eifert, G. H., Davies, C., Vilardaga, J. C. P., Rose, R. D., & Craske, M. G. (2012). Randomized clinical trial of cognitive behavioral therapy (CBT) versus acceptance and commitment therapy (ACT) for mixed anxiety disorders. *Journal of Consulting and Clinical Psychology, 80*(5), 750–765. https://doi.org/10.1037/a0028310

A-Tjak, J. G. L., Davis, M. L., Morina, N., Powers, M. B., Smits, J. A., & Emmelkamp, P. M. G. (2015). A meta-analysis of the efficacy of acceptance and commitment therapy for clinically relevant mental and physical health problems. *Psychotherapy and Psychosomatics, 84*(1), 30–36. https://doi.org/10.1159/000365764

Bai, Z., Luo, S., Zhang, L., Wu, S., & Chi, I. (2020). Acceptance and commitment therapy (ACT) to reduce depression: A systematic review and meta-analysis. *Journal of Affective Disorders, 260*, 728–737. https://doi.org/10.1016/j.jad.2019.09.040

Bluett, E. J., Homan, K. J., Morrison, K. L., Levin, M. E., & Twohig, M. P. (2014). Acceptance and commitment therapy for anxiety and OCD spectrum disorders: An empirical review. *Journal of Anxiety Disorders, 28*(6), 612–624. https://doi.org/10.1016/j.janxdis.2014.06.008

Ciarrochi, J., Bailey, A., & Harris, R. (2014). *The weight escape: How to stop dieting and start living.* Shambhala Publications.

Fausto-Sterling, A. (2000). *Sexing the body: Gender politics and the construction of sexuality.* Basic Books.

Harris, R. (2019). *ACT made simple: An easy-to-read primer on acceptance and commitment therapy.* New Harbinger Publications.

Harris, R. (2022). *The happiness trap: How to stop struggling and start living.* (2nd ed.) Shambhala Publications.

Harvey, J. C. (2015). *Red: A history of the redhead.* Black Dog & Leventhal.

Hayes, S. C. (2005). *Get out of your mind and into your life: The new acceptance and commitment therapy.* New Harbinger Publications.

Hayes, L. L., & Ciarrochi, J. (2015). *The thriving adolescent: Using acceptance and commitment therapy and positive psychology to help teens manage emotions, achieve goals, and build connection.* New Harbinger Publications.

Hayes, L. L., Ciarrochi, J. V., & Bailey, A. (2022). *What makes you stronger: How to thrive in the face of change and uncertainty using acceptance and commitment therapy.* New Harbinger Publications.

Hayes, S. C., Strosahl, K. D., & Wilson, K. G. (1999). *Acceptance and commitment therapy: An experiential approach to behavior change.* Guilford Press.

Hayes, S. C., Strosahl, K. D., & Wilson, K. G. (2011). *Acceptance and commitment therapy: The process and practice of mindful change.* Guilford Press.

Hours, C., Recasens, C., & Baleyte, J. M. (2022). ASD and ADHD comorbidity: What are we talking about? *Frontiers in Psychiatry, 13*, Article 837424. https://doi.org/10.3389/fpsyt.2022.837424

Jansen, J. E., Gleeson, J., Bendall, S., Rice, S., & Alvarez-Jimenez, M. (2020). Acceptance- and mindfulness-based interventions for persons with psychosis: A systematic review and meta-analysis. *Schizophrenia Research, 215*, 25–37. https://doi.org/10.1016/j.schres.2019.11.016

Jiménez, F. J. R. (2012). Acceptance and commitment therapy versus traditional cognitive behavioral therapy: A systematic review and meta-analysis of current empirical evidence. *International Journal of Psychology and Psychological Therapy, 12*(3), 333–358.

Lin, J., Scott, W., Carpenter, L., Norton, S., Domhardt, M., Baumeister, H., & McCracken, L. M. (2019). Acceptance and commitment therapy for chronic pain: Protocol of a systematic review and individual participant data meta-analysis. *Systematic Reviews, 8*(1), Article 140. https://doi.org/10.1186/s13643-019-1044-2

Meier, S. M., Petersen, L., Schendel, D. E., Mattheisen, M., Mortensen, P. B., & Mors, O. (2015). Obsessive-compulsive disorder and autism spectrum disorders: Longitudinal and offspring risk. *PloS One, 10*(11), Article e0141703. https://doi.org/10.1371/journal.pone.0141703

O'Neill, L., Latchford, G. J., McCracken, L. M., & Graham, C. D. (2019). The development of the Acceptance and Commitment Therapy Fidelity Measure (ACT-FM): A Delphi study and field test. *Journal of Contextual Behavioral Science, 14*, 111–118. https://doi.org/10.1016/j.jcbs.2019.08.008

Polk, K. L., Schoendorff, B., Webster, M., & Olaz, F. O. (2016). *The essential guide to the ACT Matrix: A step-by-step approach to using the ACT Matrix model in clinical practice.* New Harbinger Publications.

Ruiz, F. J. (2012). Acceptance and commitment therapy versus traditional cognitive behavioral therapy: A systematic review and meta-analysis of current empirical evidence. *International Journal of Psychology and Psychological Therapy, 12*(3), 333–358.

Soondrum, T., Wang, X., Gao, F., Liu, Q., Fan, J., & Zhu, X. (2022). The applicability of acceptance and commitment therapy for obsessive-compulsive disorder: A systematic review and meta-analysis. *Brain Sciences, 12*(5), Article 656. https://doi.org/10.3390/brainsci12050656

Stoddard, J. A., & Afari, N. (2014). *The big book of ACT metaphors: A practitioner's guide to experiential exercises and metaphors in acceptance and commitment therapy.* New Harbinger Publications.

Strosahl, K. D., Robinson, P. J., & Gustavsson, T. (2012). *Brief interventions for radical change: Principles and practice of focused acceptance and commitment therapy.* New Harbinger Publications.

Tonarelli, S. B., Pasillas, R., Alvarado, L., Dwivedi, A. K., & Cancellare, A. (2016). Acceptance and commitment therapy compared to treatment as usual in psychosis: A systematic review and meta-analysis. *Journal of Psychiatry, 19*(3), 1–5. https://doi.org/10.4172/2378-5756.1000366

Trindade, I. A., Guiomar, R., Carvalho, S. A., Duarte, J., Lapa, T., Menezes, P., Nogueira, M. R., Patrão, B., Pinto-Gouveia, J., & Castilho, P. (2021). Efficacy of online-based acceptance and commitment therapy for chronic pain: A systematic review and meta-analysis. *The Journal of Pain, 22*(11), 1328–1342. https://doi.org/10.1016/j.jpain.2021.04.003

Twohig, M. P., & Levin, M. E. (2017). Acceptance and commitment therapy as a treatment for anxiety and depression: A review. *The Psychiatric Clinics of North America, 40*(4), 751–770. https://doi.org/10.1016/j.psc.2017.08.009

Tyng, C. M., Amin, H. U., Saad, M. N. M., & Malik, A. S. (2017). The influences of emotion on learning and memory. *Frontiers in Psychology, 8*, Article 1454. https://doi.org/10.3389/fpsyg.2017.01454

Veehof, M. M., Oskam, M.-J., Schreurs, K. M. G., & Bohlmeijer, E. T. (2011). Acceptance-based interventions for the treatment of chronic pain: a systematic review and meta-analysis. *Pain, 152*(3), 533–542. https://doi.org/10.1016/j.pain.2010.11.002

Villatte, J. L., Vilardaga, R., Villatte, M., Vilardaga, J. C. P., Atkins, D. C., & Hayes, S. C. (2016). Acceptance and commitment therapy modules: Differential impact on treatment processes and outcomes. *Behaviour Research and Therapy, 77*, 52–61. https://doi.org/10.1016/j.brat.2015.12.001

ACKNOWLEDGMENTS

This book wouldn't be possible without the help, guidance, and support from so many. I will be forever grateful to Kayla Church, my wonderful acquisitions editor at PESI, for reaching out and asking me to write a book on ACT. Kayla and the entire PESI team have made this process so enjoyable and have been supportive—even when I haven't always met my deadlines. Huge thanks to my editors, Marisa Solis and Alissa Schneider, for their expertise and skill at helping me transform this book into its best version. I'm proud of what we've created here. This book wouldn't be finished without the encouragement of three of my favorite people: My best friend, Lainie, who constantly checked in on my progress and celebrated my small wins with me. My loyal canine companion, Oliver, who kept me company on early morning and late night writing sessions. And my husband, Eric, for encouraging me, being my accountability buddy, and picking up the slack around the house when I was busy writing. Thank you!

ABOUT THE AUTHOR

Jessica Borushok, PhD, is a psychologist in private practice specializing in anxiety and chronic health conditions in adults. She received her PhD in clinical psychology with an emphasis in behavioral medicine from Bowling Green State University. She trained in a variety of clinical settings, including inpatient and outpatient hospitals, chronic pain clinics, primary care, group practice, long-term acute care, weight loss programs, and a nursing home before starting her private practice. Jessica is a peer-reviewed acceptance and commitment therapy (ACT) trainer. She is an award-winning author and the coauthor of three ACT books and one card deck. In addition to training mental health professionals, Jessica teaches ACT to the public through her YouTube channel, *The ACT Therapist*. Jessica lives in the states with her husband and adorable pup.